T0163871

Let's All Hold Hands and Drop Dead

*THREE
GENERATIONS
ONE STORY*

Elaine J. Cooper

NEW YORK

Let's All Hold Hands and Drop Dead
THREE GENERATIONS ONE STORY

© 2015 Elaine J. Cooper.

All rights reserved. No portion of this book may be reproduced, stored in a retrieval system, or transmitted in any form or by any means—electronic, mechanical, photocopy, recording, scanning, or other,—except for brief quotations in critical reviews or articles, without the prior written permission of the publisher.

Published in New York, New York, by Morgan James Publishing. Morgan James and The Entrepreneurial Publisher are trademarks of Morgan James, LLC. www.MorganJamesPublishing.com

The Morgan James Speakers Group can bring authors to your live event. For more information or to book an event visit The Morgan James Speakers Group at www.TheMorganJamesSpeakersGroup.com.

A **free** eBook edition is available with the purchase of this print book.

CLEARLY PRINT YOUR NAME ABOVE IN UPPER CASE

Instructions to claim your free eBook edition:
1. Download the BitLit app for Android or iOS
2. Write your name in **UPPER CASE** on the line
3. Use the BitLit app to submit a photo
4. Download your eBook to any device

ISBN 978-1-63047-360-0 paperback
ISBN 978-1-63047-361-7 eBook
ISBN 978-1-63047-362-4 hardcover
Library of Congress Control Number:
2014945319

Cover Design by:
Rachel Lopez
www.r2cdesign.com

Interior Design by:
Bonnie Bushman
bonnie@caboodlegraphics.com

In an effort to support local communities, raise awareness and funds, Morgan James Publishing donates a percentage of all book sales for the life of each book to Habitat for Humanity Peninsula and Greater Williamsburg.

Get involved today, visit
www.MorganJamesBuilds.com

Habitat for Humanity
Peninsula and
Greater Williamsburg
Building Partner

Let's All Hold Hands and Drop Dead

I dedicate this book to the survivors of disasters
manufactured by humans and to their children,
grandchildren, and great-grandchildren.

*I the LORD thy God am a jealous God, visiting the
iniquity of the fathers upon the children unto the third
and fourth generation . . .*
—Exodus 20:5

Table of Contents

Acknowledgments

There were two major drafts of this book, each reviewed by a circle of gifted friends and colleagues. This book would not have been possible without their input. Each person encouraged me and gave me constructive criticism. This brilliant group of people taught me how to write. They are Geraldine Alpert, Lurline Aslanian, Susan Brand, Dorene Butler, Lee Butler, Nina Cooper, Lila Coulter, Sara Emerson, Leslie Goldner, Les Greene, Paula Harrington, Sari Henry, Brenda Hillman, Barbara Ilfeld, Mark Johnson, Priscilla Kauff, Bette Korman, Ivan Kramer, Jeannie Little, Emily Loeb, Kennie Lyman (my editor), Edmund Lonergan, Kenneth Lonergan, Peter Lonergan, William McClung, Leonard Michaels, Lucia Milburn, Rita Moncrief, Pam Ozaroff (my copy editor), Cecilia Pinto de Maura, Helen Roberts, Enid Schreibman, Patricia Stamm, Ira Tager, Jillian Tager, Charlotte Togorovitsky, Rita Wohlfarth, Alexander Wolf, Dennis Zeitlin, and Josephine Zeitlin. I acknowledge them with my whole broken-and-put-together heart.

Introduction

A fire burned my house to the ground. I built a beautiful new house, brick by brick. Now I want to build a book, putting the bricks of my life together, layer by layer. I sit on the floor and surround myself with the items I grabbed from my house during the fire. They are items from three generations but one story: a Jew from Ukraine, kids from East L.A., and members of a therapy group.

First there is my father's unpublished book about his experiences in Ukraine, starting in 1916. Ivan emigrated to America in 1923, soon after his fourteenth birthday. He wrote this eyewitness report of the beginning, middle, and end of the Russian Revolution as soon as he was fluent in English. The book sits on the floor in a three-ringed binder with a worn blue canvas cover. The pages are typed, double-spaced, and faded. The book is dedicated to my mother, Gazelle, who corrected some of my father's English. My mother's corrections are handwritten in black pen that has not faded. My father handed me this book when I was thirteen years old; it made a big difference in my life. Suddenly things that had been senseless before made sense.

The next items are my diaries from junior high and high school. Like my father, I felt compelled to write. I can feel the raw, up-and-down emotions of my preteen and teenage self as I read the pages—elation and rage. Next to my diary are my brother Arnold's personal notes. Long ago I'd gathered them together in a manila folder because most were scribbled on bits of paper that happened to be within his reach. His notes are searching, trying to make sense out of a world that made no sense. Like my father and me, Arnold was compelled to pour out his heart and thoughts on paper.

The last item is a box full of countless process notes from group therapy sessions I've led. The members of the therapy groups are the third generation. They are not biologically related to me, but they are the generation that I mentor; in this sense, they are my progeny. Witnessing my parents' strong ability to survive and nurture their children despite their emotional pain and limitations led me to have an overwhelming desire to understand *all* human beings. What makes us all act and think the way we do? I don't know anyone who hasn't experienced both love and hurt in some way. How do we acknowledge the love and heal the hurt? Is there a way to heal wounds inherited from previous generations? With this goal in mind, I have immersed myself in sociology, psychology, and psychiatry for the past half century, practicing group, couples, and individual psychotherapy.

The two group therapy meetings that I share in this book, chronicled over several chapters, are sessions in which I had strong emotional reactions.[1] To fulfill my goal of mentoring with wisdom, I realized that I had to face how my own history was affecting my work. I began to see that there were links stretching from my father's history to my own childhood to the subjective reactions I was having in the group. To help my group members with their own healing process, I had to understand myself.

All of our brains and hearts are wired to love and hate. Throughout our human history, there have been heroes and monsters. Human beings love heroically and kill unabashedly. In this book love and hate are expressed differently by the three generations. In the first generation (my parents'), love and hate were unrestrained. They were acted out courageously and violently; there were no controls. In the second generation (my siblings' and mine), my brothers and I were affected by the violence and heroism of the previous generation, but we had no conscious awareness of it; we were simply enveloped by it. In the third generation (my therapy groups'), members know that extreme hate and love exist, and they are extremely frightened by both. As

---

1   In Parts 1 and 2 of this book, I chronicle the first half of a single group therapy meeting and describe several members of the therapy group. In Part 3 I flash back to an earlier group therapy meeting that occurred four weeks before and chronicle this single meeting. In Part 4 I flash forward to the current group therapy meeting and chronicle the second half of that meeting.

a result, they keep these emotions bound in knots inside themselves and are not able to have healthy, intimate relationships in which love and hate take constructive forms. They experience outbursts of anger. They become symptomatic, developing eating disorders, depression, and anxiety. They don't feel free to be themselves because they are afraid they will be instruments of destruction, whether through loving or hating.

Think of this book as a patchwork quilt. All the patches belong together and make a beautiful pattern in my psyche. They interact spontaneously with one another. Each patch is alive and has its own unique voice.

Cast of Characters

First Generation

Ivan Sbritsky Abrams: my father, who was born Ivan Sbritsky but adopted the last name Abrams when he emigrated to the United States from Ukraine in 1923.

Gazelle Abrams: my mother, whose grandparents emigrated from Hungary.

Second Generation

Elaine Abrams Cooper: the author and narrator of this book.

Arnold Abrams: my brother, ten months and twenty days younger than I am.

Gary Abrams: my brother, ten years younger than I am.

Jerry Cooper: my boyfriend and first husband.

Third Generation: Members of the Therapy Group

Robert: forty-seven, oldest member of the group, distinguished looking, tall, red hair, dresses in a suit and tie, conservative, divorced and remarried, has child, trains new staff at a large real estate firm. Grandfather was a Nazi who emigrated from Germany in the 1940s. *Presenting complaints*: social withdrawal, loses temper, relationship problems.

Tim: thirty, liberal social activist, long brown hair in ponytail, premature grey strands, dresses sloppily in jeans and a flannel shirt, manages a cooperative bakery, thin, single. Ancestors emigrated from Ireland in the late 1840s during the Potato Famine. *Presenting complaints*: depression, loses temper, relationship problems.

Linda: forty-five, farmer and artist, good marriage, dresses in jeans and a flannel shirt, thick brown curly hair that covers most of her face, introvert. Descended from freed slaves. *Presenting complaint*: depression.

Elizabeth: twenty-nine, works in animal rescue, usually dresses in her work overalls, short blond curls around her face, quiet, chubby, single. Grandparents emigrated from Poland after World War II. Parents are practicing Catholics. *Presenting complaints*: eating disorder, forming relationships.

Hugo: forty-two, former creative software engineer for a large company, now self-employed and designing an electric car, thinks "outside the box," single, large man, muscular, dresses in sporty carpenter pants. Ancestors emigrated from England in the 1700s. One relative was burned at the stake for being a witch. *Presenting complaints*: depression, social withdrawal.

David: thirty-nine, medical equipment salesman, single, obese, wears a suit and tie, wants to please, low status in the group. Grandparents were Holocaust survivors from Poland. *Presenting complaints*: forming relationships, eating disorder, depression.

Cheryl: thirty-eight, accountant for a large firm, dresses in a suit and heels, wears makeup, divorced, attractive and likeable, the group wants to please her. Parents emigrated from Iran in the late 1950s. *Presenting complaint*: panic attacks.

Harry: thirty-two, newest member of the group, doctor, forced friendliness, good marriage, boyish appearance, short, chubby, dresses in a pressed short-sleeved cotton shirt and new jeans. Grandparents and father emigrated from India around the time of independence in 1947. *Presenting complaint*: difficult relationship with his parents.

PART 1
PRELUDE

Man is an island, in an archipelago.
—Arnold S. Abrams

From My Father's Book: Ukraine

1916

As the sun is rising on the Ukraine horizon, another child is born to the Sbritsky family. The rooster in the barn is stretching and spreading his wings; with his powerful screeching, he wakes up the neighborhood. It is six a.m. in the month of July, the year 1916, in the small city of Elisavetgrad (now Kirovagrad) on the outskirts of Russia. The six little houses in the "Dome" are surrounded by a wooden fence with a rusty iron gate. A lamp with a broken glass and a candle inside hangs from a bar above the gate. In the sputtering light of the candle, the number of the house underneath the lamp is hardly visible; it would be hard for anyone to determine if it is the right "Dome." In our house six children are lined up in front of the bedroom door, in order of seniority.

Father is a man of forty-eight, medium height, stately, and quiet. His general appearance is that of his king, Nicholas the Second, who is presiding over the deteriorating Russian empire. Father knows that his country is in a chaotic state. He has one eye set on a portrait of his czar and the other on the door of the room where his beautiful wife lies with another child in her arms. He is more sad than happy; he knows this is no time to bring a child into world.

Walking slowly across the room with his usual aristocratic air, Father whispers to his oldest son, Dmitri, who is first in line, "It's all right, son. You can go in now and say *mazel tov*."

Dmitri is fifteen years of age. He says *mazel tov* to his mother, as he has said so many times before when his brothers and sisters were born. Dmitri looks worried. He is nervous and impatient, giving very little thought to his mother and the new arrival. His mind is on the revolution that is to come any day. Dmitri looks at the portrait of the czar—the czar that he despises. Dmitri is a revolutionary, and Karl Marx is his idol.

He stands before his mother, solemn and emotionless, grasping her hand and squeezing it tightly. His mother looks at him and whispers faintly, "Dmitri, you look so sad. Are you all right? You are studying too hard." He gives her a light kiss on her forehead and without answering her, walks out.

Misha, the second son, walks in. He stands before his mother and smiles, asks her how she feels, kisses her, and then departs. Misha is a lanky boy of thirteen, shy, and always ready to smile whether the occasion calls for it or not.

Ida, the oldest girl, walks in quietly. She is eleven. Ida tells her mother she should get well fast because it is hard for her to care for the whole family alone. "Father is never satisfied with my cooking," she says. Just then, Father opens the door and calls Ida back to work. Ida kisses her mother feverishly and walks out. Ida has full responsibility when Mother is ill. She is dependable, jolly, always smiling, and loves all her brothers and sisters. Her mother looks upon her as a partner to shoulder her troubles.

It is my turn to go in. I am seven years old. I hardly ever smile. I am very serious, ambitious, and independent. Not only do I look like my father, I have inherited his character. The reason for my father's fondness for me is that he sees himself in me. Here the primitive instinct to reproduce oneself is at its highest peak; he watches every move I make.

My mother's love for me is also strong. As she looks at me she sees her son, as well as her husband. We look and act so much alike. Father walks toward me, showing favoritism before his other children. He speaks in a low voice. "My boy, your mother is waiting for you. You may go in now."

I stand before my mother, whom I love with all my heart. I admire her as a queen and a goddess. I whisper, "*Mazel tov, mazel tov*, how do you feel?" I have rehearsed these few words. Mother smiles.

Mother looks sad and has a worried look on her face. She wants to see her two youngest children, who are still babies and need her special care. Neda walks in slowly, as father coaxes her. She is just six. When she comes close, mother grasps her hand and kisses her cheek, straining her head over the bed.

Father comes in with the youngest child in his arms. Alex is just learning how to walk. He is the most beautiful baby in the neighborhood, and some go as far as to say that he is the nicest looking in the city of Elisavetgrad. Mother's love is at its height when she sees her baby, Alex. Her face lights up with joy as she asks her husband to let her hold him for a second. He bends the baby down to her, and she kisses little Alex and puts her arms around him. Mother tries to bring him toward her, but her husband's powerful arms pull the baby away so she can rest.

Dmitri is in an underground cellar planning and organizing with his friends. They are rehearsing the parts they will each play in the revolution that is expected to come within the year. There is talk among the youngsters that a Red Army is gathering in St. Petersburg and Moscow; it will be ready to strike any day and liberate the people from despotic rule. There is also talk of a Prince Lvov, who is trying to form a democracy. There are rumors that the Duma will disband and Russia will quit the war. Dmitri gives all this information to Father.

Father refuses to listen and constantly stares at the portrait of the czar that hangs in the large living room. Every day Dmitri says, "I will tear this tyrant to pieces as soon as I am able. Our day will come. While I am tearing this portrait, the Red Army will tear his rotten flesh to bits." Father has difficulty stopping such talk, even though he knows he will find his son in Siberia if anyone from the government overhears him.

Misha is in school. He is fortunate to get two years of education in a dilapidated school with an ignorant and superstitious faculty. More fortunate is Dmitri, who graduated from the gymnasium (high school) and is apprenticed to a pharmacist. Misha and Dmitri are lucky indeed, as there is talk of closing all schools.

Mother begins walking about the house, recuperating from giving birth. The new baby is named Sonia, but mother calls her Sonechka, and in time everyone calls her by that name. Mother is thinking about better days, when she used to walk past the neighbors in a fine fur cape with a matching fur hat. Her husband gave her expensive jewelry from his shop—the largest in Elisavetgrad. I was the youngest boy at the time, and on many occasions I was with her, wearing my royal blue Kazak suit with imitation bullets stitched on the front and a silver dagger attached to my shiny red belt. I also wore a white fur hat with red velvet hanging on the side. The boys envied me, and the women, Mrs. Sbritsky. This was only four years ago, and yet such realities seem to recede into the distant past at an astonishing pace.

A few months later, Father walks into the house with a worried look. His wrinkles are more visible than ever as he sits down at the head of the table. His hand moves over his balding head, and then, pulling his beard, he says, "I moved my store to the shoemaker's around the corner." The family is amazed. The shop he had moved from was on the "big street"—the street with the largest stores. We knew that he had been in that store for twenty years. His store was the pride of the city, and his jewelry shone like stars in the night on the boulevard.

Since the World War broke out, people have been too involved with the war to want any new jewelry; they buy only necessities. He sells no jewelry now; he only repairs watches. He can no longer make a living. Father returns to the store and sadly puts his tools in a big red handkerchief and looks at the little worn table that he has used for years. This is a great tragedy for him; he never thought he would live to see the doors of the Sbritsky Jewelry and Repair Shop close forever. In the past many folks offered him a great deal of money to teach their sons his trade, but he turned them all away, hoping his three sons would carry on the business. It is clear to him now that they are all headed in different directions.

In the store he turns to take the large clock from the wall. This clock is over one hundred years old and a gift from his employer when Father left to open his own shop. Father is highly sentimental and prizes this rusty clock with a ten pound lead weight on each chain. Antique dealers offered him sums of money to buy it; he chased them all out of his store.

And so in the presence of the barber and the dry goods merchant, who have rented his space, he moves his belongings, looking fatigued and miserable. He settles in a new place around the corner that is the beginning of the slums. He shares a little store of forty feet with a shoemaker who eats and sleeps there. The shoemaker's name is Bulba, meaning "bubble."

Before helping my father move, I collect the sack of vegetables and black bread that I bought in the market with the little money we have left. It is a big supply, since we do not know when we will have money again. There is talk that soon even money will not be able to buy food, since the farmers have complained of a bad year. I throw the sack over my shoulder, and we start for home.

On the way we pass the pastry shop where we do our shopping. We walk in; Father asks for credit but is refused by the snarly woman behind the counter. She says we owe fifty rubles already, and she does not see how we can even pay that, since we moved our business into Bulba's little hole. This almost brings tears to my father's eyes. He holds them back; he does not want to show his son that his pride can be injured so easily. He smiles with his eyes aflame. We slowly walk out.

Father is bursting with pent-up emotions. Perhaps if he talks of the past to his son, he can forget the future. Things look very dark, and he fears he will not live long. His stomach cannot bear the ordinary food he is consuming. He can no longer afford the delicacies he is used to, such as olives from Italy, figs from Crimea, oranges from California, or peanuts from South America. Such luxuries are available only to the rich. He was never wealthy, but he felt that nothing was too good for himself. He bought all these things even if he had to deprive his family of necessities. This part of my character I inherited from my father; self-love is evident in many generations of men in the Sbritsky family. His mind is now full of thoughts of days gone by. He begins to talk to me about them. He has never spoken to his children about his family, but it is different now.

"Ivan, my boy," he begins. "It's a cruel world we live in. I am sorry I cannot give you the things you should have, the things all the other Sbritsky children had, but one thing you can be certain of always having: dignity, pride, and self-respect. That is something no one can take away from a Sbritsky because it is in our blood; it flows from generation to generation.

Your great-grandfather came to this city 150 years ago, when it was practically a wilderness. The people who lived here were barbarians—

Tartars and Mongolians. Your great-grandfather became a farmer, and through hard work and honest effort, he advanced rapidly. He helped build the first school and first synagogue. He was a pious Jew but also gained the respect of gentiles because of his desire to contribute to the community. He had serfs, but they loved him because he treated them like human beings. He thought a great deal of his religion but did not worship it fanatically, as many did in those days. He donated money to his synagogue (the only one in the city), but he did not forget the city's schools and churches. He became the richest Jew in Elisavetgrad. Before he died, he willed his entire estate to your grandfather. It was an enormous estate, consisting of flour mills, thousands of acres of land, plenty of cattle, and a fortune.

Your grandfather wasn't a good businessman. He hadn't had to work for his wealth, as your great-grandfather had. The lack of this ability caused everything to dwindle away, but the dignity of his father was still strong in him. He focused his energy on better preparing his children. He gave his children an education unparalleled by any other Jewish family in our community. He sent all his sons to the gymnasium; the oldest was sent to the Imperial Medical University in St. Petersburg to become a doctor. This was the highest honor a Jew could acquire in the imperial government. This took most of his wealth, but he considered nothing too much to have his son become a doctor; he wanted him to be of service. Unfortunately, to get his doctor's degree, my brother had to convert to Christianity. My father never knew this; the shock would have been too much for him. My son, I hope you will live to see the day that such stupidity and prejudice will no longer blacken this earth.

Your other uncle went to the university to become a lawyer. He graduated with honors, and this town gave him the greatest celebration ever bestowed on a Jew. He went to Moscow to further his knowledge and later remained there, never to return. He wrote many letters to our father informing him of his success as an attorney for the imperial government. Unfortunately, he was forced to marry a Christian girl in order to gain this position in the government. This was also kept a secret from our father.

Your grandfather was religious, and his great desire was to see one of his son's become a rabbi. He sent your Uncle Aaron to the finest rabbinical school in the country. My father got the greatest joy in his life when his son received a rabbinical diploma. Your uncle is now a rabbi in the United States. Your other two uncles, the doctor and lawyer, have been dead for some time now.

You also have an aunt in the United States who is married to a rich businessman and enjoys the better things in life. They have seven children, and we haven't heard from them for over three years . . . but in these troublesome times, no one gets mail. I need not tell you much of your Aunt Catherine, since she is the only one you know. She is the eldest, and she made my father unhappy because she was mean, selfish, and unwilling to go to school. She is now fanatically religious and is most unkind and ignorant—that is why I never allow you children to go to visit her. She is the only one in the immediate family that I can turn to, but I do not want to see her. She is miserly and has been hoarding food for years.

As for me, I was the youngest of them all, and when my time came to go to the university, there was no money left. My father sent me to a jeweler as an apprentice; in those days it was considered a good profession. I took great pride in fixing watches; the mechanism of a watch is almost as delicate as the mechanism of a human being. I still take much pride in my work, even though it brings little or nothing now, but I was considered well-off in days gone by.

So you see, my son, I tell you all this to let you know something of the family you descended from. I want you to know that you are a Sbritsky, and it is up to you to carry that name with the dignity and pride of your great-grandfather, grandfather, and me. In these troublesome times, with a revolution knocking at our door and the world going mad . . . it is unfortunate, indeed, that we have to live in such an era . . ."

His voice trails off. I listen intently. Tears are rolling down my face. I feel so sorry for my father, who is losing weight and getting paler every day. It is the first time I have any good feelings for him. We all fear him as a master rather than loving him as a father. He shows little consideration for his beautiful wife and often drives her to tears.

After listening to my father, I am willing to forgive his faults. I see a better side of his character. I realize that nothing in this world is perfect, so why should I expect him to be perfect?

A Letter to My Four-Year-Old Self

2

1945

At four years old, you find yourself in a huge room with a glass wall between you and your brother. You are struck by the oddness of it. Then you are taken to a large, warm swimming pool. You have never been to a pool before, and you can't help smiling with pleasure when you enter it; in fact, you can't help smiling most of the time because everything is new and interesting. The doctors and nurses smile back. You sit in your bed and learn to pick up your shoes with your feet. Climbing ladders is better than being in bed. You are meeting children other than your brother. You don't like the girl on your left because she cries a lot. You have a contest with the girl across from you: Who can learn to say the words *infantile paralysis* first? You win and are proud of yourself.

You must have been perplexed when you woke up one morning and couldn't walk, and you saw a worried look on your father's face. Then the rare doctor visit (because it cost so much money) and the doctor coming out and saying, "I'm sorry, Mr. and Mrs. Abrams, but your daughter has polio." Your mother's face is always optimistic and reassuring, but there is a strange look on your father's face. Soon after, in the middle of winter, you are taken to New York State Reconstruction Home in West Havestraw, a two-hour bus ride from your home in Astoria, Queens, in New York City. Your parents leave; this hospital is your home for the next four months. You have no memory of your father visiting, but your mother comes on the bus with your brother a few times. The bus fare from Manhattan is $1.88 for a one-day round trip. Coming off the bus with a three-year-old in hand, she falls in the snow.

Up until now, you have spent your life with your brother as your constant companion. He is ten months and twenty days younger than you. Your mother has a twin brother, and she raises you as twins. She sews matching clothes for you. Since Arnold is a boy and smart, the two of you communicate as equals. Everything he wants to do, you want to do. He runs; you run. He goes to kiss your mother; you go too. He is picked up by your father; you say, "me too." In fact, "me too" are the words you both say the most. The two of you are in perpetual motion. Your earliest memory is of falling down the stairs of your small, two-story house in Astoria and watching the spokes of the staircase twirl—fascinated. It must have been a daily activity for both of you. Your names could both be Elaineandarnold because they are seldom spoken alone.

You are sitting on your bed, and you can see the other children in the hospital playing outside on the playground. You can't take your eyes off them. You have never seen anything like it. You sit up in your bed to get a better view and study them. Little do you know that your training as a group therapist has begun.

Lucky you! You are one of the first children to receive the Sister Kenny treatment. The only unpleasant part is the steaming hot pads that are put on your paralyzed leg. One day the nurses and doctors form a circle around you, and you take your first step, carefully putting one step in front of the other in a perfect straight line. Smiles come from everywhere, lighting up the room. You don't even have a limp!

Next year you will be playing in warm sand on the beach in Miami, Florida. You will be watching your slim, bronzed, blonde brother climb coconut trees. He has wide shoulders that are becoming muscular; they contrast with his tiny waist and hips. He is very high up, and you are impressed. You have a babysitter for the first time. She is young and pretty. Your parents have a juice stand across from the Blackstone Hotel. They look beautiful. You feel content, complete. The sand and sun are a constant caress.

3

Getting Ready

My office is beautiful. It is a box but a box with new furniture and a window that looks out at the New York City skyline. I have never had an office like this. I am starting a private practice, and this is my first all-my-own office. It is a bit outside the city, in New Jersey, so the offices are more roomy than those in Manhattan. My group is arriving in twenty minutes. I have to lie down on my couch, close my eyes, relax the muscles in my face, breathe deeply, and try not to think too much.

Tomorrow I will teach a class on group therapy for the psychiatric residents at the medical school. There are several concepts that I want to get across to them: the social unconscious, systems theory, and leadership roles. I think I'll start with the social unconscious. Some people confuse this concept with the collective unconscious, à la Jung, which names the qualities central to all human beings—namely, our abilities to be both loving and hating, heroic and demonic, masculine and feminine, aggressive and passive. We are all of these qualities and many more. We are part good and part evil.

The social unconscious, also called the generational unconscious, has to do with a buried memory from past generations of a trauma, especially one imposed by our fellow human beings. It could be the Missing in Argentina or the pogroms in Russia and Ukraine. The list is endless, and it can be found in most human societies. These events might have occurred one or two generations before, and we are unaware that they propel our thoughts and actions. The survivors typically have no idea that their children bear their suffering, since they themselves rarely speak of their past, if at all. The children pick up their parents' pain unconsciously.

I hear Cheryl walking outside my door to the waiting room. Her step is distinctive because she wears high heels. Everything about her is feminine and sensual; she couldn't hide it if she tried. She does try to underplay it, but group members can't help being attracted to her. She has the irresistible combination of Iranian beauty and vulnerability. She is coming to the group because she is desperate for help with her anxiety attacks. She is divorced and wants to make a better choice the next time around.

Everyone in this group functions well in the world, but even those who are married feel blocked from real intimacy. I believe that Cheryl's anxiety attacks and intimacy problems are related. In fact, I think that all the symptoms the members have presented are related to their intimacy problems. Growing up, they did fine with one-to-one relationships, but they got into trouble when they had to negotiate triangular ones. Triangular relationships are more complex. Two parties want to possess the object (the third); one pursuer wins and the other is killed off. The desired object and the winner have to live with the fact that in the process of acquiring the intimate relationship they yearned for, they killed off a person they loved. This cruelty causes guilt and fear, sabotaging intimate relationships and making them conflictual. Neuroses are born. The conflict between the desire of winning and the fear of winning often keeps people from even attempting intimacy.

Cheryl is one of the Emotional Leaders of the group. Because she is likeable, attractive, and open in sharing her emotional pain, the members want to please and help her; they open up more of themselves in order to join her. They don't want to fail her.

I hear David's footsteps. David probably came early in hopes of finding Elizabeth. He is always trying to befriend her. She usually ignores his overtures, looking down as she walks past him. She does not want to be associated with him. He has the lowest status in the group and is the Scapegoat Leader. She is worried about her own status. Cheryl is quite friendly to David because she does not have to worry about her status in the group.

Back to my class: I'd also like to cover systems theory tomorrow. I want the trainees to see all the groups they have ever been in as concentric circles, with the innermost circle being the group in their heads or the bacteria in their bodies (yes, bacteria form groups) and the outermost circle being the society they live in and ultimately, the planet. A thread runs through all these circles. I will mention John Muir, who wrote in 1916, "When we try to pick out anything by itself, we find it hitched to everything else in the universe." I suppose this means that there is a thread that connects the circles in my head: my group, myself, my brothers, my mother, and my father.

Time to get up and usher my group members into the group room that all the therapists in the building share. I guess I didn't do too well with not thinking, but I feel rested—just shutting my eyes and lying down helps. I walk to the mirror and push my hair around. I put on fresh lipstick. Taking a moment to look more carefully in the mirror, I see a woman in her late fifties with short, curly, black-and-gray hair and small brown eyes. A round, baby face stares back at me. She smiles and says, "Good luck."

A Letter to My Six-Year-Old Self

1947

4

At six years old, you are one sad little girl. It's too bad, but your parents didn't like the humidity in Florida. The doctors had told them that they should move to a warm place for your recovery. Now they think California might be a better place to live. So you move back to New York—to that small, dark house—and your dad leaves for California to scout it out. I know, dear child, that when he leaves, the light goes out of your life. You have been such a trooper, but this separation breaks your heart.

Your mother is a rock, and you and your brother never question her constant presence; you take her for granted. Mothers are for security, but they're boring company. Fathers add excitement. They know the ways of the world. They can throw you up in the air and catch you and introduce you to new ideas and adventures. Your dad has grand ideas about socialism. He pickets for the labor movement. You've seen the picture of him where he's holding up a sign, visible in a crowd of people. He also dances in vaudeville. He can leap up and touch his toes in the air. Most of the time, he's grumpy, tired after working—but occasionally, wonderful colored lights shine through. Life without him is a life without color and fun. The most fun is when he does tricks with you. When he has a day off, you and Arnold come to his bed, and he holds you both up on his feet—one foot for each of you. When he is up and out of bed, you bend over and put your hands between your legs. He grabs your hands and flips you up in the air. Every night he gives you a piggyback ride to bed, tucks you in, gives you a big kiss on the forehead, and says, "Pleasant dreams." He promises that someday he is going to take you to the theater to see the dancers from Russia. You can't pronounce "Moiseyev" or "Bolshoi," but you know they are the greatest ballet companies in the world.

Perhaps you sense that your parents are not getting along and that your dad is thinking of breaking up your family forever. Who knows? But you and Arnold miss a lot of school because you are sick all the time; there was one month when your mother could not even leave the house. The only thing you will remember about this school year is the dark red brick wall of the school on a dark, winter day. It is hard to imagine your mother (with her beautiful smile and easy laugh) truly unhappy. You lose your appetite and get very skinny.

My Brother Arnold's First Letter

1948

5

Dear Cousin Enid in New York,

    I am in California.

    I hate girls but I like you.

    I love Uncle Paul because he pulled my sled up the hill in the snow.

    Arnold

    (six years old)

Wanting
and Fearing

*Current Group
Therapy Meeting*

The room is large and square. It is an excellent room for group therapy: large windows to let in the light; chairs that are not too hard or too soft, with armrests on them, arranged in a perfect circle; a coffee table with a box of Kleenex on it; a tall fichus plant; framed prints on the walls.

The members are following me to the group room. Linda and Cheryl follow close behind me. They are giggling and chatting and sit together. Hugo, David, and Robert follow. Soon the women have men on both sides of them. David sits across from them, watching. Cheryl looks bright and beautiful. Her black hair hangs down her back. She is an accountant at a well-known firm and comes to the group from work. She uncrosses her legs, takes off her suit jacket with a stretching, seductive move, and hangs it on the back of her chair.

Harry comes in quietly and sits next to David.

The cheerful chatter ends abruptly as people take their seats and it becomes clear that the therapy meeting is beginning. Members are silent, tense, and uncomfortable.

David tries to make light conversation. His attempt falls flat. Everyone's eyes roll as he talks, but Cheryl responds in a friendly fashion. Despite his effort to groom himself nicely—a suit and tie, hair carefully cut—members do not find him appealing. He was responding well to a weight-control program when he joined the group, but then he quit. He talks in a monotone. He always seems to be on a different wavelength from the others; he wants to learn their language but keeps failing. He wants to please and earn some points in the group, but no matter what he does, he can't get recognition. The others try to like him but can't.

Hugo saves the day. Everyone looks at him with eager anticipation. He is shy and usually doesn't talk much, but when he does, he says fascinating things in interesting ways. He is a big man, with a muscular body and—when he lifts his head up—a handsome face. He can't hide a winning smile, even though he tries. He usually sits doubled over as though he is in severe pain or in deep thought, like Rodin's sculpture *The Thinker*. When he moves, it's in slow motion, staying doubled over to guard his pain. Right now his face has a deadpan appearance, and his voice is teasing: "I think we missed a big opportunity last week. It was Halloween, and we could have worn costumes."

Linda starts to giggle, and Cheryl and Robert smile delightedly. Linda blurts out: "So what was going to be your costume? I'm just sitting here bubbling over with curiosity."

She continues to grin, surprising herself, since she's usually fearful of people. She is sitting between Cheryl and Hugo, wearing her usual farmer's work clothes—jeans and a plaid flannel shirt hanging out. She crosses her legs at the ankles, her feet shod in work boots. It's hard to see her face, with her brown hair falling over it. She usually looks down at her lap, but today she is ready for some fun and continues: "Do we have to wait until next Halloween to find out what your fantasy is?"

Hugo continues to tease. "I didn't have a costume. I was just musing."

I turn to Hugo. All eyes are on me. I speak quietly and choose my words carefully. "Are you sure you didn't have a fantasy?"

Hugo answers, faltering. "Well, my fantasy, really? I guess, I would create a video game."

Robert is puzzled. "A what?"

Hugo answers again, "You know, a computer game?"

"W-e-e-e-ll," responds Linda in a playful way.

Hugo continues, and people are beginning to sense that he's serious. "Strangers would join me in creating a fantasy."

Hugo realizes that he has everyone's attention. People are watching him; they are grinning, friendly, and interested. Linda asks, "So what would you do?"

"I would be a perpetual teenager and a graphic designer, like Walt Disney."

Linda squeals, "Oh, I'm starting to get it!" Cheryl laughs.

Hugo shifts his weighty body, getting ready for more attention. "I would dress up in different costumes, depending on my mood. I would draw a fantasy, and strangers could join me and alter it. One moment we would be in an underground cave and the next, in a galaxy." Hugo uses his hands as though he is drawing the picture for the group. Everyone seems to be hanging on his every word; he has them mesmerized.

Hugo is animated. "We could have a computer club where anyone could add ideas for an imaginary, weird utopia. There would be no boundaries to the creativity. One person would be making a waterfall, and another would turn it into a falling star. Pure creativity. No thinking allowed."

Hugo turns to me, remembering that it was I who asked him the question. "I don't know; it's the first thing that popped into my mind. I'm thinking: if I wanted to be a fantasy character, who would I be? A perpetual teenager who creates a fantasy universe." His voice starts to drift off as he dreams of a fairyland.

Linda starts to look at her lap, her curly hair falling over her face, as she drifts off into her own dreamland. Cheryl eggs Hugo on with her steady, delighted stare and her giggles over his images. The other men look on.

Hugo continues, saying his words very slowly. "All the creatures would get along with one another. There would be no war and no conflict."

Suddenly everyone looks serious, and there is a long silence.

Robert can't stand the silent rumination and breaks it, trying to get the group to return to its former joviality. "Thought about that all week, huh?" he says teasingly.

"No, I didn't," Hugo says defensively. "Actually, by the time I got down the hallway last week . . . " The group's laughter drowns him out.

Another silence. People are serious again. They know why they're in the group. They can't escape thinking about it for too long. Hugo started all this fantasy "stuff," and now he's trying to make a bridge to reality. Maybe they can take something from dreamland to make real life more palatable. As it is now, they are stuck and looking for a key to a satisfying life.

Hugo speaks. "I think it would be the greatest thing in the world if we could all lock up the creative process within us and then let it go." He pauses. "We'd be spontaneous."

Linda lifts her head. "I don't think I could stand a steady diet of constantly being spontaneous." She laughs self-consciously.

Hugo is astonished, "Really?" He is so tortured—trying to figure out the meaning of it all—that he can't imagine there could be a different kind of torture at the other extreme: spontaneously letting go without thought.

Linda has been in the group for over a year, but only now does she reveal to the group that she is a painter. She felt too much pressure from her parents when she was young and had a negative reaction to their high expectations and control. It was a relief when she found farming as a career after college. She could be artistic and deal with the creative process on her own terms. Her artistry often comes through in her words. She has no idea that she possesses a clarity of thought that most would envy.

Linda answers Hugo. "No. I've gone through long periods of painting with no other stimulation. I get physically very tired. I go to the Adirondacks for a week at a time. As soon as it gets light enough to see what I'm doing, I start painting."

Tim enters and slips into a chair closest to the door next to Robert.

Linda ignores the interruption and continues talking to Hugo. "Paint until it gets late in the afternoon, until the light is just too dim to do any more painting. And, yeah, I lose track of everything—time and space. When I finish, I'm tired. I fall asleep immediately."

"Yeah, but doesn't it feel great?" Hugo asks. Linda is describing his dream.

"Yeah, except by the end of the six days, I always have the sense that I concentrated entirely on one thing to the exclusion of everything else. There are still all the things that are going on in the real world and in the rest of my life." What I believe she means is that she needs people. More specifically, she needs to love and be loved.

Elizabeth comes in quietly and takes the last empty seat.

Hugo asks hesitantly, sensing that he is about to lose the stage: "Yeah, but what if you really had a passion for it? If you felt everything else was extraneous?" He is persistent, but Linda has already shattered his dream; he knows he is in the group because he also needs connection with real people.

The group has to move on, but everyone politely listens as Hugo and Linda prolong their conversation, giving the others a chance to catch their breath before tackling the hard issues. The conflict has now been resolved for the group. Linda is right. They need to loosen up and be less fearful and more spontaneous—but they shouldn't go off to never-never land. There is an important place for imagination and fantasy, but it needs to be combined with reality testing. They are in the group to learn to cope better with real, present-day life.

I look around the circle, saying little but meeting each person's eyes. The circle is complete; everyone in the group is here. Its members vary in age, size, shape, and ethnic background. The oldest is Robert at forty-seven, and the youngest is Elizabeth at twenty-nine.

Leading this therapy group is the highlight of my work week. I am attached to the members, seeing them every week for an hour and a half and watching them build relationships with one another. Tailgating on Hugo's fantasy, I muse that this is the creative process I love to observe. I provide the material (the people and the structure), and then I watch the magic of relationship occur.

All eyes are on me. They wonder what will come out of my mouth today. I usually make comments that seem "off the wall" at first but after a while make sense. To the group I appear majestic and powerful. They look at me as though I am their last hope. Trust in me is what is going to lead them out of the mire in which they find themselves. They believe that if they only listen carefully and are patient, I will show them the way. No one notices the deep lines in my forehead from frequent headaches. When I lead this group, a calm comes over me; I step into the role of a guide and soothe myself in the process.

I focus on the conflict that I feel is the most prominent at the moment. I don't realize that I am using my hands to accompany my words. Again, I speak carefully. "You seem to wish to be spontaneous and creative in your personal lives and in here as well. How are you doing with that today?"

Linda starts to put her head down in her lap but then looks up as Hugo quickly responds. "Actually, sometimes I feel like I'm too involved with the group. I mean, I am too involved in talking."

"What do you mean?" I ask, knowing that talking is a necessary step to making connections with others.

"Well, I feel that not everybody gets the same amount of time to talk." Hugo is reluctant and vague.

"Do you feel you talk too much?"

"Sometimes." He pauses.

"Do you feel that your talking takes time away from other people?"

"No, I'm not sure I feel exactly like that."

"What about with the group getting larger now that Harry has just joined the group? That means each person has less time to talk. Does anyone have a reaction to that?" I am hinting at competition, which I know is ever present and can be challenging.

Harry squirms a bit, since he is the new member. This is only his third session. There is a long pause that seems to go on forever.

Linda finally says, "Time, as far as I'm concerned, doesn't seem to be much of an issue, because when I'm willing to say something, I say something. There's always time to speak." This response doesn't help Hugo with his basic dilemma. How can so many people compete for time and have the outcome be truly fair to everyone? Someone is going to get cheated, and he does not want to be the one doing the cheating. If he doesn't watch himself, he could be abusing people right and left. He's never hurt anyone, but who knows what he might do if he doesn't watch himself every minute. Maybe he'll be violent—as in his dreams—or maybe he'll get so involved with others that he'll lose any sense of himself and forget who he is.

Hugo begins apologizing to the group for going off on intellectual tangents and not using his talking time in the group productively. He is self-effacing and embarrassed by his own behavior. What I asked resonates with him. Now that there's an "additional mouth to feed," he has to be especially careful how he uses his time.

"Sometimes a good way to use the group is to check out whether other people see you the way you see yourself," I suggest. The more I encourage Hugo, the more he squirms in his seat, moving from one side of the seat to the other.

Hugo nods.

"If you want feedback, you might as well ask for it. That is a good way to use the group," I repeat.

"Well, how do you respond to that?" Hugo finally asks the group.

Linda responds immediately. She has a friendly smile. "No way do you talk too much." She's laughing in her quiet way but at the same time reassuring him that not only is he acceptable—but they all might be. Perhaps they don't have to worry so much about being dangerous or, at the other extreme, losing their essence in a relationship.

I persist. "But are people in here generally open, spontaneous, and creative in the way you relate to one another, or are you uptight and only relating from your intellect?"

Everyone looks thoughtful. Linda finally admits sadly, "I think our spontaneity level is the lowest. I can't think of anything else to say."

Robert straightens in his chair and gives himself a push. If Linda is dropping the ball, somehow he has to pick it up. This group has got to move on and get someplace! He talks slowly, carefully, tentatively. It is so hard to approach these people in an honest way, but he must have courage and try if he's going to move past his fears and get better. "I just have the feeling that there are people in here that have a lot on their minds. They want to say something, but they don't know when to say it. Or maybe they're wondering if it's the right thing to say or how to say it." He takes a step in the direction he wants to go. He is surprised at how vague he sounds.

I ask, "Does that include you?"

Hugo leans forward and changes his position in anticipation of what is to come. Maybe Robert can do what Hugo cannot do yet.

Robert blushes and says that he's "damned afraid. Yeah."

Linda laughs in a friendly way and encourages him. "So say it."

The men on his right give him reassuring nods, and Harry quickly injects, "Go ahead" with a nervous laugh. Elizabeth shifts in her chair. It feels like the hardest thing Robert has ever done in his life, but with determination he begins to speak.

Lecture for Beginning Group Therapists

I am preparing another lecture on group therapy, this time for beginning group therapists I want to convey my passion for this type of therapy because I truly believe it's the best form of treatment, even though it's probably the hardest. I need to go over what I've written thus far:

> The therapy group is a microcosm of our world. If you look at it closely, you can see it all. The characters of the group are important, but what they create together is more important. If we look at the products of their spontaneous interaction, we can find the essence of all human activity.
>
> Whether we look at the group-as-a-whole (the group process that is greater than the sum of its parts); each character, with his or her own individual history; the group leader, with characters in his or her own history; the staff of the clinic where the group is held; or society as a whole, the theme of opposites will resonate. We are all variations on the same

theme. We go through life, each one of us a living system, composed of mini-systems, interacting with other systems—circles within circles, all connected, all influencing, all resonating.

Therapy groups are usually made up of six to eight members, with one or two leaders. People come for treatment when they are in emotional pain or know that they are not making the most of their lives. Almost all emotional conflicts affect our interpersonal relationships. Thus as people spontaneously interact with one another, they get stuck at certain points. In group therapy the blockage becomes clear; by relating to one another, members see the interpersonal changes they need to make. These process of change involves dealing with someone in the group in a new way. The therapy group becomes a laboratory where people practice and experiment. For this reason friendships between members outside the therapy meeting are discouraged. If such alliances form, members might not take the necessary risks within the group.

Group therapy is a much less protected form of therapy than individual therapy—and as a result, it is more effective. The leader has less control in group therapy. She has even put together the specific members of the group to provide diversity, surprise, tension, and conflict. The leader does not want the group to be a social experience devoid of frustration. Life is difficult, and members are using the group to prepare to cope with the toughest of circumstances. The therapist cannot predict what will happen in the group—a complex set of factors converge and ignite. The leader learns to move with, understand, and interpret the life forces that emerge at any given moment.

Group therapy can be quite joyous, but it can also be terrifying. There are moments when people from divergent backgrounds "hold hands"; time stands still and the group experiences a moment of peace and happiness. Someone says, "So this is what love is." There are other times when you may see the worst part of yourself reflected in another. There is no escape. You have to live with that person ninety minutes a week. At times your nightmarish experiences with family and peers are reenacted in the group. If you run away, you will never take the steps needed to change the historical neural pathways (patterns) in your brain. These are the most crucial times to tough it out and find a new way of coping. This is the road map to changing dysfunctional patterns.

When members join the group, the leader tells them that the way to work in the group is to check in with themselves and try to figure out what they are feeling at any given moment during the meeting. Once they know what they are feeling, they are supposed to try to let others know. Feelings are the most reliable path to one's inner life. They are the vehicle for getting to know oneself and others.

According to Ariadne Beck and Peter Dugo, as a group develops four implicit leaders emerge: the Task Leader, the Emotional Leader, the Defiant Leader, and the Scapegoat Leader. Why are these people called "leaders"? Because each of them is leading the group in an effort to resolve a certain conflict that everyone in the group is feeling. As they take on their roles they challenge the group to respond to them. In this way they model the conflict.

Here is where I will give an example of process from my group.

The Task Leader is the group therapist. She takes care of the organizational and structural functions needed to further the task and thus models the conflict around power and control. How much power should each person retain, and how much should be given over to the leader and other members? The group members have to give up some individual power to empower the group. They have to give up some of their *I* to become a *we*. A good therapist will take power when needed but never leave members powerless.

The Emotional Leader is the group member who most clearly models the conflict of how close a person should get to others. How involved can members get with the other people in the group without losing a sense of self and an awareness of their own needs? The Emotional Leader is well liked. This leader gets involved with the therapeutic process, is motivated to get better, cares deeply about the other group members, but still seems to hold his or her own as an individual. In my group Robert and Cheryl jointly assume this role. By watching them, members see that it's possible to be intimate yet still thrive.

The Defiant Leader models the opposite behavior. This leader is the most distant from the group and the least involved. How much independence, aloofness, and disregard for group rules can a member get away with? The person who emerges as the Defiant Leader wants to preserve as much autonomy and distance as possible and still stay connected to the group. Can the Defiant Leader come late? Miss every few sessions? Avoid thinking of group members during the week? How much detachment and avoidance of intimacy can the group tolerate? Elizabeth takes on this role in my group.

The Scapegoat Leader helps the other group members deal with their conflict about aggression and submission. This leader is attached to the group, takes abuse, and allows members to project all their bad feelings onto him or her. The others see the Scapegoat Leader as obnoxious in a way they find disturbing, compelling them to react. This person becomes the focus of their attention. Because the Scapegoat Leader never misses a session and never arrives late, members constantly have to deal with this person's insistent presence. As members become aggressive and confrontational, the Scapegoat Leader defends himself or herself against their attacks. In the process members gain increasing clarity as to what they deem appropriate behavior within the group. While sternly educating the Scapegoat Leader, they also set standards for themselves. David is the Scapegoat Leader in my group.

These leaders have varying degrees of importance depending upon the stage of the group. Most groups go through three basic stages as they are forming and dealing sequentially with three sets of opposites: Trust-Mistrust, Power and Control–Submission, and Intimacy-Distance. At the beginning of group formation, people deal with trust issues. The members ask themselves: Can I trust these people? Will I be hurt? Will others accept me? Can I belong? Once members have answered these questions to their satisfaction, they go on to the second phase—dealing with issues of power and control. This phase is painful, chaotic, and threatening as people jockey for power positions. Hostility comes out, and people become rivals. If the group survives this clamor, its members go on to the third phase—intimacy. At this point people know they trust one another, and each person, including the Scapegoat Leader, has come to accept the degree of status, power, and control he or she has achieved. Members can now begin to reveal themselves and invest in the group. The group suddenly feels like a family. Sometimes this family can feel better than one's original family; at other times, it can feel as if it is recreating the worst of early family life. Group membership becomes a powerful, absorbing, intense experience; it often feels like the single most important activity in a member's life.

I believe that the group I'm describing in this book is in the intimacy phase, but it does regularly cycle through former conflicts of trust, power, and control. This cycling occurs in some form at the beginning of most meetings. One factor that leads me to believe that that this group is in the intimacy phase is that there is a coming together of David, the Scapegoat Leader, and Cheryl and Robert, the Emotional Leaders. Their bond forces everyone else to own some of the feelings they have projected onto the Scapegoat Leader and for the Scapegoat Leader to take some responsibility for the tough position in which he has placed himself. He begins to look at whether he is repeating a pattern of self-destructive behavior that originated in childhood. The Defiant Leader, Elizabeth, has also fulfilled the group's requirements and is enabling members to deal with their fears of intimacy. The Emotional Leaders continue to lead the way in courageously opening up difficult issues to examination.

The first example I shared of the group process is typical of beginning groups. It could be called "dipping a toe in the water." Group members dip, run away, and then come back and dip again if the water isn't too cold. The group arrives at a consensus as to what is fair control (use of time) in the group, but it's a fragile consensus, and the group struggles with the question off and on. No one wants to monopolize; if one person dominates, the structure and life of the group are in trouble. Later, members will begin to share their secrets. It is important that this kind of sharing not be confused with intimacy. True intimacy includes being able to say how you feel to another person *at the moment you are feeling it.* For example, "You are making me angry *right now*" or "I feel such love for you *right now.*"

As we follow the group members, we get a sense of how hard it is for them to let down their guard, to trust, to share power, and to be intimate. The thunder of hurt and death echoes from all the circles in the group members' ears. Psychologist

Harry Guntrip describes two forms of hurt and death: You can be physically killed by the violence of another person or yourself, or you can get so close to another that you lose your boundaries and feel as though you are being smothered to death or swallowed up. The latter case is *psychic* death. You need your own personal identity to survive psychically; what makes growth challenging is that you need people, too.

Whether we look at the individual in the context of the family, the therapy group, or larger constellations (society), we see a struggle between powerful forces, positive and negative. How this conflict is resolved—one way or the other, for better or worse—results in life or death, joy or misery.

Robert: A Bad Boy

Group Therapy Member

8

Robert was a very bad boy. He lied. Lost in a middle child position between a brother who was autistic and a sister who was a star, he learned early that negative attention was all he could get from his father. His mother would only dote on him when he was sick. Robert managed to get rheumatic fever when he was fifteen and get hit by a car when he was seventeen, so he got a fair dose of maternal affection. How to get what he needed from his father became a lifelong obsession. He hated his father but also wanted him. His father was everything he did not want to be—yet Robert felt as if he was just like him.

Robert and his family lived on a farm in Iowa, and his parents worked hard. Their ill son was always seeing doctors; it was a big strain. Soon after Robert was born, his parents sent him to stay with his grandparents for a few weeks because his mother had to care for his autistic brother. Because Robert's dad worked two jobs, he was rarely home—and when he was there, he was tired and irritable. He resorted to rules and rigidity. Little boys identify with their fathers; thus his father's rigidity became a training ground for Robert to make power struggles a way of life. Whatever his father said he wanted, Robert would do the opposite. He learned to lie without hesitation. Of course, he always got caught and enjoyed his father's intense rage. It was more important to have negative attention than be self-protective. He would do stupid things to hurt himself, and his father's view of him as a "fuck-up" would be validated. In this way his father remained powerful to him, giving him a sense of security. He rode his bicycle at night against his father's orders and got hit by a car. He accidently burned part of the house down when he was playing with matches. This time he was terrified and hid out at his grandmother's for three weeks so that his father wouldn't kill him.

At the same time, Robert had an opposite wish to prove to his father that he was not the good-for-nothing his dad believed him to be. He felt that he had to go to college and succeed but at something his father might not be crazy about. He succeeded and ultimately became a trainer of new staff at a prominent real estate firm, but his father wanted him to be a scholar. He married a woman he loved. Nevertheless, Robert remained an angry, rigid man. He was afraid that his anger would get out of control and that he would destroy the people around him. He was mortified at how disparaging he was toward new staff members when they had trouble grasping a concept.

Robert was afraid of his loving feelings because they were foreign to him; it was easier to suppress them. He never saw his parents being affectionate with each other or expressing good feelings. His grandfather had been a Nazi and was never loving to his wife or children. When holiday time came and there were office parties, Robert called in sick. He never socialized with anyone from work.

Robert allowed himself to fall in love with a young woman with ALS—a disease he knew was fatal. He was completely devoted to her. They were married for one year when she started to get sick and the numerous hospitalizations began. One day he got the call that he was dreading. "You need to come to the hospital right now; we believe these are her last hours." He procrastinated, finding one thing or another to delay him. When he arrived at the hospital, it was too late. His opportunity to say good-bye was lost forever.

Two years later he blindly chose a second wife. They created a nightmare together. She would attack him irrationally. He would become paralyzed with fear and withdraw. This distancing enraged her even more. He would then become controlling and lash back with whatever sadistic verbiage came to mind. It became worse after they had a child. One day he was changing his daughter's diaper when his wife yelled that she knew he watched child porn. He ignored her.

After the divorce, Robert and his ex-wife settled into a pattern of co-parenting. Robert saw his daughter during vacations. He adored her, as he had his first wife. Yet he was too afraid of his "shadow" side to discipline her—so the more complex his feelings became, the more he indulged her. He spent most of his money on his daughter.

Trouble started when Robert included his girlfriend on weekends. His ex-wife formally accused him of watching child pornography, and the lawsuits began. Robert was thoroughly investigated by the courts. He was accused of watching child porn on a regular basis, even when his daughter was around. His nine-year-old daughter was forbidden to visit him; she also testified against him. The psychologist who interviewed the daughter said that the girl told a consistent and credible story.

All Robert's energy went to defending himself. Every penny he had or could get his hands on went for legal fees. He was in terrible debt. He defended himself for ten years. No case could justifiably be made against him. He passed the lie detector test. There was no proof—it was his wife's and daughter's words against his. The judge forbade him to see his daughter again.

Robert is motivated to gain insight and be less explosive. He has remarried, and his new wife has been loyal through the worst of times. This time, he wants his marriage to be a healthy one. Robert knows that he must work on his anger if he is to fulfill this wish.

When he comes to the group and tells his story, people are terrified at the danger of a bad relationship. It verifies everyone's worst fear. You fall in love, marry, use bad judgment, and your life is ruined. For ten years your ex-partner assaults you, takes your child away from you, and exhausts all your money so that you can't have a future, either. But when Robert looks at people's faces and sees that no one is convinced of his innocence, including the leader, his rage starts to mount. He wants to walk out and never come back.

I encourage him to articulate this rage, but I don't reassure him that I believe him. Instead, I say, "You are a stranger to us. How can we know that you're telling the truth?" Even though this comment makes sense, it does not quell his rage. Members tell him that they don't like it when he says, "My daughter is dead." His first lesson in frustration tolerance ensues, and he toughs it out. The more commitment he displays in staying in the room and saying how he feels, the more people start to respect and like him (even though they are still not convinced of his innocence). As he begins to feel their admiration for his courage, his self-confidence improves. He becomes a dedicated member of the group and thus part of a benevolent, constructive community. He can be angry, fearful, loving—all he needs to do is put words to these feelings, and he will keep his status.

He has remarried and feels that he is a new person with a new life ahead of him. We learn that his ex-wife is suing him again for a million dollars. The ex-wife is with her eleventh lawyer. Robert realizes that he now has supports that he did not have before. His insurance company says that his umbrella policy will cover his legal fees. He has his devoted wife and the group.

From My
Father's Book

1917

9

October 1917: Russia is in a revolution that we have long expected. Men go to war with enthusiasm and hysteria. In Moscow and St. Petersburg, the czarist regime is overthrown, and the palace is invaded by the masses. A new regime is established by Kerensky, only to be overthrown again by the Bolshevik government. The revolution in the heart of the nation rages for a long time, and different powers attempt to take over. Monarchists, democrats, socialists, and anarchists try to take over the capital. Some succeed, only to be overthrown again. Finally, the Bolsheviks and the Red Army gain control and establish the U.S.S.R. (Union of Soviet Socialist Republics), with Lenin and Trotsky at the head of the government.

Things are different in Ukraine, where we live. People are backward and ignorant. Communication is bad, and the Moscow government does not reach these parts for many months to come. Ex-officers and generals take advantage of this opportunity to establish their own government. They form little armies and come to the towns, villages, and hamlets—looting, stealing, killing, doing anything they please. Word spreads that in Proskurov, more than one thousand Jews were killed in a single day. "All right," is the reaction of the Cossack leader Semosenko when he hears the news. "It will do for today." This reign of terror is shut off from the rest of the world. Only those who witness the atrocities can attest that they truly occurred.

Fortunately, the city of Elisavetgrad is the last one hit by this terror because it is occupied by troops from different nations for short periods. During the World War, soldiers are transferred to various fronts through the railroad station in Elisavetgrad. German, Italian, Romanian, and Bulgarian troops stop for a month or more and bring some relief to the people. They give food and clothing in exchange for shelter, but in some cases they loot homes and take anything they want. A few are kind and give generously to the starving women and children.

I bring home some food and clothing that I get in exchange for cigarettes. My family is amazed to see such good woolen clothing, underwear, and boots. For the first time in a long while, they see clothing that is new. I also bring home hand grenades, gas masks, and steel helmets that I pick up in the streets. Mother and the neighbors are astonished; they never saw such things before.

The bandits from the outskirts of the other towns are now on their way to bring terror to our already-suffering city. The first to arrive is General Petlura, who is a tall, powerful tyrant. Like a madman, he enters the city with an army of half-crazed soldiers. Their lust for power and blood is beyond words. They immediately hang large billboards all over town reading, "Kill the Jews and Save the Country!" Many Christian Russians, who were brought up in ignorance—on superstition and prejudice—are waiting for this moment to take all they can get from the Jews. They are hungry and like beasts. All they need is a little instigation to send them on a rampage. Petlura gives them that stimulant; on his entrance to the city, our terror begins.

There is shooting, looting, and abuse beyond imagination. Children are attacked, women are raped, and the beards of all Jews are cut off and burned. The savages enter houses day and night, waking and dragging women out by the hair. The women are found on the streets in the morning, abused, cut, beaten, and in too many instances, dead.

Some Christians are kind to their Jewish neighbors. They put a cross on their door and stand watch there. When Petlura's soldiers come, they say that no one in their household is a Jew. When the soldiers leave, they call their Jewish friends from their hiding places and give them some food and clothing.

Our family is now hiding in a cold and dreary cellar—unsafe because sometimes the soldiers search the cellars also. We are huddled with some neighbors, praying and shivering, awaiting the same fate that has overcome our fellow townspeople. The older children squelch the cries of the babies by covering their mouths with their hands. The hysteria of old men and women is quieted with a sock on the jaw. Many are unconscious from lack of food, while others cough from colds, pneumonia, and tuberculosis. A few die, and many whisper that they are better off.

Suddenly we hear a noise as someone climbs in from a small opening. We see a uniform and think the end has come. We all start praying and crying but stop instantly when we see who it is. It's my brother Dmitri. He goes to our frail mother, whose eyes are now sunken. He gathers her in his arms and kisses her, saying, "I have joined the Red Army and am going to meet them in Kiev. You won't have to hide long; it will be over soon. Don't expect any mail because it is impossible to send news." With these words he departs. Mother starts to cry violently; the children beg her to stop. Mrs. Lubanka, witnessing all this, says, "He is better off. My two boys left yesterday, and is it not better than this hiding?" Mrs. Jacobson also cries that her sons are gone and that only God knows where they are. This gives slight relief to Mother, who now cuddles all her children around her, caressing each one fondly. She puts Sonia to her breast to keep her from crying.

We hear another noise, and this time it sounds like the real thing. We all gather in one corner and await our doom. "This is Mr. Karlenko," says a voice, and we all shudder, as he is the Jew who converted to Christianity. We all think he has given us away to gain favor with General Petlura. "My friends," he begins, "do not be afraid. I have come to take you to my house. I have a big cross on my door and a good place for you to stay. We keep my mother-in-law there, who is sick and out of her mind; they will never suspect you there." This makes us very happy. Some of the neighbors had lost respect for him when he converted, but we never did because we are broad-minded.

Hope and courage fill our hearts. We are cold and hungry, but the desire to live is strong. We pack our belongings and one by one enter the dark but warm cellar, where the sick and crazy old woman is kept. She is deaf and half-blind from old age and lies on a bed surrounded by all kinds of icons. She is more than one hundred years old, and it is rumored that she does not die because she is very religious.

The place is mysterious looking, with spiderwebs all over the concrete walls, but we are certain we will be safe; the old lady will frighten them away. The soldiers come often, but seeing the cross on the door, they leave. After a while Petlura and his henchmen start for the next town.

Admiral Kolchak enters the city, and after an all-night battle in the bitter cold, thousands are found dead, and the city lies in ruins. Kolchak is more anti-Semitic than Petlura and crueler to women and children. Most of the shops are empty and the homes shattered, but he finds enough to fulfill his cruel desires. He loves to attack women, and his soldiers share that lust with him.

After Petlura leaves, I start to sell cigarettes again. I look more like a Mongolian than a Jew, and I master all the test words that are used by these tyrants to differentiate a Jew from a Christian. I know I am risking my life to get some food for my family, who are still in hiding at the home of the kind Karlenkos. I have many stories to tell them when I come home.

I see the Kolchak army enter the rich Rosenfelds' home and break priceless vases, tear up all the paintings, loot the house, and upon leaving, set their beautiful home on fire. After drinking plenty of wine and eating good food, the soldiers begin their search for women. I see them enter a Jewish grocery store that is run by a widow who has three beautiful daughters. The girls are in hiding, but when they see their mother being molested by these men, they cannot bear it and come out to defend her. The soldiers are drunk, and when they see these young girls, they laugh like maniacs and attack and rape them. I witness all this and cannot believe my eyes. I try to do something to help them but realize that such actions would mean death—and my family needs me. Without me, my family would starve. This incident is so horrible that I cannot relate it to anyone; it makes me sick. I walk around in a daze and cannot eat for a few days.

The Bolshevik government in Moscow is the only one that can stop this reign of terror. They are on their way to destroy these bandits. Lenin and Trotsky are the leaders of these Bolsheviks and are worshipped as saviors by the victims of the terror.

I am dodging bullets in front of the theater as another battle rages. Kolchak is retreating, and Madame Marushka is coming. She is a woman of two hundred pounds and has an army of men and women. They are all armed with guns, hand grenades, and machine guns. She enters the city in a large limousine, yelling and shouting orders. She is followed by other cars and wagons filled with food and clothing that are taken from other towns. She is an anarchist and hates the Bolsheviks, so she starts her search for them. She rounds up fifteen young Communists in the outskirts of the city. She has them brought to Imperial Park, where the Royal Calvary once gave exhibitions. There they are hanged; she leaves them for the public to see. They are young boys ranging in age from seventeen to twenty-three, and it is a horrible sight. Many people in the crowd know them, but to try to do something would be fatal. They are left hanging there for three days. On the fourth day, the Bolsheviks enter the city with heavy artillery. After one week, Madame Marushka evacuates quickly.

It is an unforgettable day when the Red Army enters the city. Their guns are of all shapes and sizes, and their clothing is tattered and torn. They are disorganized as they march, carrying all sorts of posters with different slogans of the revolution. They look upon the capitalists and aristocrats as beasts and tyrants. The czar is pictured as a dog who is cut up and crawling with agony. They are shouting and singing. There are thousands of them. To their surprise, they find few people to greet them; many are still in their hiding places, afraid to leave.

After much persuasion, people are reassured and crawl out of their holes, their eyes burning from the light of day. They have been shut in for three months, and now that they are free to leave. Their poor souls are broken, their stomachs empty, and their hearts shattered from constant fear and worry. They come out into the streets one by one and walk slowly, with no energy to spare. Although they meet the Bolsheviks with little enthusiasm, the people are happy to be free. Their voices fail them when they try to cheer. Some frantic mothers begin hugging their small children, afraid they may get lost in the confusion. Other mothers look for their husbands and sons. Many are thrilled to find them safe, while others weep with sorrow when they cannot find them. The young boys and girls are excited, looking over the strange uniforms, asking for food, and stealing it when no one is looking. The entire city is filled with hysteria, joy, and sorrow.

Father runs to Bulba's shoe shop, where he has left his few belongings, while Mother searches for Dmitri. With tears rolling down her sunken face, she asks all the soldiers, "Have you seen my boy? Do you know my son Dmitri?" She finds Mrs. Lubanka embracing her own son, and she shouts to him, "Have you seen Dmitri?" He replies in a low, choking voice that he saw him in Kiev just as he was leaving for the front with his battalion. He looked like a general in his uniform. "Never mind that," replies Mother. "Where is he now? Where is he?"

"I don't know." he replies. "That's the last I saw of him." Mrs. Lubanka interrupts, asking her son all sorts of questions. My mother walks away, weeping like a child.

Mother then goes with her children to see what's left of our belongings. She enters the house, which is shattered with bullets. The back rooms were hardly touched, but the front entrance is demolished. She finds a few things and begins to fix them as best she can. The children help her put the house in order and clear away the debris in front of the house. The czar's portrait, which hung in the dining room, is torn to shreds; she can't help but think it's Dmitri's work. "He always wanted to do it," she murmurs, "and he finally did it. My poor boy."

My cigarette business is picking up now, and I am not afraid to be recognized as a Jew. I am happy because there is more to eat. I get high prices for my cigarettes, since they are scarce. After my stock sells, I spend the rest of the day talking to soldiers and asking them my many questions.

Father finds Bulba sitting near the stove. They are glad to see each other, and Bulba immediately tells him everything that occurred while Father was in hiding. The monsters entered his shop and took all the shoes away. They broke open Father's desk and took all his precious possessions. They saw the big clock on the wall and smashed it into pieces. Tears come to Father's eyes. He gets up to leave and says to Bulba, "I am hungry and weary, and I may never see you again. I can't bear to see my family suffer any longer. I never thought my life would end like this. I feel very weak, so I better be on my way. Thank you for all you have done." Shaking hands, they part, and he slowly walks away.

Father hasn't eaten anything substantial for twenty-four hours. He is used to the finest food, and his stomach is revolting against the crude black bread that I bring home daily. As he walks he looks pitiful. His aristocratic features are still present, and he tries to keep up his neat appearance despite his shabby clothes, but his eyes are sunken, his cheeks are hollow, and his beard hasn't been trimmed for months. His eyes have a faraway look as he thinks about his youth, his better days, and the dim future. Stumbling as he walks, praying occasionally, he finally reaches home.

Sex and STDs

10

Current Group Therapy
Meeting Continued

W HERE WE LEFT OFF: *Hugo described his fantasy computer game. Linda revealed that she is an artist and thinks that being lost in creativity isn't all positive. Dilemma: How to be less fearful and loosen up in the group and be more spontaneous but not go off to never-never land. With new member Harry, members now have to compete for time—but competition is dangerous. Robert has decided to jump in and expose himself.*

Robert is trying to get the words out. His perpetually red face is redder; it overpowers his closely cut red hair and blue eyes. He always looks neat, dressed in a suit and tie.

All eyes are on Robert; he can feel the coaxing. He begins slowly and painfully. "Well, it's a subject that I've avoided because I didn't want to talk about it. I'm running through a phase right now in my life that . . . " He pauses and starts to use his hands to help him. "Sexually, I'm just not all there. I'm turned off to some extent. I don't know if it's a combination of . . . " He sits back. "See, I work a lot, especially this time of year. Maybe I'm tired because I've lost twenty pounds in the last three months. Maybe the sex allegations against me have something to do with it. I don't know." He gathers his courage to continue. "I'm wondering if anyone else has gone through a phase like this in your life at any time . . . and what you did to snap out of it. I just don't have the desire. I withdraw. It's very hard on Sally—it's not fair to her. We talk about it all the time. I just, I don't know. I don't know what to do about it. I mean . . . so Sally and I talked about me bringing it up here."

Cheryl moves her hand to hold up her chin and has to turn slightly to rest her elbow on the other side of the chair. No one else moves as they listen to Robert.

"I developed herpes six years ago. The doctors feel it came from all the emotional stress that I've had for the last eleven years. There was a period of time this past year before I was served the most recent summons when I didn't have an outbreak of anything. I thought it was gone for good." He rubs his eye and puts a finger up by his mouth. "It's never gone. Within a week after I got the summons, I broke out. It only lasted a week, but then a week later, it came out again." He scratches his ear. "I know when it's going to come out because I get terrible backaches, and that's a typical symptom. I really withdraw. I feel filthy inside. Sally and I have learned to deal with it. That part we can handle, but I've never been turned off sexually before the way I have been these past few weeks. It really scares me."

Linda astonishes herself by responding immediately. If she had thought for a second, she would never have disclosed her feelings. Robert sits back and listens. "Well, I understand what you're saying because I'm in the same position right now. What's puzzling me is that I keep getting sick. I got one cold, which is no big deal. But then I caught another one about a month ago and was too busy to deal with it, pretending it wasn't even there. Now I'm stuffed with tetracycline. But I don't have any, you know, desire for men. I feel like it takes so much energy out of me. And when I get under a lot of stress, I break out with herpes, and my skin gets so painful to the touch that I don't want to, you know, I feel, not unclean in the sense of being a leper, but I feel so unattractive. My skin feels like sandpaper."

Linda starts to talk about pressures at work that are affecting her. A restlessness starts to ripple through the room. The first sign of it is that David starts slinking his heavy body in his chair. He puts his head back and drapes his arms on the back of his chair. He scratches his neck and then grabs his hands and starts to crack his knuckles where no one can see. Elizabeth coughs. Harry moves forward, then back in his chair.

Linda concludes, "Right now I'm sitting here itchy and tired. It's good that you can talk about your problems, Robert."

Robert starts to respond, but Linda wants to continue. Cheryl tilts her head and absentmindedly starts twirling strands of black hair around her finger. David caresses his head.

Linda continues: "The hard part is that it hurts my husband. He says, 'Well, is it something that I do? Is it something I'm doing that you don't like?' Fortunately, he doesn't sit there and try to pep talk me out of my feelings." Linda becomes excited and animated. "Those pep talks drive me crazy, like when someone says, 'Well, don't be depressed! Look at all the things you have going for you!' It's so insensitive. If I could help it, I wouldn't be this way! If there was something I could do, I'd do it!"

Harry is adjusting to the group, and he begins to participate in a familiar manner. He leans forward, focuses on Robert, and asks in his most saccharine, doctor style, "Is there something more that you're afraid of Robert, something more that's bothering you?"

Robert answers respectfully, acknowledging that Harry is a member of the group, "No, it's just not fair to Sally."

"Tell us more about it. Be more specific," Harry urges. He looks like a beautiful grown-up boy, with black hair, huge brown eyes with long eyelashes, and little hair on his face. He is small and a bit chubby, qualities that enhance his baby look. To everyone's surprise, we learn that he was once anorexic—skin and bones. Like David, he was used to being excluded, the kid others laughed at. Five years ago he started gaining weight. Harry feels a painful kinship with David and wants to protect him, even though it might alienate him from the others.

Robert starts tapping his fingers on his chair, "I know age must have something to do with it. I'll be forty-eight. Maybe that's bugging me too—I don't know. For some reason I was never a stud. That used to bother me. I was not a trophy hunter like the other guys I knew. I never felt sex was something to flaunt; it was something personal and something to save. I was like a virgin trying to save myself." His voice is serious; he speaks slowly, purposefully. "Of course, I had the drive and desire the other guys had, but I never wanted to climb in bed with somebody different every night. I don't know how I ever got herpes."

Linda takes a deep breath and quickly continues: "I got herpes when I was in graduate school. I was under an enormous amount of pressure. I thought I had a second degree sunburn. And then I had all these sores over me. I got it every six months for the two years I was at the school that I loathed. Soon as I left that school and started making changes in my life and got out of the mold that I'd been put in and started to do the things that felt right to me, I didn't get it again until the past few years. It's horrible though—my face, lips—you get this ache right under your skin and then you go, 'Oh, no!' And two days later, these things start appearing on your skin."

My Father's Drive to California

1947

imagine the thoughts that went through my father's head during his drive out to California to find our family a place to live after my parents decided to leave Florida.

As I drive out to California I like the feel of being a free man. It's hard to choose between my own needs and those of my family. I want to get divorced. I had such a good time in my twenties, before I met Gazelle, but it was such a brief time. I met Gazelle at night school. We were both working during the day and going to Manhattan's Washington Irving High School at night to get our high school diplomas. Why did she have to ask me, "How was the dance?" as we were walking down the school staircase? That one sentence sealed my fate. I like women, and I know women like me. I'm lucky that I'm very masculine. I have a handsome face and wavy black hair on my head and curly black hair all over my muscular body. I am a great ballroom dancer. I lead firmly, so that even the most untalented partner feels graceful. If a woman is hesitant, I say, "Just listen to the music, and it will tell you what to do."

Once I walked Gazelle home to her tenement in the Lower East Side. When I walked into that building, I never saw such poverty in my life. (Coming from a tiny house in a courtyard in Ukraine, that's saying something!) She said it was terrific now that they had plumbing and garbage collection. When she was young, there were piles of garbage under their window, and they'd have to walk up and down three flights of stairs to get water from the pump or to use the outhouse. There were two outhouses for ten families, and you had to time your use for when the line would be short. Now there is one toilet for every two floors. The place doesn't stink anymore.

Gazelle says that her family is cold, not warm like mine. Her parents are from Hungary; they speak Hungarian and Yiddish at home. Her older brother and sister are the stars of the family. Her mom was exhausted from raising children when she found herself pregnant with twins. The story goes that Gazelle took her brother's bottle in the crib. That pegged her. She became the black sheep of the family. It was an unhappy childhood. She always thought she was ugly, but I think she's prettier than her sister. It's hard to imagine her mother participating in the scapegoating. She was the family slave. At the end of a typical day, her mother would say, "I can't believe I'm so tired." Her kids would laugh and say, "Mom, you've been working for fifteen hours!" (At least they noticed!) When I met her mother, she was homely, heavy, and very good-natured. She and Gazelle seemed to enjoy each other.

It is nice being alone with my thoughts. Yes, this would be a good time to divorce. But what about my duty and responsibility? I really love the children with all my heart. Arnold is an anomaly: Even though Gazelle and I have black hair and brown eyes, Arnold has blond, luminescent ringlets. I couldn't bear to cut his hair. Finally, I had to because he looked like a girl. I put the cut ringlets in an envelope so that I could always look at them and touch them. Arnold has my eyes, but instead of beady, oriental brown eyes, his are deep blue. A woman will have to look hard to find them, but when she does, she will find a pool of deep blue reflected back at her. Arnold has a spread-out nose, unlike his parents' small, nicely shaped noses. He was born sickly—with a cold—so maybe his nose just stayed swollen. Before he was two, he had to have his tonsils out and then he got allergies. It's amazing that Arnold fought off the polio bug and Elaine did not.

Elaine: She has the most beautiful brown wavy hair. I will never let her cut her hair. I love to brush it and look at the way it shimmers in the sun.

They are not the most gorgeous children in the world, but their little bodies are works of art: one budding with masculinity and one delicate and curvy. My son will be everything I am not. Elaine has the sweetness and beauty of my mother and little sister. I remember being a kid and a big brother. Once when Sonia smiled and kissed me and I held her close to me, I realized how much I loved her.

I am now driving on the long freeways. I can imagine Elaine as a teenager. She will be as beautiful as my little sister. The boys will flock to her. I will need to protect her. I can imagine her going off to study one summer, having gotten a scholarship because she is smart and works hard.

Now I am singing "Let Me Call You Sweetheart." When I find a place to settle, I will record myself singing this song on a record and send it to Elaine and Arnold. It will make them happy.

How could I desert my wife or children? Gazelle might not be perfect, but she has always stood by me; her devotion is unflinching. I can picture her. She has wiry, curly black hair and is "zaftig." Along with everyone else, I love her smile. It is a broad smile, with the most beautiful teeth I have ever seen. She has a generous bosom and shows it off in a tasteful way. As I picture her head to toe, I come to her legs. On her legs are all the marks of suffering. They are covered with ugly varicose veins from standing and ironing handkerchiefs for nine years before we had children. I admire her fortitude and good nature. As long as she is appreciated, she is happy. I know the problems in the marriage are due to my difficult nature. I'm such a selfish bastard.

I am smiling again as I think about how Gazelle handles her rage when I pick on her. She will say, "You're going too far. If you continue, I'm going to scream." Then she will put both fists up in the air and let out a bloodcurdling scream. I can't help but think, "Boy, she is one person who will never have a nervous breakdown." Not like me. I keep things inside. When I hurt, I feel it so deep inside that I can't reach in and scoop it up. Gazelle is shallow because she lets all her feelings out instantly; I am deep because I carry around weights in my gut.

Gazelle is so honest and hardworking. I could never find as good a business partner. I can't help chuckling as I picture her waiting on customers in our luncheonette, always smiling; the busier it is, the more she likes it. She is a real good worker.

The plan for when the children are old enough to go to school is that Gazelle will work the busy lunch shift and then go home and clean, take care of the kids, and cook dinner. She makes me the exact meal that I request. No one can make my dinner the way she does. I cook all day, so when I come home, I don't want to go near the stove. I always have the exact same thing, except for the entrée. We may be poor, but we never skimp on food. We are health conscious and only eat fresh, healthy food. I allow no sweets in the house. I eat alone. Every night when I come home, my salad and rye bread are on the table; the salad has no dressing, and there is a flowered radish that has been cut and put in ice water to open up. No butter on the bread. Then corned beef and cabbage or lamb chops or veal cutlet or stuffed cabbage or breaded filet of sole. Fresh spinach is mixed with mashed potatoes. Gazelle does real well on the measly allowance I give her. She never complains. All she wants is a "thank you"—and yet, louse that I am, it is impossible for me to give her that.

When we were dating, I had a job spraying gold dust on fabric for pennies a day. For a while I coughed gold dust, shitted gold dust, and had gold dust snot. Gazelle had a job ironing handkerchiefs. She always loved me and helped me even though I had very little to give. Gazelle is the only person in this world I know I can trust.

A Letter to My
Seven-Year-Old Self

12

1948

At seven years old, you are at the airport in New York. You are going to California. Your dad rented a home in Culver City, in greater Los Angeles. Your aunts and uncles and cousins are with you, saying good-bye. No one in the family has traveled as far as California; it's very far away. They bring presents. I don't think you have ever gotten presents before. You get on the plane for your first airplane ride. You sit by the window with Arnold next to you, and you both cover yourselves with boxes of unopened presents. You look outside and see fluffy clouds. You think you are in heaven. The light in your life is back.

Your father is rocking you in a rocking chair in the small living room. Your mom is sitting across from him. He says, "Gazelle, she eats like a bird. She is so skinny. What are we going to do?"

You get to go to school! A real school! It's a bright room with real desks. You are in the second grade. The teacher is tall, slim, and attractive with long dark hair in a ponytail lying on her back. She gives you bright, white index cards and your own new box to put them in. She writes beautiful letters on the board, and you copy them on your cards over and over again. She comes around and looks and smiles in approval. You are happy. Everything is bright and shiny.

Linda: An Alien

Current Group
Therapy Member

13

No one in the group could quite appreciate what it took for Linda to dismiss her parents' expectations and pursue a career in farming. Her parents were frustrated academics. Both of them were descendants of freed slaves who would have given anything to have had an education. Her great-grandmother was the first person in her family to go to school to the eighth grade and learn sewing. Her grandparents were both teachers. Linda's parents knew they had a talented daughter and always expected her to achieve. The problem was that this expectation was the only message Linda got from them. Her father was an alcoholic, but he was good at concealing it. Her mother always smiled and said everything was fine when she was angry and unhappy. Her mother told Linda that whenever you talk to another person, you just listen to them and learn what kind of person they are, so you can protect yourself. One must always be in control, watching every step, or the results could be catastrophic. Family members were allowed to express only nice feelings. Since everyone in the family was walking around in a rage, the only solution was distance. They talked to one another in platitudes, exchanging the niceties that make it possible to live in the same house.

Linda retreated to her room. Aloneness became both a solace and a prison. She said she retreated to her room the way a dog uses a crate after being in a storm. But this storm was voiceless. She felt that her mind came from an alien and was put in her body. She often thought about wanting to return to the land of the angels where she came from. She felt as if she had been dropped in the middle of France and didn't know the language. She had never felt like a child. She didn't belong with her family or her peers. Sometimes she pulled her hair out; the *real* pain of it felt good.

At school she was frightened. She was taught not to have any feelings, and it was intolerable if she had one and people knew it. She couldn't go to the movies because once, while viewing a film, she had cried. To cry or be sad was forbidden. Her parents never cried and were never angry or sad.

Linda tried hard at school. She was mortified when a teacher reprimanded her for not telling her that she couldn't see the blackboard. She wanted to say, "But doesn't everyone see blurry like me?" The words wouldn't come out. It didn't help that she was never in one school for more than two years because her family kept moving.

When Linda was old enough, she began babysitting for her little brother. She was always afraid her parents wouldn't return and she'd have to take care of him forever. She was too consumed with worry about her current circumstances to dream of what she wanted.

Yet there were some adults who intrigued her. Since she couldn't ask them for anything, she'd try to be near them and wait to see if they would notice her. A few teachers and friends of her parents did just that and set her up with various projects that they supervised. These moments were the closest to happiness she'd ever known.

Linda joined the group because she had been getting bouts of depression two times a year for six years. She cried spontaneously. Needless to say, she found these outbursts very disturbing. When depressed, Linda felt as if she were in a maze, trying to get out. She described her work situation, where she was the only female farmer. Her male boss kept demeaning her; she couldn't figure out how to get his approval. When she finally escaped the maze (work and boss), she still felt deep despair. By this time her father had become a vegetable from alcoholism and her mother was still smiling—but Linda wasn't aware that these things might also be bothering her.

Coming to the group and trying to identify and express feelings was like learning a new language for Linda. Every time she started to talk about herself, she would blush. Finally, she said she saw the group as composed of wildcats, with me as the leader. Each cat's individuality was encouraged. I kept them from killing one another. (This description was very different from David's. For him the members of the group were all rowing together in a canoe, and I was at the rudder.)

Soon Linda felt free enough to cry at a funeral. When she felt depressed after a group meeting was cancelled, she couldn't believe me when I suggested that she might have missed us—and that she might have feelings and reactions to the events of the group and the people in it. More recently, she declared that all the strings attaching her to the wall were breaking; soon she would be free to be herself. She was scared.

A Letter to My Eight-Year-Old Self

14

1948

Y ou are eight years old, and you have finally gotten your wish—to have friends. You are sick of playing (really fighting) with Arnold all the time. Now you have a chance to engage in fantasy play with two girlfriends.

Other girls play school or dolls. I am stunned by your fantasy play. *How in the world did you come up with the idea of going through rubble after a town is decimated and trying to find personal items of value???* You don't realize it, of course, but you are acting out a psychoanalytic concept known as the generational unconscious. Your father never talked about his traumatic history. The only hint you might have gotten is the cardboard picture of his mother in the hall closet. The woman is dressed in a fur coat and hat and looks robust and proud. She has a slight smile on her face. Once you saw your father look at the picture for a second, and you might have seen a look of great longing on his face. Once when you were fighting with Arnold (a daily occurrence), you pushed Arnold into the closet and the picture tore. You knew you had done something terrible. Your father didn't say or do anything, but the look on his face is too painful to remember.

During the summer, your parents bought a house in Monterey Park, California, in a new, homogeneous suburb: white, Christian, working class. Everything is new, even the plants in people's yards and the elementary school. You and Arnold are excited about going to brand new Bella Vista Grammar School. You both walk over every day and peek through the window to watch the pretty teacher set up her classroom. She looks like Snow White. One day she sees you and invites you to come inside and watch. You sit quietly, in awe. Years later you thank her for this generosity, but she doesn't remember. School will always be your favorite place.

The Wonder
of Discovery

1949

15

I t's a new neighborhood with wide streets, sidewalks, simple white houses with large front lawns, and an alley that runs along the backyards. Our house is modestly furnished with the cheapest furniture available—no charm whatsoever. Arnold and I share a bedroom. The wallpaper is a dull blue with clowns on it. We lie in bed and pick our noses and put the snot on the wall next to our heads. No adult ever comments on this practice, so we think it's normal. Arnold still wets the bed at seven years old; no one makes a fuss over this, either. Our mom just puts a rubber sheet on his bed and changes the bedding matter-of-factly.

There is one room in the house that is beautiful—our parents' bedroom. I assume my mother used her waitress tips to buy a special bedroom set. It's made of sturdy blonde wood with squares interlaced together. It has a tropical look. One piece is a chest with drawers on the bottom and a cabinet on the top. In it is the most exotic thing I have ever seen—a flat box with a royal blue velvet-covered top. I touch it, feel the soft velvet, and open it. It is a manicure set. I have never seen her use it. It must have been one of the few presents my dad gave her a long time ago. My mother makes her bed perfectly. I can't figure out how she does it. The woven mustard bedspread she picked out suits the room perfectly. It is smooth all over—not a single crease. I keep trying to make my bed that way, and I never can. I contribute something wonderful to this room. I enter a talent contest at our local movie theater and get second prize for doing a tap dance that my father taught me—the time step. My prize is a set of two large lamps with painted ceramic Arabian figures. My parents love the lamps, which are simple and dramatic. My father makes up a certificate saying that this event was my debut on the stage.

Arnold and I argue about stupid things, hit each other, and lock our bodies together, wrestling. I can't wait to be friends with a girl. Abby lives two doors down, but there are no boys that close by. Arnold doesn't know what to do. Our parents work all day; he is bored and has no one to play with. I go to Abby's house to play, and he sits on the steps and waits for me to finish playing. I try to pretend that he isn't there on the steps, but I never succeed.

My mom likes to sew. When I was little, she made us matching mother-daughter dresses. When I desperately wanted to be a ballet dancer, she sewed me a tutu. We picked out light-blue satin and a string of braided pink cloth roses for the bodice and light-blue organdy for the tutu. She also made intricate clothes for my secondhand dolls. I wish they were new dolls, but I still love them. Now she makes matching dresses for me and Abby.

Finally, Arnold makes friends, and I am truly free to be with a girl. During the week Abby and I play all day, but we also fight. We pull each other's hair and stare at each other; when one pulls harder, the other one does too. Finally, one of her parents finds us and breaks us apart. Sometimes, Abby is nasty to her mother, and her mother washes her mouth out with soap. I wonder what that tastes like. I want to learn everything about Abby. We talk all the time. I even keep her company when she is on the toilet making a "duty." (I hate this word that my parents use. What do other people call it?)

Now that I have a friend, I can learn about another family. Abby is an only child. On weekends her parents teach us how to play cards. Later her father tells us interesting and funny stories from his tour in World War II. He is passionate, and I am fascinated. There is only one thing that really makes me jealous of Abby. Her father works in the produce department of a supermarket, and on Halloween he brings home pumpkins that he embellishes with vegetables as hair, ears, nose, and mouth. They are incredible.

In the morning Abby's mother makes bacon and saves some for me. I've never had it before, and I love it. Somehow my mother never serves bacon or avocado, which is also delicious. My father doesn't believe in religion, so even though we are Jewish, he eats pork chops. Maybe he thinks pork chops are healthy and bacon is not.

My food at home is always the same and boring. Everyone in my family eats separately. My mom eats while she cooks, tasting things. Food is put on my plate, and I have to eat it. I have to wait to drink my milk so I will not be too full to eat my dinner: usually lamb chops and spinach mixed with mashed potatoes. I know I have to eat because the one book my parents have in the house is *You Are What You Eat*. Arnold, on the other hand, loves my mother's food. Our parents joke that he eats as much as our dad. He is skinny too. It's a mystery—a puzzle. Once my father announces that for the first time, he is going to take us out to eat. He takes us to Clifton's Cafeteria in downtown L.A. It is magical—all that different and delicious food. Arnold is walking down the line with his tray and spills his peas. An old lady slips on them and falls. Dad says, "I'm not taking you to a restaurant again for five years." Five years later he takes us to a Chinese restaurant. Arnold looks at the menu and orders ham and eggs. "How can you go to a Chinese restaurant and order ham and eggs? That's it. I give up on taking you both to restaurants," says Dad.

The ice cream truck comes by. Children gather around to get their ice cream, and we stand there. Once in a while, an adult buys us one. Our father is against all sweets. There are two exceptions. One is when his sister sends him Barton's miniature chocolates from New York. He puts them on the top shelf of the closet, and a few times a year, he says, "Let's have a Barton's chocolate," and we each get one. Then he puts the box back on the top shelf of the closet. The other exception to sweets and restaurants is when he decides to have Arnold work at his restaurant. Arnold is the cashier at ten years old; he takes the money and makes change instantly. I watch the customers save their largest bills to give him. I am happy that Arnold gets this attention. When we are at Dad's restaurant, he lets us share a large oatmeal cookie from a big glass jar. He also lets us share a milkshake—but this is a problem because I like chocolate and Arnold likes vanilla. We decide to alternate each time we go.

Vanilla isn't so bad. In the restaurant my mother waits on customers. The truck drivers tease her, and she smiles and laughs a lot. I like to see her happy. My father says that truck drivers know the good restaurants, and he is the only cook he knows who will eat his own food. His chili is a favorite. My mother makes the potato salad and coleslaw. He says he went to the meat factory across the street, and after seeing how a hot dog is made, he would never eat one. The restaurant has beautiful lit-up pictures that Coca Cola and a beer company made of waterfalls and forests. The waterfalls actually move.

My mother makes a friend, and she is so happy. Her friend's husband is a furrier, and he gives me a real present: a box with scraps of fur. I have fur from a rabbit and even a lynx. My box is full of different shades of brown, black, white, and gold. Each one feels different. The lynx is my favorite because it's so soft. It feels good to stroke my face with it.

I'm supposed to go to the doctor for follow-up from polio. My mother, Arnold, and I go to the public hospital and wait six hours for my appointment. It is so boring, and then the doctor sees me and gives me exercises. We make this long excursion several times, and it's always the same. Finally, we agree that it's a stupid waste of time; I know what exercises I'm supposed to do. They don't do any good, anyway. Once we have to go to the hospital for Arnold, not me. He has an allergy where different parts of his face swell up. His lips are huge. He looks like a freak. He says to me, "If you tell anyone or bring a friend over, I'll kill you." I'm more frightened by how he looks than by his threat.

Tim: A Dropout

Group Therapy Member

16

I look at Tim. He is sitting across from Linda. Even though their skin color is different, they look to me like brother and sister. They sometimes dress alike—with torn jeans and flannel shirts. They are both average height and slender. They both wear the same expression on their face. Tim has a brown ponytail, streaked with grey, hanging down his back. He refers to his "pubic" beard, because unlike his pony tail, it is curly and reddish.

Tim's ancestors emigrated from Ireland in the late 1840s during the Potato Famine. Tim describes his parents as boring and staid. His father is also an alcoholic, and just as in Linda's family, no one acknowledges it. Tim's mother also smiles and says that all is well and good in the family. Like Linda, Tim was a terrified child who spent a great deal of time alone. He read. He was a very good boy and would do anything to please an adult—anything to avoid a look of disapproval from the teacher. When he found an adult he admired, he would stand nearby, hoping to be noticed but not saying a word. Since he was a smart and cute little boy, he often got a response. He lied out of desperation because it was better than getting a dirty look from his father. His father believed in the paddle, but Tim felt that his angry look hurt more. Tim describes his father as "a little guy in the US Army." The fact that Tim's family moved every year didn't make his childhood any easier. Tim felt that he was dressed inappropriately for every new school he went to. He was a constant target of ridicule.

Some of the family's moves were to other countries. Once they lived in Warsaw. His parents told him what a wonderful country Poland was, but he thought their Polish neighbors were mean. Years later he learned about the atrocities that had been committed in that very town. Hypocrisy is the banner Tim carries around to describe his parents. Leftist politics are a natural for him.

Even after he grew up, Tim continued to go through the motions of being a good boy. He went to a major Ivy League university to get a PhD in physics. Soon he realized that he was surrounded by the same hypocrisy he saw in his parents. He felt that his teachers' values "stank." They preached "peace on earth" but demonized all the Communist countries. He fulfilled all the requirements for the PhD in record time but then quit without graduating. He believed that there was no point in making goals for his life because he lived in such an insecure world. Logically, the only goal worth his energy was to change society. The threat of nuclear war seemed to make his worldly efforts a joke.

He took a job as a filing clerk for seven dollars an hour. He liked it because he didn't have to relate to people. Most of his energy went into political organizing. He helped plan demonstrations at nuclear power plants. He worked with real dedication on these projects, and his peers respected him. The work gave him a way to be with people without having to be intimate with them. He considered himself an observer of people. In fact, he couldn't imagine that there would be any value in sharing his feelings with people, even if he could figure out what his feelings were.

Tim came for help because he had temper outbursts, and they embarrassed him. He is a manager of a cooperative bakery and is impatient with the young employees. He can be testy over petty things. This behavior is incongruous with his values; he sees himself as the type of person he doesn't like. He says he looks at his life as though he were watching a washing machine in motion. Every time he blinks, he sees a new pattern—now blue jeans, now a green shirt. He can't keep up with it or sort it out by himself.

When Tim first came to the group, he was afraid the others would denigrate him, as his father had. He was nervous and frightened. It wasn't long before his temper flared in the group, just as it did outside the group. He thought I was a "passable leader," but I wasn't good enough for the group. I let people waste time during our meetings. I made good interpretations but not enough of them. At other times he felt judged by me. He had some trust in Robert, but Robert betrayed him by making a comment in a sarcastic tone when Robert mentioned that he'd gone to a ballet class. At least his father was direct and predictable in his put-downs, whereas Robert is indirect with his hostility and nice on the surface.

Curious Exploration

1950

I am in the fifth grade. I make more new friends, and that means more families to learn about. Angela is the most beautiful girl I have ever seen. She has soft blonde curls that blow in the wind, big green eyes with long black eyelashes, and a perfect nose. To my surprise, she is not conceited. She has a sweetness about her; I can tell that she is truly a good person. I go to her simple home, and I can feel a gentle kindness in the air. I realize that it emanates from her mother, who looks like a movie star (maybe Grace Kelly), even with no makeup and everyday clothes. They have a new baby, and Angela's mother kisses her bottom affectionately before giving her a bath. Angela and her mother both delight in their baby girl's beauty. The baby looks perfect and sweet, just like they are. I am surprised to meet the father, who works at a gas station and is not very friendly. I can't quite put it all together. My mother comes by to pick me up, and she and the movie star talk and laugh together. I am surprised that the movie star talks to my mother.

Ruthie's mother is from England. Their home looks like all the others on the outside, but when you go in, it's formal with furniture from an old country. The living room and dining room look like pictures in a magazine. Ruthie's mother has delicate, tiny features and a thin figure. She wears a dress with a belt and a full skirt with crinolines underneath. Her hair is perfect, with curls carefully placed on her head. She always wears lipstick. Her husband comes home, and he is ugly and looks a bit like a slob. I can't picture him in this house, but I guess he works and pays for all the fancy things I see around me. He mumbles a few words and doesn't eat with us. Ruthie's mom decides that she has to teach me how to eat properly. I am supposed to keep my mouth closed when I chew and talk only between bites. I know this already and do it because my father eats nicely. But now I also have to switch the fork from my left to my right hand when I eat—fork in one hand when I cut and in the other when I take the food from it. I am happy to learn these new things.

Rachel's father died, so she lives alone with her mother and sister. She is my very best friend and is everything that I ever dreamed a best friend could be. I share my whole heart and soul with her—and she, with me. I don't hold anything back. I am sure she will be my best friend until I die, but grown-ups tell me that that won't happen because I am only ten years old. This makes me mad, and I don't believe them. I am fascinated by Rachel's mother. On Sundays she listens to opera on the radio. Rachel doesn't like that music, but I do. Her mom looks the opposite of Angela's mother—actually, a bit homely—yet she got married and had children. How can that happen if you aren't pretty? Rachel's mother is smart; she talks fast and thinks fast. She is the one I would ask any question and trust that I would get a good answer. Finally, Rachel and I ask her about sex. "How does a man know where to put it in?" She says, "You know when you go into a drawer in the dark and you're trying to find something? You have to feel around until you find it, right?"

Rachel is smart too. When I run for a student body office, she is my campaign manager, and she writes and designs the most clever campaign posters. She writes enticing poems for the posters. I'm sure that's why I win. Rachel says that she doesn't want to go to college, and this drives her mother crazy. Her mom knows that I could never imagine not going to college, and she likes this about me. I can't understand why Rachel wouldn't want to go to college, either. I know she's smarter than I am.

My father says that Arnold and I are so lucky that we'll get to go to college. All we have to do is work to make money and study so that we'll get scholarships. I ask, "But will you help us pay for college?" He looks at me incredulously: "Are you kidding? Do you realize how lucky you are? I was fourteen and put in the second grade when I came to this country. I was so humiliated that I ran away to Manhattan as soon as I turned sixteen. I didn't have a penny, so I took any job I could get and then went to night school to get a high school diploma. I wanted to be a doctor, but it was impossible. *You* can be the doctors, if you want!" I say, "I'm a girl. I don't have to be a doctor. Arnold has to be the doctor." Every time we go to the beach, nine-year-old Arnold collects bags of soda bottles and gets five cents a bottle to start his college fund. My father is proud of him. He says that we have to work hard in order to have character.

Now that I have a group of friends, I see that they have birthday parties. My mother sees this too. When I ask for one, she says, "Sure, I can do that." My father thinks having birthday parties is stupid. He says, "I will make you two parties: one when you are sweet sixteen and one when you get married. I will do all the cooking. When you are sixteen, I will make you a party in my restaurant. I will cook a ham with pineapple on it. You can invite your friends and teachers. Everyone can get dressed up. Your mom will make a birthday cake." Mom smiles. "When you get married, your mom and I will cater it, even if you have one hundred people. We will make a ham, a turkey, chopped liver, potato salad, coleslaw. We will make the dishes look professional with decorations on the platters. I will even do my Russian dancing at your wedding."

My mother enjoys having fun, and she enjoys seeing me have fun. She says there is no point in cooking unless people like it; this is why she cooks something different for each of us. "I can cook anything you like, just tell me. If you can read, you can cook. The whole point is seeing a happy face and getting a thank you." Doing things for people is what makes Mom the happiest, but only if we say thank you. This is the only thing she wants from us. Arnold and I are happy to oblige, but my father, for some reason, cannot. His inability to say thank you, combined with not giving her a big enough allowance, causes daily fights. Mom is no match for my father. It's not a fair fight. Mom fights like a child and ends up screaming with frustration. Dad says in a calm voice, "Why do you yell? See how quiet and calm I speak. You are turning the kids against me. It is not good to yell in front of the kids." At the same time, he needles and instigates and says hurtful things. He sounds rational, but what he is saying is mean-spirited. Mom has no tools to understand or return his meanness, except to scream in frustration. I start to defend her, explaining that things cost money and that she shouldn't have to work at the restaurant. She should stay home with her children; we need her. We don't even know how much money we have. Are we rich or poor? Do we really need to scrimp, or is there money in the bank? Mom has a right to know. We would all understand and be willing to help if we were convinced that we were poor.

A Letter to My Ten-Year-Old Self

18

1950

You share a room with your brother. He has allergies, so you go to sleep being entertained by a multitude of patterns of his snoring.

You spend hours playing with friends on the front lawn. You do acrobatics, and Arnold wrestles. You like to watch him. He is good. He likes to watch you too. At night, you take turns looking under the bed for the bogeyman. It's very scary when it's your turn. Do you know why? It's your sexuality that's under the bed. You can't help being stimulated by each other's bodies. Sometimes you have a race to see who can get into pajamas the fastest. The idea is that you race so hard, you don't have time to look at each other. Other times you practice falling face down on your bed without bending your body. Not easy: try it. You'll end up sharing a room until you're fifteen years old.

Like son, like father. Your dad has a gorgeous body, all covered with black hair. Your friends call him "the gorilla." You're lucky—you have the perfect father for a preadolescent girl. He is physical with you. He has been throwing you up in the air and catching you since you came home from Boulevard Hospital, where you were born. He made everyone nervous, but you loved it, and so did he. You never had a doubt that he would catch you. As you get older he'll do tricks with you. This will eventually lead to your performing at Muscle Beach in Santa Monica, where muscle men will throw you from one end of the stage to the other. You will love every minute of it.

More about your dad: you are lucky because you will be very seductive with him and he won't show a trace of sexual interest. When you start to develop, you'll parade around him, bare breasted, trying to get his attention. He will only say, matter-of-factly, "Arnold, your sister is becoming a woman. You have to be careful when you fight with her." You're also lucky he isn't attracted to skinny women, as so many American men are, causing their daughters to have eating disorders. He thinks skinny women who drink coffee and smoke all day make good waitresses because they are nervous and wired and can wait on several tables at once.

The incest barrier in your household is like iron. It has to be, given the close quarters you all share. It's peculiar, but the only time you felt an actual sexual feeling was when you were seven years old in Culver City, and you and Arnold made friends with a little boy. You went behind the house and pulled your pants down together. That feeling of naughty excitement was a sexual one. It didn't matter that you saw Arnold naked all the time. Hiding where no one could see you changed everything.

Do you know what I think is the most intimate moment you've ever had with your father? It's not what you think. You provoked him to hit you. You pushed and pushed until he took his belt off, threatening to hit you with it. I think you found this sexy. Last week you actually physically attacked him, and he grabbed your hands to contain you. You fought with him so hard that your hands were bleeding. You believed that you really were his match! How absurd. Your father is an athlete and a muscle man. He allowed you to have a run for your money and to feel powerful. Arnold wasn't so lucky. Your father won the fight with him, and it made Arnold cry. I know you felt terrible for Arnold. You saw that he was heartbroken, and you will never forget his pain in defeat. You can't remember if you comforted him.

I understand that it's hard not to fight with Arnold. Every morning you say to yourself, "Don't fight with Arnold today," and every day you do. You feel like a bad person, being so mean, but you are probably copying your parents, who fight every day—about money. Your father is, in truth, a miser. He cannot part with money, and your mom needs money to buy food. He gives her an allowance, and she doesn't think it's enough. They both work like machines at their restaurant. Your dad is worried about not having enough money for now and the future. He gets up at five a.m., goes to work, comes home at six p.m., reads the paper, has dinner alone, and goes to bed. Every day the same. Your mom just wants to be loved and appreciated, but he cannot give that to her.

Your parents are unhappy and mean to each other. It's confusing because they love you and Arnold, and you know that they sacrifice everything for you so you can have food and a roof over your head. They never criticize you or Arnold; they just criticize each other. You have never seen them sick and staying home from work, and you have never seen them buy anything for themselves. They have no friends, belong to nothing, have no family around, have no religion, have no holidays, and never go out. They get no magazines in the mail except *USSR*. There is no music except a record of the Red Army, which they do not play. They are good parents, but they don't know how to create a good family. Of course it's confusing. There is so much love in your family, and it exists side by side with cruelty and deep unhappiness. I am *so* sorry for all of you. You are all good and are trying hard and you love one another, but it is not a happy home. You all deserve better. If only you could have family therapy, but in your world no such opportunity exists.

The older you get, the more you and Arnold are going to want to fix this family so that your parents can be happy. In high school Arnold will come home and study probabilities for blackjack, so he can make a fortune for his father and solve his problems. His room will be strewn with papers covered with numbers. Arnold will actually figure it out, but your dad will not give him any money to bet with. The rules for blackjack will change a few years later, and Arnold's system will no longer work. You will go to social work school, telling your mom that you want to figure out what's wrong with the family, so it can be fixed. Your mom will say, "Thank you, Elaine."

Movie Stars

1951

I know I use superlatives a lot, like *beautiful* and *horrible*, but I am writing the way I feel. I seem to be more intense than any of the other kids. I feel things in the extreme. When I have a crush on someone, it almost hurts. My first fantasy love is Shirley Temple—the grown-up Shirley Temple. My friends and I each pick a movie star to idealize—someone we want to be like. We pick a movie star who has a vague resemblance to us. Abby picks Piper Laurie because her nose is similar; Angela picks Mitzi Gaynor because of her high cheekbones; I guess I pick Shirley Temple because she has a kind of baby face. We pick movie stars because going to the movies is our only entertainment. We especially love musicals. The words to the songs in *Annie Get Your Gun* are so profound, like "Got no silver, got no gold, / What you've got can't be bought or sold" and "with the sun in the morning / And the moon in the evening / I-i-i-m a-a-l-r-i-i-ght!" I am going to remember them all my life, as a guide. The words in the musicals teach us what's most important in life. I hope I don't forget what I'm learning.

So we all love our favorite movie stars and read articles about them in movie magazines. But I go to the extreme. I not only buy every movie magazine I can find that has an article about Shirley Temple, but I memorize the articles and think about them all the time. I have a record album of *Bambi* that Shirley Temple narrates. I memorize the entire album, music, her voice, her narration, everything. This way, when I'm waiting for the bus, I can listen to the album in my head from beginning to end.

Hate, Anger, Despair

1951

20

Dear Diary,

Please let me pour my heart out to you. Right now I feel like I'm going to bust. I feel like every muscle in my body is going to collapse, that I can't stand another second longer of life. That's just how I feel this minute. The only reason I can explain this is that in the past hour, I have felt Hate, Anger, and Despair. I'm trying to be at peace with my family, but it's just no use. I finally told my brother that I hated him, and I meant it. Then he said, "We hate each other." It's just talk, I think.

Oh, God, take me out of this house!!! I wish I was eighteen, so I could move out. In my heart I imagine such a wonderful world—a world of love and no harsh words—where people don't go out of their way to hurt one another. I wish I was on an island with only my best friend.

We just can't stop fighting. I mean, I can't stop fighting. Every morning I say to myself, "Don't fight with Arnold today," and every day after school, I can't help fighting with him. My mother is at the restaurant, and we're alone. The house is a mess. I'm getting scared. Once I hit Arnold over the head with a skillet. Once I locked Arnold out of the house until dinnertime, when my mom came home. Arnold was enraged and shot arrows into the screen windows, hoping one would get completely through and kill me. This is why I need to get out of this house.

We're Going to Have a Baby

21

1952

Everything is different now. Arnold and I are going to have a baby. As soon as our mom told us, we were so excited that we started planning. We are going to be much better parents than our parents. We will protect our baby from our parents' fighting. If it's a boy, Arnold will teach him how to fight to protect himself, and I will read to him and give him love. A girl will sleep with me and a boy will sleep with Arnold. We vow with all our heart that we will love this baby with all our might and cross our hearts that we will be bound together for the benefit of this child as long as we live.

We finally see a father with a big smile on his face, proud of our mother. We are in bed. He appears in the doorway and says, "Your mother has given birth to a beautiful baby boy." This is the happiest moment of my life. I want to hold on to this image forever. The next day we all rush to the hospital. We are not allowed inside; our radiant mom comes to the window and holds up this precious baby boy. We name him Gary Michelle, and we already love him with all our heart.

Junior High

1952

I am old enough to go to Eastmont Junior High School in Montebello. I take the bus. It's totally different from my grammar school. It's kind of scary because of the *pachuca* girls. They have black hair in beehives; makeup with red lipstick; dark eyebrows and black moles on their cheeks; leather jackets and short, tight skirts; and oxford shoes with white bobby socks. I get the shivers when they pass me in the hallway. I never know if one of them will stop me, glare, and say, "Meet you after school." Every day at lunchtime, a group of boys form a circle, and two come out in the middle and fight with knives.

It is easier for me than for Arnold because I'm a girl. Arnold has to be tough enough to be respected by the gang members but liked enough by them that they leave him alone and don't expect him to join them in a gang war. He has to downplay his straight A's so that he won't be considered an alien "brain." Somehow he succeeds and begins speaking Mexican English.

About half of the kids are Mexican. No one has much money. Except for the *pachucas*, everyone is sweet and nice. There are no Jewish people here. The kids don't mind that I'm Jewish; they're just curious about me.

Crushes On Teachers

23

1953

I have enough change from babysitting to buy whatever I want for lunch. I choose the same thing every day. I can't believe how delicious it all tastes. I get cherry cobbler, a box of Cheez-Its, and a carton of milk. Now for the real treats. On the way to school, I join my friends for a Winchell's donut. Every day I try a different one. I finally settle on the long bars with thick maple or chocolate frosting. Then there is after school. We get flavored cokes: cherry, lemon, chocolate, or vanilla. I try them all.

Something mysterious is happening to me. The same thing is happening to a few other girls in the school. We see each other at lunch time, and we start laughing hysterically. It is hard to stop when the bell rings. We wipe the tears off our faces and try not to choke as we swallow to control ourselves.

I want to be popular. I want everyone to like me, and I want to like them. I want to walk down the school hall and smile at everyone I pass and have everyone smile back at me. I also want to be friends with them and learn about them—how they are like me and how they are different. I can listen to my friends talk forever. Angela and her friends make fun of me because I am naive and don't know about sex the way they do. I am definitely not in the "in" group. But Rachel isn't either. As long as I have Rachel, I feel lucky. Is it all right to want everything?

I get crushes on two teachers. I have no control over these crushes; they consume me. Neither of these crushes is sexual. I never think about sex or have sexual feelings when I think about these teachers. More than anything, I just want to be in their company and learn how to be like them.

First is my gym teacher: a chubby, muscular, round-faced woman with short, curly, dark hair. She's a jock—a bit masculine. She is the opposite of me. I'm not athletic in the least. I'm always the last one to be picked for a team. I used to want to be an actress and took drama. The teacher told me to play the part of a boy athlete. I couldn't do it no matter how hard I tried. That failure ended my acting career.

My other crush is on my music teacher. I wish I had musical talent so she would like me. Other people may not consider her beautiful, but I think she is. Her skin is creamy and looks soft. She is soft-spoken and looks like she would be wonderful to hug. She is the first Negro I've ever seen or met. I mean, I think she's Negro; none of us are positive. Her skin is as white as mine, but there's a rumor that she's Negro. She is also not married, which is most unusual. People say she lives far away from school and goes to an evangelical church called Four Square. I can hardly contain my curiosity; I wish she'd take me home with her. This is not as bizarre a thought as it may seem. From the time I started school, many of my teachers took me home with them or tried to teach me something special. The drama teacher took me to the Philharmonic in L.A. to usher with her. We saw Barbara Cook in *Silk Stockings*. I'll never forget it. I know going home with my music teacher will never happen. I will never get to know the mysterious world she lives in.

My Father Gives Me His Book

1953

had my first kiss with a boy at a "make-out" party. Wow! How can I describe this extraordinary experience to Rachel? We share everything; I wish she'd had her first kiss at the same time. I've got it: "Put your lower lip over your top lip. Now you know how it feels."

Hate, hate, hate—that sums up what it's like to be thirteen years old. I am consumed with hatred for my father. I am suffering. I cry on my bed every day. The minute my father comes home from work and opens our front door, I scream at him, tears running down my face, saying, "I thought you loved me! I thought you were my friend! I thought you trusted me! You have turned to stone! I don't even recognize you as the same person! Why can't you understand me? I can't believe this is happening! Suddenly I have a different father!" My mother, who never says anything deep, watches me cry and says, "Elaine, I think this has something to do with your father's past."

I have never had a boyfriend. No popular boy has liked me before. It's time for graduation, and I'll be moving to a new city. The popular student body president asks me to go to the graduation party! My father says, "No. I told you that you cannot go on a date until you are fifteen years old." I cannot believe it! This is the most important event of my life. Doesn't he understand what this means to me? All my friends' parents call my dad on the phone and beg him to let me go to the party. He says no to all of them: "She is not fifteen yet." I see that I do not have a normal father. He is rigid. He truly does not care what anyone thinks of him. The president of the United States could call, and it wouldn't matter.

My father seems to be unaffected, no matter what I say to him or how loud I scream or how hard I cry. Today is different. He looks at me helplessly and hands me a faded three-ring binder. It looks old. He says, "Maybe this will help you understand. I wrote this book as soon as I learned English, before you were born."

PART 2

AN UNRECOGNIZABLE WORLD

Though the strength of others is not known to you,
it does not mean it does not exist.

—Arnold S. Abrams

Arnold's Short Story

1958

The Winning Ticket
By Arnold Abrams
Junior, Excelsior High School

Bob Wertz's swollen eyes perused *The Daily Racing Form*, his bible for many years. His worried mind gathered in every word, number, and symbol. He had eliminated the first seven races, not finding any horse he liked. He was looking at the eighth and final race when he saw it: a horse that could not lose. He had not slept many nights, waiting for this. Of course, number 1, Mr. X, was a determining factor in the race, but it was quite obvious that Mr. X would fold in the drive to the wire and be easily passed by Indianola. He hid his tip sheet, form, and scraps of paper where his wife would not see them.

Sleeping pills helped him sleep three hours. At ten a.m. he woke and went into the kitchen for a good breakfast with his wife and two children. As he entered the kitchen, he said, "I think I'll go to the track today. I've been away for so long, I don't think I know what it looks like." His wife gave him a quick kiss, sent the children off to play, and asked him how the midnight movie had been. "I fell asleep halfway through it," he said, trying to lie effectively.

He found his binoculars and headed off to the races. After four blocks, he made a detour and headed for Joe Ranse's luxurious apartment. As Bob walked in, he was greeted by Joe's ugly smile and the dejected faces of many another horse player. He pushed his way through a thick blanket of smoke and a group of men until he was in front of Ranse's desk.

"Hi ya, Bob, " bubbled Joe. "Haven't seen ya for two weeks now. I guess ya didn't have enough guts to quit the ponies, huh?"

"I never planned on quitting, Joe—and I'll show you who's got guts," spoke Bob, his voice slowly rising.

The sudden outburst was heard above the low murmur in the room. Everyone turned to where the voice had come from.

Bob dug into his vest pocket and drew out a heavily padded wallet and removed ten thousand dollars. He threw the bills on the table and spoke quietly: "Number 9, Indianola, to win, Mr. Ranse, in the eighth."

A gasp was heard as Joe slowly counted the bills and handed them back to Bob saying, "You're not serious, are you?"

"The hell if I'm not, Joe!" yelled Bob. "You've been taking my money for nine years now, and today I am going to get it all back, times five."

Joe was not the kind to back out; if he did, his booking days would have been over, so he was almost forced to accept the bet. Ranse slowly recounted the money, put it in a steel box, and gave Wertz a slip of paper that had on it the terms of the bet and both their signatures. As Bob left the room, the other horse players patted him on the back, wishing him luck, and assured him that there was nothing they would rather see than Ranse lose a small fortune. Wertz was different from the rest of the men; he did not blame Ranse for his losing money on the horses—he blamed himself. He would have just as soon bet this money at the track except that his heavy wager would have brought down the odds on his horse.

With the clang of the opening gates, the horses were off to the roar of the crowd and the announcer's smooth call of "They're off—and—running!"

Bob's heart pounded like a trip hammer, and then there was a large thud, like that of a fast ball meeting a catcher's glove; it sent him reeling from his seat. When back in his seat, he took stock of the chain of racing events that had brought him to this day. At first the horses were a game to him as he made an occasional visit to the track. But one day he met Joe Ranse, who invited him to come to his bar and place a bet. He took Ranse up on it once, and from then on he was hooked. At first he would just bet a little, but soon he was betting a week's salary on one horse. All this took place without his wife knowing about it. Soon he was behind in his car payments, his house was totally mortgaged, and he lost his job. He pleaded with these men not to let his wife know of his difficulties. He got up every morning and left for work, even though there was no place to go. It soon became evident that his wife would find out if he did not do something drastic. So before going to Ranse's apartment, he removed all of the ten thousand dollars from their bank account. If Indianola won, he could replace the money in the back account, pay the mortgage on the house, make up the back payments on the car, have enough money left to open his own little business, and tell his wife that he had quit his job. But if Indianola lost, everything would be lost.

He put his hands on the arms of his chair, pushed himself up slowly, and put his binoculars to his foggy eyes, filled with sweat and tears. His horse was running eighth in a field of ten. He thumbed nervously through the form to the page with his horse's statistics on it to reassure himself that his horse was a come-from-behinder. He had read that his horse had come from behind no less than fifty times, but when everything is at stake, one is not even sure of one's own name. Bob looked at the tote board and under number 9 saw the odds of ten to one. He then took a deep breath, steadied himself as much as possible, and looked for his horse; he had moved up to fifth. As he had expected, the favorite, Mr. X., took the lead at the beginning of the race but was dropping back steadily.

"The horses are turning for home!" screeched the announcer. "It's Dabber by three-quarters of a length, Nemesis second by a length and a quarter, Two Ton third by a nose, Indianola fourth by a head, and Little Jess. Coming back to the leaders, it's Dabber by two lengths, Two Ton second by a nose, Indianola third by a neck, and Nemesis dropping out of contention. Into the stretch it's Dabber by one and a half lengths, Indianola second by a length, and Two Ton six lengths ahead of the rest of the pack. At the eighth pole, it's a two-horse race with Dabber under a drive and Indianola closing ground rapidly. It's Dabber and Indianola. It's . . ."

The announcer's voice was lost in the roar of the crowd, and Bob Wertz's hands were shaking the binoculars so vigorously that he could not see. Even if he'd had a perfect view of the finish line, he still could not have picked the winner because not more than a pinpoint separated them. He turned to the people around him to see if they knew who had won—number 7, Dabber, or number 9, Indianola. Each man declared that he had never missed a call in a race, but each one gave a different answer. The steward's ruling on who had won the race was exceptionally long because there was a dead heat. The numbers of the horses' finishes finally appeared, and there was a great roar emitted by the winners in the crowd. Those who lost turned aside and spewed profanity.

Bob heard the roar of the crowd and knew the numbers had been posted. He made a silent prayer, gathered up all his virility and courage and turned to face the numbers as a man who stood in front of a firing squad, waiting for a bullet to end his life. The winning number was 7. He stood there, stunned, and did not move an inch or utter a word. There could be an inquiry, he thought prayerfully. But his last hope, like that of a man on a steep ledge holding on with the little finger of his left hand, was shattered with the official sign. Dabber paid a fabulous $109.80.

Bob remained in such a dazed condition that when he came to his senses, most of the people had left the track; the track was calm after the storm. He walked drunkenly to the train even though he has had nothing to drink and got on it just as it was ready to pull out. He slumped in his seat, a hopeless mass of flesh, defeated and pulverized. "What is the use of living?" he thought.

It was at this time that an expensively dressed gentleman staggered up to Bob, inquiring about the result of the last race. Bob kept repeating over and over the name of Indianola, so the man in his drunken state thought that Indianola was the winner. He took ten tickets out of his pocket and threw them happily in the air, saying, "It's good to lose once in a while." The tickets floated down into Bob's lap, each one labeled "$100 to win, number 7, eighth race."

Bob, undisturbed by the man or the tickets in his lap, took the familiar bottle of sleeping pills from his pocket and ate several hungrily, muttering, "If only I had enough money to square my debts with the world, I would be happy."

From My Father's Book

1920

2

The people of Elisavetgrad are returning to their ruined homes and trying to put things in order once more. But winter is approaching, and there is little food, fuel, and clothing. Two summers ago the wheat was burned by the scorching sun, and last summer's crop was ruined by the rains.

The new government tries to organize, but they face an awful task—there is no gold to import food from other countries, and no credit is given to them because they are not recognized by any country in the world. Famine results, and it turns out to be the greatest famine Russia has ever known. The law of self-preservation is invoked by all, and people begin hoarding the little they have and will not part with it for all the gold in the world. The dreadful cholera is spreading through Ukraine, and deaths are common—at the rate of hundreds every day. There are sights beyond human comprehension.

Our family suffers a great deal, but we have too much pride to beg and steal. We just sit around and wait for what fate has in store for us. The children cry for food, and Mother cannot stand it any longer; she takes all the belongings that are left and runs to the market to exchange them for food. She brings back a little bread, some corn, and rice—just enough to keep the children alive.

Father lies down for his usual noon nap; he does not wake up. After many hours, mother tries to wake him, but it is in vain. She gathers all the children around him, and we stare at our father with wonder. He resembles a clay figure—that of a nobleman. His face is swollen in proportion to his body, like those of all the people who die of starvation. There is little weeping by the children, since they sort of expected it; they are used to death by now, having witnessed it all over town. The children are starving themselves and can only pity their own existence. Mother weeps and weeps. She always cries when someone dies, and now it is the man she loves.

The neighbors all feel he is better off; there is an air of envy in the room where he lies. Mrs. Kapaloff brings a little corn to us when she comes to pay her respects. Mother tells her kind neighbor how peacefully he died: "He wasn't sick at all; he just walked around the house not asking for anything, and then he took his usual nap, never to rise again. May God bless his soul!" At this time a man walks in wearing a heavy coat, burlap bags wrapped around his feet, and a fur cap. Icicles hang down his long mustache. "Where is the body? I have orders to take it away!" Mother sadly directs him to the room, and among much weeping, Father is carried away. The man throws the body over his shoulder and dumps it into a wagon with hundreds of other dead people. Where he takes them, no one knows. He is from the government, and it is said the bodies are all buried in one large grave.

Life goes on as usual. Mother is the only one who stays home these days. Since Dmitri left with the Red Army, she has lost fifty pounds and aged twenty years. She sits around all day, and the children try keeping her alive with the little food they can get.

Alex is now six, and Sonia is four; they are a great help to the family in getting food. They are the sweetest-looking children in the neighborhood, and people feel sad when they see their appealing look as they beg for food. With two little bags on their shoulders, hand in hand, they walk to the wealthy section of the city. They knock on doors and ask for anything at all to help them. Some people are kind to Alex and Sonia because of their age and pitiful appearance and give them bread, corn, and sometimes candy and other delicacies. They fill their own little stomachs before they come home. Mother is always glad to see them; they always save enough for her. The other children beg them to save some for them next time, but Alex replies, "Go out yourself and get it. You're old enough to take care of yourself!"

Mother cooks the corn in water and bakes bits of bread from the flour they bring home. She shares it with her other children, much to the dissatisfaction of Alex and Sonia. I ask how they manage to get food while the other children are unsuccessful. "You try it," Alex replies. "Just stand in front of the bakery until someone orders a pound of bread. Sometimes a little piece has to be added to make a full pound. If you're ahead of the other boys, you can beg for the piece."

"Can you always get the leftover piece?" I ask. Alex answers that sometimes when they refuse, they have to follow them, and after much persuasion, they might get it.

I decide to try it. I start going around to the same people that my sister and brother have gone to, but they chase me away, calling me a bum and loafer. I am so hurt that I want to cry, but my pride won't let me. I try again and again, but no one will give me anything. Then I realize I'm too old to get any sympathy. I try all the bakeries, but only once do I get a piece of bread. After much heartache I give up. Many times I grab the bread from Alex before he has a chance to give it to mother, while Misha in turn takes it from me. Then mother takes it and gives it to Neda, who is very sickly.

Neda is shy and afraid to go to people to ask for food. She has tried a few times, but can't keep it up. She leaves in the morning and pretends she is going to beg but only walks the streets and comes home at night. Mother knows she is shy and cannot get food, so she gives her as much as she can.

I get a little bit of money—a pound a day—from my new job selling *machucha* (a hard bar of crushed sunflower seeds, husk and all). The news of my job is a relief to mother and Alex; it means I can feed myself. Ida gets a job in a slaughter house for a few pounds of bones a week. This is also a great help, as soup can be made from these bones. These soup bones bring the flavor of meat into the house for the first time in two years.

Misha spends his time on bread and soup kitchen lines. Sometimes he stays there day and night because the lines are so long. Several times when his turn comes, there is no more left. Many people faint on these lines, and some die. Only the young men and women have a chance to withstand the strain of these lengthy lines. There are thousands of people, and those in front of the line are offered clothes for their place, but nothing can take the place of food. The people almost freeze to death waiting their turns, and after much suffering they get a quarter of a pound of bread and a bowl of soup. This ration is a luxury and worth enduring all kinds of suffering for, even if it means death.

High School

1954

We are now at Excelsior High School in Norwalk, a small city in L.A. County. We looked for the perfect, most beautiful house we could find. It cost sixteen thousand dollars and is in a new tract next to cattle feedlots. My mother is excited that she can go to the dairy to buy milk and to the farmer to buy corn. I am excited because I finally get my own room. I am going to make it special and not let anyone in it, except my precious five-year-old brother, Gary. My mother is going to help me. She is going to work and use her tips to buy furniture for the house. She says I can pick out anything I want.

Our new town is called La Mirada. It doesn't have its own high school, so we have to go to school in nearby Norwalk. There is one huge problem for me: I don't know how I will live without my best friend, Rachel. There is a Market Basket two blocks away that has a pay phone. I will go there every day and talk to her for hours.

Excelsior has a reputation for being one of the most dangerous schools in the state, but it is actually a very nice school built by the WPA, and all the kids are friendly. It is nothing like Eastmont Junior High, where there were knifings every day at lunchtime and *pachucas* walking down the halls, saying, "I'll meet you after school." That was scary. At Excelsior, like at Eastmont, we are all white, except for one Asian. Half of us are Mexican. There are no Negro people in our neighborhood. Arnold and I are the only Jewish students. No one has much money. We all get along. Kids are curious about Arnold and me. One boy comes up to me and says, "What is a Jew, anyway?"

I say, "I don't know."

He says, "Didn't they kill Christ?"

I say, "No." This ends the conversation.

I really want dickeys (fabric that fits around the neck and chest to look like a shirt front or turtleneck), but they are expensive. My mother says, "I can make those. What colors do you want? Pick as many colors as you like. It's easy to make them." For my mother, everything is easy. When I need a prom dress, she says, "Let's go to the cheap store and buy a basic dress, and we'll embellish it. It'll be easy." My prom dress is as pretty as the other girls'. But there are two things my mom doesn't think she can make for me. We both fall in love with two garments in the expensive clothing store at Knotts Berry Farm, a working farm that is becoming a tourist attraction, with a restaurant, several gift shops, and a replica ghost town. One garment is a pink cotton sundress with little roses on it. It is delicate and highly styled. The other is different from anything we've ever seen before. It's a black gathered wool skirt with small colored squares woven into the wool and a red-and-black fringe at the bottom. We go back several times and drool over the dress and the skirt. Finally, my mother says, "You know what? Gary is in school now, and Dad has a good waitress, so I'm going to get a job at a fancy restaurant and buy these for you with my tips." She does this, and I treasure my expensive clothes.

Another time my mom walks into a neighbor's house, and classical music is playing on a stereo in a cabinet. She says to me, "Elaine, the music is beautiful, and it gives the home such a good feeling. I'm going to get one of those, and it's going to be in a good piece of furniture just like hers." She waitresses, saves her tips, and buys it.

Once, in an argument with my father, she says, "I want and need a car. If you want me to work, I have to have a car." He shoots back with sarcasm, "When you get a driver's license, I will get you a car." Six months later she hands him her driver's license. Since he is a man of his word, he buys her a car.

I am babysitting and making money. I am a popular babysitter because I do whatever dishes are left in the sink. My mother likes to do dishes, so I never get a chance. I also learn to sleep and stay awake at the same time because I want to be awake when the people come home. I don't want them to think I could sleep through their children's crying.

What fun. I get to think about what I want to spend my money on. Whittier Boulevard is the place where my friends and I go when we want a diversion—which is often. I look at the sweaters in Abby's clothing store every time I go. The colors are beautiful, and the yarn so soft. I think my favorite color is coral—halfway between red and orange—but it's hard to choose. The cheapest sweaters are Lanamere. Lanamere is the thickest knit and has some coarse hairs in it. I can afford a Lanamere coral sweater. I put it in a special drawer and savor it. I feel like a million bucks wearing it. It's not long before I graduate to Wondamere. It's not cashmere, but it's almost like cashmere. I pick different styles and colors. These are my treasures. When my cousin visits from New York, I say, "Do you want to see my sweaters?" She says yes, and I never guess that she is not the least bit interested in sweaters.

My father can't understand any of this. He says, "I am wearing the same sweater for twenty years. Why do you need more than one sweater?" He and my mother never buy any clothes for themselves. Once my dad takes Arnold and me to buy a rhinestone necklace for our mother. It is stunning. Arnold saves up his money and buys my mother a fashionable dress. He gives it to her with such love and pride in his eyes. I want her to jump up and down with joy, but her response is muted. I will never understand her reaction. By now I know that all my brother's hurts are my hurts also—they are permanently lodged inside me.

Meet My Friends

1956

4

During the summer my friends and I do something exciting. We take long drives to Balboa or Newport Island. The beaches are covered with teenagers. For the first time, I taste a Napoleon French pastry, a chocolate éclair, a frozen banana covered with chocolate, and an ice cream bar dipped in chocolate and covered with nuts. I can't believe anything can taste so good. The rest of the time, I lie on the beach in the sun and read *True Story* and *True Confessions*. I learn about unwed mothers, hermaphrodites, homosexuals, orphans, child abuse, and divorce. In these magazine articles, people tell their stories, and no one judges them. I realize that there is a whole world of people that I know nothing about. I want to meet and get to know them.

In my new school, I make friends and meet their families. Dorene is my best friend. She is always there, supporting me and believing in me. She says I am the first person to tell her that she is pretty and give her confidence. I marvel at her long, blonde, wavy hair and Betty Grable legs. She is a gifted dancer and choreographer and directs the drill team. She comes from Texas and has moved many times. This is the first time she has been in one place long enough to make a best friend. We join countless clubs at school and take every opportunity to be in leadership roles. We act, dance, and write—whatever the school has to offer us. Our pictures are in the school annual more than anyone else's. In every picture, if you see Dorene, you'll see me. The trust is mutual, the admiration is mutual, and the desire to be popular and learn is mutual. Dorene is competent and reliable. She is a good driver and drives us everywhere. When we take Christmas vacation jobs at Knotts Berry Farm, working on an assembly line packing their famous jams, Dorene does her part packing and then helps me with mine so I don't fall behind.

I spend many hours at Dorene's house. She lives closer to the school than I do. Actually, the hours are spent in her kitchen. Dorene lives in a small house that looks poor to me. But when you sit in the small kitchen, it's full of warmth. Her mother is like the fairy godmother in *Cinderella* with her magic wand. She cooks weird southern food like grits and collards while Dorene and I talk and talk. We can say anything in front of her. She listens, sometimes with a little smile on her face. I can tell that she totally accepts us, and we cannot say anything wrong around her. There are moments when we all chuckle.

I look around and see that this family doesn't have the pretty furniture my mother bought for our house, but Dorene keeps telling me how blessed she is. She explains that she is blessed because she is loved—because she has a family in which people love one another. Well, I know that my parents love me and I love them, but my home is not happy. In Dorene's house people talk about how lucky they are. *That's the difference!* My parents just talk about what makes them mad. They never say what they like about each other. It's strange because we have as much love as Dorene's family, but because no one talks about it, we all feel miserable. Maybe when we all go to heaven, we'll talk nicely to one another and say how blessed we are to have one another.

Valerie's house has an ice-cold feeling. This is odd to me, because it is as beautiful as mine. Valerie is tall, blonde, blue eyed, and big breasted (which fascinates all of us). My father says that she is the most attractive of my friends. She is outgoing and laughs easily, but we all sense that she has a dark side. Her father is a huge, handsome man who looks as if he jumped off a movie screen. He has a charming and boisterous personality, unlike any I have ever seen before. Her father introduces us to a real party. He and his friends gather on the patio, barbecue, drink beer, and laugh about stories they tell. Everyone is glad to include us. Valerie's skinny, sad-looking mother sits quietly in a corner, smiling a little. She is kind and sweet but almost invisible. Finally, Valerie confides in us that her younger sister cut her wrist in the bathtub. The water was full of blood, and she died. Valerie loves her mother, but her dear mother is mentally ill.

Mari is the only Asian person in our school. She is Japanese and lives on one of the farms near me. She is always sweet and smiling—a very pleasant person to have around. She joins in all our fun but never tells us anything intimate about herself. She never invites us to her house or farm, and we never ask to go.

Lela is a friend who intrigues me. I can tell she's intelligent and a deep thinker. She's attractive too. She tells me that she used to live in a garage with a dirt floor with her grandmother, who does not speak English. Now she lives in a small house in Norwalk that her father bought with a veteran's loan. He wanted to buy a house in Lakewood but was turned down because his last name is Chavez. She says that no Mexicans, Jews, or Japanese are allowed to live there. She always keeps some distance from me even though I know she likes me. She never invites me to her house. Like me, she is going to go to college. Dorene is going to college too.

Wait'll You
Hear This!

1956

5

Dear Diary,

   If you are about to eat, wait until you're through before reading this.
Our club had an initiation, and guess what we did? The initiates come to
my house, and one at a time we bring them to Denise's because she has a swimming
pool. We blindfold them and tell them to put on this gunny sack on top of their
underwear. Then we hand them a bowl of noodles and tell them one of them is a
worm. When they pick one up we shake it with our finger and they scream till we
think we'll split from keeping our laughter in. Then we take them to the bathroom
and in the toilet we put fertilizer and some bananas. We make them pick it up and
when they drop it, we give them a clean banana but squashed a little. They think it's
the same one and we make them eat it. You would have died if you'd seen it. Then
we take them outside by the pool and twirl them. Two feet in back of them is a piece
of newspaper with noodles and bananas and they have to walk in that and then they
walk straight in to the water. That isn't all! We make them lie down, and we get some

ice and a potato masher and pretend that we are branding them, and we even put a bandage on them. You never saw anything so funny in your life! Sherry and I made up the whole initiation. Isn't it a good one?

Making Out
and One Dollar

1957

6

Dear Diary,

We sit out in the car for about a half hour, and here's where the problem begins. He insists on lying down when we make out. I keep arguing and arguing. Finally, he pushes me away and says, "Why don't you let me make love to you the way I want to?!" I feel real bad because I know a boy takes a special pride in being sexy. So before I know it, he's on top of me and getting hot. But as soon as he does, he sits up. I just about die. I don't know what to say.

The next time we go out is Christmas Eve; we look at Christmas decorations. He acts different. He is driving, and he hardly puts his arm around me; he seems to have made up his mind that he isn't going to kiss me. But of course he can't stick to that. When he takes me home, we begin to talk and make out a little. He kept trying to go "up," if you know what I mean.

I explain to him how I feel about it and reason with him. I just about die! He then says his motto is "Never give up." I don't know what to do. Then—prepare yourself—he puts his hand right smack on my breast! It's the first time I ever get mad at a boy, and I say, "Open the door, I'm going in." He says, "Don't get so silly," but he doesn't argue with me. Then he says, "I'll see you." Then *I* kiss *him* goodnight.

In grammar school Arnold and I wanted to learn more about sex—what men and women actually do together to have babies. Arnold quizzed his friends, and I quizzed my friends. Then we put our stories together. What we came up with was disgusting. We decided that it was too repulsive to be true and certainly too degrading for either of us to ever consider. Well, now it's high school, and it's all different. Arnold and I are well liked, but he doesn't have a girlfriend and I don't have a boyfriend. We both get crushes on the best-looking, most popular people, who would never be interested in hanging out with us.

I have a couple of dates with a football player—the one I wrote about in my diary. The next time we meet, he says in a sensible tone: "You have to face it. We're not a good match. You get A's and I get D's." I see his point. Arnold has his eyes on the prettiest girl but can never approach her. He says that he couldn't bear a rejection. I believe him.

Arnold is not large enough to be on the varsity football team, so he has to be on junior varsity. His friends are impressed by his strength on the football field, and the varsity guys include him in their inner circle. For the football guys, eating psychedelic morning glory seeds—dope—is the way to be cool. Arnold eats just enough seeds to be one of the boys but not enough to risk losing his judgment or health (our father has taught us to be health conscious).

The guys' fascination with Arnold increases when they hear about his summer adventure. Early in July Arnold appears in the kitchen one day and says to me unceremoniously: "Give me a dollar and I will go cross country. I'll find my way without anything else but one dollar in my pocket." I am stunned and give him the dollar. After horrendous hitchhiking experiences that he never describes, he arrives at our relatives' house in New York with jeans so stiff from dirt they cut his legs. Our aunt and uncle get him a summer job running the elevator at the Essex Building.

Arnold is smarter and more sensitive than I am. These traits makes it harder for him to understand the world around him, but he keeps trying to make sense of it. The rest of our family doesn't bother thinking about such things. We don't even read the newspaper; my father thinks that's awful. Arnold and my father are the only people I have ever seen read a newspaper.

Ever since Arnold and I read our father's book, we have understood that terrible things happen "out there." People can hate and persecute others who are different. Now when we read about prejudice against Negro people, we feel pain. We know in our gut about poverty, intolerance, and war. We don't even know how we know, and we don't talk about it to anyone. My dad teaches us that everyone is the same and should be treated the same. He says he's an agnostic, not an atheist, and a socialist, not a communist—but we shouldn't tell anyone because no one here will understand. (I used to think that the only difference between my family and everyone else's was that we yelled at one another!)

Arnold is almost paralyzed by rage and fear and love as he mulls over the crude events occurring in places far away. He begins writing his thoughts down. He calls them "Thoughts That Come from Nowhere but Feel Good."

Arnold's Thoughts from Nowhere

1957

I have thoughts that come from nowhere but feel good:

I love to say, "Man is for shit," but then I have known too many exceptions.

Even the most despicable ignorance has some basis in fact—albeit a tremendous distortion of it. For the weak this distortion becomes easy, even natural, and its mastery makes one strong among the weak, who through numbers dominate almost everything.

I marvel at my internal ignorance, externally manifest in others.

My father asks me, "Do you think you'll ever be a success?" His question demonstrates that at least one member of the family is not.

I dislike violence, but injustice more.

Well, I'm kind of worn out, so I'll stop here. Not all of it may make good sense. Each one isn't meant to encompass all truth on the subject discussed but a point of view, an individual experience, or thought felt by me. The best example of this is "Life is a degrading experience." Right now I don't feel that way, but I have and surely will again. Some of my ideas come less from rational thought than a momentary impulse; they are sayings that came from nowhere and felt good.

I'm So Happy!

1958

8

Dear Diary,

Its five p.m. now, and at nine p.m. we'll know who the Homecoming Queen is. I know that in years past, it has never been like this year. Halftime at the football game is so beautiful and perfect that you just get a lump in your throat watching it. You don't think it can get any better, and then the lights go out and with red, white, and blue lights, the drill team makes an American flag! It's breathtaking. Then the lights go on and the princesses (ME) come out on this float. Rodney, our Student Body President, is handed an envelope with the queen's name in it, and then he crowns her and kisses her. It's going to be just like a fairy tale! Then afterwards the princesses (ME) and the queen are escorted in to the dance one by one with a fanfare, and then the queen and her court dance while everyone is seated. You should see the crown. It is too magnificent for words. Oh,

I'm shaking so much!!! I'm just so thrilled to be out here on the float. I just can't believe it.

I'm so popular now. When I walk down the school corridors, everyone smiles and says, "Hello, Elaine." I don't even know half of them. Oh, all my dreams have come true. All the school activities I have planned have been a success. We've been excellent in football, and song leading is too wonderful for words. Even some kids from Montebello who came to one of our games said our pepsters made theirs look sick. I can't wait for that game. We're going to give them a tough fight.

I hate to stop writing, but the excitement is just too much. I've never been so excited in my whole life!

By our senior year, I am Girls' League Secretary, Student Body Song Leader, Homecoming Princess, and an honors student. In Arnold's senior year, he is Student Body President, Valedictorian, and a junior varsity football player. It is Dorene's idea for Arnold to be Student Body President. She has leadership skills. She says Arnold is smart, and we need a smart president—also, the football players like him. She is his campaign manager. We are all having such a good time. The faculty chooses me to go to Girls' League, and the student body votes me Song Leader and Homecoming Princess. Each time I say to my mother, "This is the happiest day of my life!" She says, "Do you realize how many times you have said this to me?"

Dorene is a serious Catholic. She and I are idealistic, and for me this means believing in God, contrary to my father's agnosticism. My father doesn't say anything. He watches me the way someone would watch a flower start to bloom and not know what it will look like. When we exchange presents, I give Dorene a statue of the Virgin Mary, and she gives me a *mezuzah*. This is a cylinder with a three-thousand-year old Hebrew prayer inside. Arnold gets such a kick out of doing weird things. He has always kept his middle name a secret. Now he insists that the school newspaper put it in the headline of the paper: "*ARNOLD SBRITSKY ABRAMS IS VALEDICTORIAN.*" Then he walks down the aisle at graduation with a big *mezuzah* bouncing off his chest.

Summer Camp Job: A Letter from My Father

1958

9

Hello Sweetie Pie,

I just read your nice, long letter. I enjoyed hearing from you. It is the first informative, good letter since you went away eleven days ago. I was hoping you would write. Every night I came to the kitchen to look for the letter, and finally, today it is there. Don't feel bad for not writing sooner because I know you were too busy the first week enjoying yourself, and I am glad that you did find time to write when you did. (I'm really not being sarcastic.) I kept thinking of you all the time since I left you, wondering if you will have as wonderful a summer as I thought you would. Elaine, dear, I am so happy to hear that you are enjoying yourself. For a person like me who has had so little happiness, it is hard for me to understand how you can be so happy. It gives me so much pleasure and happiness to read of your joys and how you feel. It really exhilarates me to see you so happy. Keep it up and try not to let anything mar your happy feelings. I told Ma when I left you that no matter where you are, you shine like a ray of sunshine on a rainy day. Stay happy, healthy, and pretty as you are, and the boys will come to you. Don't feel bad if they choose you over others. Just be glad you have good fortune. You can't tell the boys to pay attention to someone else if they want to be with you. You all have the same chance, so don't feel that you are greedy.

So long, my dear daughter. Again I want to stress to you that I am very happy for you. I want you to enjoy life as you do. Have a good time, and be careful at all times. Write when you find time. We all like to hear from you.

Your scribbling old Dad,

Love and Kisses

P.S. It is getting dark, and I cannot see what I am writing. I gave up my whole evening for you and I'm not sorry.

Arnold's Notes and Yearbook

1959

10

have one friend who calls me "God" in all company. I like it. In my yearbook varsity football players write:

It's been real great knowing you, and it is a real privilege for me to know a guy as great as you are. There are not many guys in this world that has the athletic ability, scholastic and leadership ability as you. It's a guy like you that makes a guy like me want to come to school.

• • • • •

Through the years I've known you, you been the nicest guy I know. You haven't any idea how much I respect you.

• • • • •

If you want an MD, I'm sure they will allow you to get it.

• • • • •

If all big men had as much guts, desire, and determination as one little man I know (you), the world would be a better place to live.

• • • • •

Do a favor for me, and do your best in college. Don't goof off like me. Make something of yourself.

• • • • •

I don't think I could have gone through school without your inspiration. You gave me very much confident. You are the best all-round football player I've met. I wish I had the guts you have so I would be a better player.

Arnold's Notes at UCLA

1960

E veryone here is rich and white. I have nothing in common with them. I miss my East L.A. friends; they are real people. Elaine is at Whittier College. She says she doesn't fit in there, but she is still getting good grades. She says she is going to work and study for two years so she can go to Berkeley with Jerry Cooper, her fiancé. She is working at the Chicken House Restaurant at Knott's Berry Farm with Dorene. They work as a team and are making a lot of money. If I don't keep putting my thoughts on paper, I will go crazy. I used to feel bad, but then I would feel good. Now I am at the bottom of a big hole.

The greatest sorrow is when you have all the requirements for what you desire, except the mechanics.

I am negative possibly because I have been hammered out a little differently than most; that makes me more sensitive to society's ignorance or perhaps makes me a different perceiver. I *attempt neutrality*, which reflects reality— the most inhuman of attempts.

The Struggle
for Relationship

Current Group Therapy
Meeting Continued

W HERE WE LEFT OFF: *Robert and Linda talked about herpes and their lack of interest in sex.*

In previous meetings Tim and Robert were bound to clash. Politically, they are on opposite ends of the spectrum. The impending explosion between them was almost impossible for both of them to bear, but they had made a commitment to stay in the group no matter how much they wanted to flee. They believed that they could get better and have a happier future. Usually when members don't want to come to a meeting or want to quit the group, it's because they have to face themselves in some kind of new and elemental way. They have to face what they most don't want to see—they have woven a lifestyle and personality designed to avoid just such a confrontation. Sticking with the group during these crises is typically what spurs the breakthrough that everyone seeks. The best example that I can think of is when Tim and Robert sat red with rage, feeling that they were going to explode or disintegrate if they couldn't leave the room. Robert was angry about Tim's "loose morals" and "un-American" sentiments, such as not supporting the US military. Tim was angry at Robert's bigotry: "He looks and talks like a nice guy, but he doesn't care if the human race blows up from a nuclear war!" Both men have been known to be walking time bombs.

In the group meeting, I do not allow name-calling or cruelty. They both had to put into words what had honestly angered and offended them. With incredible strain the words of anger came out; actions were no longer necessary. Afterward, Robert and Tim felt tremendous relief—they had survived. This shared, horrible experience gave them a new bond.

I had the passing thought: If only more people with different belief systems could be reconciled through interaction. Studies show that the more real-time contact people have with one another, the less prejudiced they are. Tim and Robert demonstrated how peace can be made. They moved from difference to commonality.

Tim turns to Robert and speaks in a peppy tempo. He laughs nervously, and so does Robert. "I'm going to say that you might be able to stand by the excuse of old age, but I wish I could say I didn't have the same problem. It's a little different with me. I mean, a lot of the stress has gone out of my life, but it's . . ." He pauses. "Well, it reminds me of Woody Allen's *Everything You Wanted to Know about Sex but Were Afraid to Ask*. One of the skits is about this guy who's going out on a date. He has these guys in his stomach with little bulldozers. They flit around and move to weird parts of the body; some go up to his brain. It's like we should control what we do and think, but these weird little guys are running around inside us, calling all the shots. They're speaking into microphones, 'Okay, do this, do that.'"

Cheryl starts to laugh and covers her mouth to stop. Linda does the same thing, and they both keep their hands over their mouth to keep from giggling out loud.

Tim seems pleased with the response he is getting, and his voice gets louder. "Then all of a sudden the guy is about to have sex with this woman, and everything falls apart. The little guys inside him have pressed the panic button. That's the end of that."

Robert says, "I'd like to see this movie."

"There's this Catholic priest in a black smock going around inside him, tearing the wiring out. It's this little homunculus, this little kid, and the guilt thing. It's like, with the whole issue of sex, it's like, there's something in there that pulls the switch and says, 'No, uh-uh, no way.'"

Tim can see that everyone is focused on him. He risks it. "Remember the discussion I brought up a couple months ago? It seemed to me that even though I had gone through the motions of saying that everything was fine with my old girlfriend, everything probably wasn't. Because something in my brain, something down in there is saying, 'Uh-uh. Don't trust. Don't take a chance, 'cause, to me, with sex, it's real important that I know the person—that there's some kind of interchange. If there's not any kind of interpersonal meaning to it, it's a real drag."

Linda coughs, and everyone looks serious.

Tim continues. "So I'm linking sex to a relationship and a relationship to being burned. I guess it's that little guy in there, mission control, tearing up the wiring. And the problem is that everything seems okay to me up front, so I don't know how to get at it."

Tim glances at Harry to his right. "For the benefit of the folks who don't know: I lived with a woman for one year, and she became a lesbian."

Tim continues. "I understood what she was going through; I understood who she was. There wasn't anything personal. We still talk to each other. She said there was just this urge in her for a long time, and she still liked me and all that. And so it wasn't like some sort of stereotypical, horrific story of rejection. And I didn't feel bad about it. I don't feel personally slighted. My masculinity doesn't feel pulled out from under me."

Robert challenges, "It did not bother you one bit?"

"Oh, it did when it was happening. But I think most of it was jealousy. But eventually it got to the point that other relationships have, where to have it end felt better than going on with it—just by default. And once I was out of it, there was a feeling of relief. It isn't a complete loss because she's in the same political organization, so I run into her a lot. I didn't know her lovers or anything. So it isn't quite like she just walked out of my life. It isn't quite like she told me to go to hell. It isn't quite like she said, 'I don't need men.' So to me, the sense is that it is simply and purely a relationship that I value that was taken away. I don't feel bitter."

I cross my arms. I'm thinking: Tim doesn't realize that loving someone and having that person close is one of the essentials of human happiness, and losing that someone is one of the harbingers of human misery.

Tim continues. "I don't feel any loss or anything. So the long and the short of it is that I sense that's what's bothering me. It's funny, the ambivalence toward sex takes a couple of different forms: one is just generalized lack of interest. But also, the closer it comes to actual sexual intercourse, the more repulsion there is. When the moment of physical closeness arrives, I have this deep-seated, unconscious inhibition. The wiring gets ripped out or something. It's very hard to describe."

Robert replies without hesitation, "Yeah, but I don't even get that close. I can't even get my interest going."

Both Robert and Tim start talking at once, but Tim prevails. "I understand what you're saying. That happens to me. I can tell you how I deal with that: I take an attitude that I'll just do whatever is fun. I have a friend now, a girlfriend, whom I've told about my problem. She's real cool, and we're good friends as well as lovers and stuff. She's basically an understanding person."

Tim looks around and sees that he has everyone's attention. "What we've done about it is to say, 'Let's just do whatever is fun.' I say to myself, 'If all else fails with me, I'll do what I can to satisfy her.' We just do whatever feels good. Slowly, I reacquired that sense of pleasure: physical pleasure and psychological pleasure. And that has helped a lot. Just to back off and say, 'Okay, look, forget it. Whatever is going to happen will happen. Just take it from there.'" He uses his hands to emphasize his point. "I guess what I'm trying to say is that the worst thing in the world is to make performance demands on yourself, especially with sex. I don't know what it is about sexuality, but it's a special psychological niche."

Robert puts his hand on his nose and responds readily. "You're making a good point when you say that even if you don't feel like doing it—going the full way—you can still help your partner."

Tim nods. "Yeah."

"I don't have the tendency to do that. I back off completely," Robert adds.

Tim is taking to the role of being a helper to an older man. "It would be frustrating if it stayed that way forever. But what it does is, it reestablishes a sense of giving. It's a start; it's better than nothing."

Robert starts to chuckle, and others follow.

Tim speaks timidly because he is beginning to remember that he and Robert are competitors. Robert might react badly to being in the lower position. "It worked for me, anyway. But nonetheless, there's still that little monster guy in Woody Allen's movie—that saboteur is still up there in my head."

Linda clarifies, "You're taking conscious control of a problem that you have, and that makes it less disturbing." She doesn't understand why he is starting to hedge.

"Seems a helluva torment, though," Robert comments.

Cheryl giggles without meaning to. She is not used to hearing this kind of honest talk between men.

Tim says apologetically to Robert, "There are differences in our situations. I didn't mean to be giving you advice."

"Taking conscious control is the only idea I've heard," Cheryl states straightforwardly. People smile, and Robert adds, "Right."

Robert pursues: "My roadblock is trying to figure out what's going on inside me. Is it bitterness in me, or what?"

"Yeah," says Tim, "like did I really get burned from that old relationship? Did I have some kind of Pavlovian conditioning and then I mistrust relationships? Did past traumas plug my memory?"

David stretches his head, trying to stay awake. Robert notices that David is having trouble keeping his eyes open but doesn't say anything. I imagine what Robert is thinking: "I bet he's thinking about going out and getting a hamburger." David is the perfect scapegoat. It's hard for everyone to see that a part of them would like to go to sleep also. The task at hand is a hard one.

Linda is thinking about what Tim said. "Maybe you're stuck because of a relationship with someone in your family? That may be the Pavlovian conditioning you talked about."

Tim negates her within a second. "I've never in my life experienced that!" Then he retracts what he just said. "Oh, that's an untrue statement if I ever heard one." They both laugh.

Linda proceeds. She can think clearly in this open and nondefensive atmosphere. "Maybe it's like Robert's herpes and my herpes—it just took an extraordinary amount of stuff to make it happen. It's like a tree root. It'll grow along until it hits a barrier, and then it will eventually bend down. But as it bends down, it will build up this big knuckle of tissue. In reality the tree root is only that big around, but the knuckle is that big around." She uses her hands like a Hawaiian dancer and shows the large circle of the knuckle and the small circle of the tree root. "And maybe you go along, and whatever the negative little voice inside is that you can't identify . . . Well, as you're digging, you get to something that brings it up."

Tim feels close to Linda. "I understand. I know what you mean. That's real possible. Because my parents just never taught any kind of openness or . . . "

Linda interrupts, "I know we talked about that before—about whether our parents ever talked about sex."

Tim adds, "I'm wondering if I even know what a relationship is. Maybe I haven't had one, because I don't know who I am."

I notice that he is starting to turn to Elizabeth. I ask him about it. He makes an excuse, saying that he wanted to include more of the group. I persist. "Maybe there's a reason you were looking at Elizabeth as you were saying that."

Elizabeth is startled. She thinks she's invisible. Robert scratches his shoulder, and Tim looks puzzled.

Tim stammers, "What exactly am I saying? Now I'm distracted. I can't remember what . . . "

I fill him in. "Not being a real person when you are entering a sexual relationship."

Linda helps Tim out. "You were wondering what kind of person you were in relationships prior to . . . "

"I remember now. Right. I don't know if I looked at you for any reason," he says to Elizabeth.

Robert shifts his legs, crossing them in the opposite direction. He is uncomfortable with my pursuit.

Tim tries to ignore me and says, "My lesbian friend is the only girlfriend I've lived with. It's the longest relationship I've ever had. After the breakup weird changes happened in me. I just don't understand."

"Is that when you started to have a problem with anger?" asks Robert.

"No, I've always been angry."

Harry is tired of not fully understanding what's going on. "What are all these changes? I'm sorry, but I wasn't here when you talked about them."

Tim answers: "I had no sense of humor. I felt isolated. I felt lonely. I felt depressed. There didn't seem much point to anything. I didn't feel like changing the world anymore. I didn't feel like doing a damn thing. Nothing was fun. No sexual interest. I was absolutely paralyzed socially. I'd go up to somebody and stand there and fumble around and pretend that I'd forgotten something important and just walk away."

As she listens Linda holds her forehead with her arm and gets lost in thought about her own history of social paralysis.

"Do you feel that it shouldn't take you any time to get over a relationship that meant a lot to you?" Hugo asks.

I cross my feet slowly and slide them under my chair. I do this when I'm thinking about an intervention.

Hugo sits up straight. "It takes time. It can take years. It can take a couple of years to get over a relationship. It doesn't matter what you understand up here." He points to his head with authority. "It's a healing process; it is some kind of cataclysmic lethargy."

I begin to speak. The air in the room seems to stop moving. "Somebody mentioned Elizabeth. It may not be a coincidence that the subject of sex is coming up again today, given that no one has voiced any feelings about the meeting where Elizabeth was hurting and then rejected the group. For the past month, topics have gone from the loss of sex drive to the dangers of sex (STDs) to managing self-destructive rage and withdrawal."

I turn my head slowly. Each person stares back at me. People sit frozen in position. I am someone they have chosen to trust, but they don't understand what I'm talking about. They wonder if I'm crazy, or if they are.

Tim takes a stab at it. "Do you mean that Elizabeth has something to do with what we're talking about today?"

"There may be a link between the meeting four weeks ago and today."

People look both mesmerized and perplexed. Harry breaks the spell. He is feeling more a part of the group, and the group seems to need him. "Tell us, what is it?"

I am respectful of his question, since he is new in the group. Others in the group have learned that it is useless to ask me such questions. I have explained that if I answer a question too quickly, the members won't have a chance to fantasize about what my answers might be. Their spontaneous guesses help me understand their unconscious. "First let's see if this idea strikes a chord with anybody."

Robert is beginning to catch on and is astonished. He protests, "But I've wanted to bring this up for a long time."

Linda takes her glasses off, rubs her eyes, and coughs.

Robert continues to reflect. "Maybe what happened with Elizabeth last month and then afterward gave me a little bit of courage to say what I did. It dawned on me the other day: I'm with people that I should tell everything to and not be afraid."

"So how was it for people last week when Elizabeth came back to the group after she'd been so upset, and she talked about what she felt had been blocking her in here?"[2]

"It sure helped me," says Harry. "I thought to myself, that is a very courageous thing to do. I wasn't here before, but I thought to myself, wow, this lady Elizabeth is—she's working real hard. I felt tingles of admiration."

---

2   This meeting is not described in the book.

I Want Sex

13

1961

I want to have full sex in the worst way. I know it's a big and important decision. I consult my brother. He says, "No, don't. If you do, Jerry won't marry you. The boys talk about bad girls and good girls. There is no in-between. Use all your willpower." The desire is so great. I will write a contract to myself.

Dear, Dear Elaine,

Please, please remember throughout the *three* years of your courtship with Jerry that today, June 12, 1961, you are making a covenant as sacred as Moses did on Mt. Sinai. It is a covenant between you, the *real* you, Elaine, your inner self that has inhabited your actions and your feelings through all your nineteen years, and with God. God put you in this society and by doing so, expects you to abide by the most prominent social mores. If you break this covenant, you will be destroying a part of yourself—a part of yourself that you have always been thankful for.

Arnold said something very impressive: "You are Elaine, and Jerry is Jerry. Until a Rabbi blesses Jerry and you, there is a 1 percent chance that he will not marry you." (Dear Elaine, *please* listen!) That 1 percent chance is not worth risking. The risk of being "had" by someone else other than your lifelong partner is too big to take. You must have this one sacred thing confined to two people who are spending a lifetime together. Remember, his mom, whom he patterns you after, didn't do it. You are strong! You are an individual! Please don't disappoint me—you have to live with me forever!

Love and devotion,
Elaine

I remember when Arnold confided in me about how to have sex. His macho friends were telling him that he had no success with women because he was too nice. Women like men to be mean to them. For example, when you have sex and the woman is sucking you, you put your hand over her head, so she can't lift it until you come. Arnold asked me if I agreed. I was adamant. He should stay just as he is—nice!

Arnold's Notes

1961

14

To be intolerant of intolerance is to be intolerant.

Feelings are as much a reality, and as worthy of consideration, as purely rational thought.

A person lives inside his house, and all others are passersby. Be wary of criticizing another's house. There are things a passerby does not see or feel.

Maturity is in the mind but appears to require time, experience, and physical development. Sad, but I think true. I never let these influence me, however, in assigning maturity.

Though the strength of others is not known to you, it does not mean it does not exist.

College Parties

1961

15

U C Berkeley, here we are: Arnold and I and my fiancé, Jerry Cooper. We are a loving threesome. Jerry says Arnold is his best friend. We are sure that Arnold is going to be a doctor and I, a social worker. Arnold is a zoology major and is getting A's, but for some reason he's rejected from medical school—so being a doctor is out. We are in one of the best universities in the world, but we get no guidance.

We have small parties; Arnold is always the life of the party. I love to watch him dance. He is fantastic—just like our dancer dad, except he's doing the twist. At the most unlikely moments—like at the moment when people are ready to yell surprise because the birthday girl is about to walk through the door, or when the table is beautifully set and we're all quietly anticipating the arrival of an important guest—he says mischievously, *"LET'S ALL HOLD HANDS AND DROP DEAD!"* Even the most uptight person in the room cracks up. I can't help laughing. However, I can never figure out what is so funny.

Arnold entertains everyone with passionate talk about the oppression in the world. Now it's Vietnam and how thousands of people are needlessly dying. He tells us what it was like in the Santa Rita jail when he was arrested for marching for civil rights in downtown Berkeley. How is this entertaining? I can't explain it, but it is. He tells our friends, "My sister and I look at the same thing, and she sees a rose and I see a pile of shit." Despite his passion for political activity, he continues with the academic grind and graduates with honors in zoology.

Arnold's Notes

1962

I feel like BS-ing a little, so I'll just free associate like I'm talking to you. Well, do you know my cousin, Alan Cohen? He wrote a paper of his ideas for school and sent it to us and I really liked it, so it kind of inspired me to write. I'll share a few of my thoughts. If they are not so good, what's the difference? Short stuff like this:

A friendship that no longer serves its previous needs should be terminated for the good of both—an anachronism.

What the world lacks in understanding, it makes up for in hatred.

Organization destroys what it is meant to create.

I am discussing Lawrence of Arabia's title of his autobiography, *Seven Pillars of Wisdom*, with my only real friend. I suggest that if I had been of consequence like Lawrence, I would title my autobiography *Seven Pillars of Nothing*. We both laugh so hard that tears run down our faces.

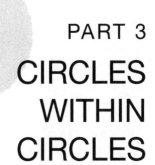

PART 3

CIRCLES
WITHIN
CIRCLES

Not to be able to blame is a hell most people escape.
—Arnold S. Abrams

One Month Ago: Anger vs. Assertiveness

Earlier Group Therapy Meeting

W HERE WE LEFT OFF: *I alluded to the previous "events" in the group one month ago. I had the following meeting in mind. I believed that there was no way the group could not be struggling with its aftermath. During this meeting the members had taken great risks—with my prodding. I was quite sure they thought the results were catastrophic. Unfortunately, at that meeting Linda was absent, and Harry had not yet joined the group. The beginning of the meeting started quite well, with Tim and Robert exploring how they dealt with anger.*

"I'm critical of people, and then I do the same thing that I'm criticizing them for!" Tim is exasperated. He pauses to find the words. "I have to give this up because people get pissed off at me for being so critical. In the co-op it becomes a big crisis, and everyone ends up with low morale. And then I think, 'Life could be more pleasant if I didn't have to go through this kind of thing." He stops and then asks hesitantly, "Does that make sense?"

"Hmmhmm," the group echoes together, thinking over what Tim has just said.

Robert nods his head thoughtfully as Tim speaks. Hugo scratches his head, crosses his leg, and then looks around at Robert, who has decided to take advantage of the fact that Tim has brought up the subject.

"My boss called me this morning, and the way he started talking to me, I knew he was going to criticize something. But he did it in a very, *very* nice way; he built up to it." Robert is serious and thoughtful. "If it had been me, I would have said, 'You screwed up! Change it!' His approach impressed me. At first I got all tight inside listening to him. And then I decided I wasn't going to defend myself at all, just let him talk. He said politely, 'Would you take care of it for me?' And I said, 'Yeah, I'll take care of it.' When he hung up, I was kind of shaky, but . . . " Robert is thinking and talking at the same time. "The more I thought about it, the more I saw that it wasn't that severe of a criticism. He was giving me every opportunity in the world to get it rectified—not in *his* time period, but in *my* time period, which made me feel comfortable." Members are quiet and give him time to process some more. "And I thought, 'Man, I wish *I* could approach people like that.'" It's hard for Robert to believe that someone can be angry yet still be in control and express that anger constructively.

I ask, "How do you want it to be in here? How do you want the control to be in here? How do you want the criticism to be in here?" My questions are clear enough, but five puzzled faces turn in my direction.

Robert is the first to answer. "I think it has to be as real in here as it is on the outside. That's my feeling." The group seems to be counting on him, so he continues, "Why should it be any different?"

"Yeah, but . . . " Cheryl collects more momentum and then turns to Robert, challenging him with fervor. As usual, she looks very glamorous. She is wearing a light green knit skirt and sweater that cling to her body. "But what does that mean? I don't criticize on the outside, even though I get pissed off. I don't take criticism well, and I don't criticize, so does that mean that's what I should do in here, too?"

Robert feels strange in the role of the authority (his father's role). "Well, I think it has to come out." He uses his hands to implore her. "I mean, I guess all of us have to see you in a situation like that once in a while to really get to know you. And you have to see me in that situation, too."

Cheryl challenges again. "So to really get to know me, I would *have* to say more in here?"

"I would think so. Right."

Cheryl's voice is beginning to have a touch of hysteria. "How do I get over thirty-eight years of being me?"

Hugo's voice is soothing. "I think the rules are different in here." Suddenly he raises his voice, sits up, and slaps his leg for emphasis. "Good or bad, I just think the rules are different here."

"Yeah, I know, but those are words, and I'm a person and not words," exclaims Cheryl. "I don't know how to do that!"

Just like Robert, Hugo readies himself to accept Cheryl's dare. He says, "The only way you're going to do that is to take a risk. Just say, 'Fuck you!' with all you've got."

Cheryl laughs. "Okay." She yells, "Fuck you!" Her laughter is infectious, and everyone joins her.

I can't help smiling and muse: "People think that if they're angry, they have to be totally out of control or totally in control. It's so hard to imagine a middle ground."

"Well, that was easy, wasn't it?" Robert asks.

Cheryl is still laughing, but stops to answer. "Oh, that's easy for me. That's never hard."

Robert realizes that the shoe is on his foot now. "That I've got to learn. I can't say that. I just can't come out with it. I did the other day for the first time in a long time—to someone who was directly under me, but . . . "

Hugo's question is almost inaudible, with his hand over his mouth: "What happened because of it?"

"Five minutes later I called him up and said I'd like to talk to him about it—that I was sorry I'd turned my back on him. I just got frustrated—just could not communicate with the person and said, 'Aw, screw it.' But then I said, 'Alex, we have to talk about this; we have to get this cleared up.' So I did. But I really felt guilty after I did it."

"Sounds like it went fine," Hugo reflects again.

Robert continues: "I don't know; I was shocked into doing something. Alex wasn't going to approach me." He hesitates and then says in a quieter voice, "I tend to withdraw. When I get upset with something, something that really bothers me, I just climb into a shell."

Hugo shifts uncomfortably as though in pain and says: "Yeah, well, withdrawal is sort of a key issue for me too." Hugo reminds me of Arnold, especially when he goes into his "thinker" position or does what he is doing now: his emotional pain literally looks like physical pain. He moves his large, muscular body as though he's just had surgery.

Hugo is sitting next to Robert; Robert can see him resting his head on his fist, ready to listen. Robert takes his cue: "I've been in a shell recently. I've tried not to let the lawsuit bother me. I talked to my attorney two days ago, and I said, 'I'm really concerned.' He said, 'I can hear it,' and then he said: 'Well, you should be. But we're going to fight, and we're going to let them know it.' I learned that the insurance company is going to back me 100 percent under my umbrella policy. It was a relief to hear that. He said, 'You've got to keep yourself together. If you fall apart, you'll never make it. We've got a long haul ahead. In the next two years or so, whatever it takes, your marriage can fall apart, your finances can fall apart, your job can fall apart, and your whole life can fall apart. Try and keep it together as much as you can.' That's one of the reasons why I'm here."

Robert's tone changes. "I've got this anger thing. I appreciate hearing you name it, Tim, that you have it too, and Hugo also. I don't feel as alone as I used to feel. I used to feel that I was the only one, the picked-on one, the only one in the room that got all the crap. That's neither here nor there. I just need to learn how to control myself. The easiest thing for me to do is to shut the world off and climb into a shell. I did this for five years straight. I climbed into a shell right after my divorce—I had nothing to do with people. Went to bed early, nipped a little wine here and there, and slept like a baby all night long. And as long as I was sleeping, I didn't have to worry about the world, and nothing could get at me. I finally decided that wasn't the way to live the rest of my life. But when you stick your neck out, then things start flying at you again."

Hugo is grimacing. Cheryl giggles and then quickly controls herself. Her laugh at such a serious moment tells me that he hit a nerve.

Robert continues, "And that's what happened when I came out of my shell. All of a sudden I started ending up in court every time I turned around." His voice goes up an octave. "And I wasn't doing anything. At least I thought so, or think so. So then I automatically started saying, 'Hey, I better climb in my shell again.' It's not as easy anymore, now that I have a wife. I can't do it anymore."

Arnold's Notes

1962

2

constantly need to clarify. I do not want discussion to be construed as dogma. But language forces the appearance of dogma where it doesn't exist.

I would rather be calm than king.

I can change my viewpoint on a second's notice and then back again. Both are me; which is more correct?

Hugo: The Search for Self

Earlier Group Therapy Meeting Continued

W HERE WE LEFT OFF: *We discussed finding a middle ground in expressing anger.*

Hugo is trying hard to find some order in chaos. He starts slowly, rubbing and patting his chest, and then says: "You can take it too seriously sometimes, in terms of the ramifications of your actions. I used to get medically ill from withdrawing. I never had significant threatening things like you do, Robert, and I don't know how I'd feel if it were a big thing like yours, like the lawsuit against you—*that* significant—but seeing that I was destroying my body allowed me to make changes in my life. I mean, I worked hard and never did the things I wanted to do like travel and take other risks—climb mountains, jump out of airplanes. Then I decided that it didn't make a whole lot of difference. If I could look at life as a joke, it would be all right. Play the game without becoming a piece in the game. I don't know if that's more avoidance, but at least it let me give up stuff that didn't seem productive."

Hugo is purposely being vague. If people knew how he was living his life, he was sure they would be critical. No one could possibly understand. His mother certainly didn't. She couldn't brag about him to her friends or show off his wealth. For a while Hugo had lived the life he was supposed to. He was a successful software engineer with a promising future. He fell in love at twenty but didn't know himself well enough to recognize it. Gradually he became aware of a lack of meaning in his life.

Hugo's father tested race cars and then had a car accident. He was left with a limp, and as a child Hugo was ashamed of him. After the accident his father went into business and made enough money for the family to move to the suburbs. His mother was happy with this increase in status, but his father became depressed.

Hugo knew he was living his life for his father—not the life that was right for himself. When his father died five years ago, Hugo decided to completely change his life and do only what he had a passion for. He had an ancestor who had been burned at the stake for being a witch. She was a rebel in the days of the moralistic Puritans. He wanted to be true to his beliefs, as she was. He quit his job and lived on the money he had already made. He took consulting jobs occasionally but only ones when he agreed with the company's values. He concentrated on hobbies the rest of the time: woodworking, music, theater. He spent time only with people he enjoyed. Despite all these changes, Hugo was not happy. He came to the clinic for help with his chronic malaise. He couldn't find his passion. He had made all the changes he thought he needed to make. He had resisted all of society's seductions toward leading a meaningless life, and yet this did not leave him brimming over with joy. He was completely baffled. He said that he no longer felt as if he was in a cage, living his life for his father, but now he was surrounded by murky matter, and he still couldn't find his way out.

"So you don't withdraw anymore?" Robert asks Hugo.

Hugo alternates between looking at the floor and looking at Robert. "Yeah, I do. I mean it's a constant thing that I have to be aware of. Once you learn those tricks, it's easy to do it."

"Right," Robert mirrors.

I ask Hugo hesitantly, "How involved are you in here?"

"Well, I don't know. I feel like I'm involved. I mean, in some ways I don't know if . . . " Hugo has started to answer without thinking first. He tries to use his hands to help him find the words. I start nodding my head to the rhythm of his words, as encouragement. "You know, I'm just saying what comes to mind. I'm definitely not thinking before I speak. I don't want to say to myself that people think I'm stupid or that this is right or wrong, 'cause I basically don't believe in *shoulds* and *shouldn'ts*, rights and wrongs, good and bad."

From My Father's Book

1921

S uch are the lives of millions of people throughout the famine that raged in the USSR between the years of 1918 and 1921. It was beyond the control of the government.[3] We knew that there had been a world war. The Russian people had sent their sons to die to defend their country; they were told they were fighting for a good cause. They were actually fighting to make the czar secure on his throne.

---

3   Although famines were not unusual in Russia, the Great Famine was the worst so-called natural disaster since the Black Plague during the Middle Ages. Five million people died, with one hundred thousand deaths in just one week. Though the famine was natural in origin, the reasons for its severity were man-made: the overthrow of the czar; the ensuing Russian civil war; the incompetence of the new Soviet government; and political enmity with the United States, which provided famine relief. Herbert Hoover, then secretary of commerce and director of the American Relief Agency (ARA), led a massive two-year humanitarian campaign that began in 1921. Ultimately, the Soviets and Americans transcended their enemy mentality, and the ARA was able to feed eleven million people every day. Source: *American Experience: The Great Famine*, directed by Austin Hoyt and Aisiyuak Yumagulov (Boston: PBS and WGBH Boston, 2011), DVD.

After a while the soldiers refused to fight and went back home to overthrow the Romanoffs and establish a workers' government. They heard that the world war was over, with millions dead, and they settled into building a new nation; little did they realize that they would have to face a famine that would cripple their entire country. The soldiers of other nations in the world war went home to their loved ones. Their hardships were partly over, but in Russia the soldiers' troubles were just beginning. Sometimes they wished they were back fighting rather than starving like dogs.

Before World War I, the people of Ukraine had always enjoyed a quiet life. They took little interest in the outside world, but now that they are in desperate need of help, they cannot understand how other nations do not offer to help. The authorities inform the people that they are doing everything in their power to locate their relatives in foreign lands. Agencies are organized, and the Soviet government asks the people to be brave; help will come to them any day now. These promises give people the hope that keeps them alive. Diseases and epidemics rage through the country, and Elisavetgrad is the hardest hit of all. Our family is recovering from diphtheria—the most common disease. Alex and Sonia make their daily rounds and bring something home to our mother every day. She is losing weight rapidly and displays slight swellings, which are a dreadful sign.

I still work in the market selling *machucha*; this keeps me alive. I come home with strange stories every day, telling my mother I saw dead bodies in the streets, swollen to three times their natural size. I tell her I met Botka, the glazier, and talked with him, asking how his family was. In the midst of our talk, he dropped the glass he was carrying and dropped dead. I tell my mother these stories because I never think any harm might come to her, since Alex and Sonia always bring food home for her.

Due to these drastic conditions, people are becoming degenerate, insane, and idiots. Mrs. Lubanka's son, who came back with the Bolsheviks, is still a soldier. He is on leave now. He gathers all the children into the public toilet and shows them how he is diseased with syphilis and says that they better keep away from him until he is cured. The children always liked to be around him to play with his guns and bullets, but after this incident they never go near him again.

The boys and girls of the neighborhood call on me to peek into the cracks of Mrs. Jacobson's door. There we see a young soldier and a woman in the midst of being intimate. Mrs. Jacob's husband is dead, and her sons have gone away, never to return; the only way she can exist is to rent her rooms to prostitutes, who manage to get a soldier in now and then. We peek until we are chased away. I am shocked to see what I witness. The leader of the gang who started this activity finds an empty house; any boy or girl who refuses to come will be beat up by the gang. These boys and girls are eight to twelve years old. After a while I have a fight with the leader of the gang; I never go near that house again. The people know of these immoral practices going on, but they are so depressed about their own suffering that they do not have the energy to stop it.

Many people go crazy. They run out of their homes, tearing their hair out, yelling. They might find an old shoe or rope and bite on it frantically. These scenes do not attract any attention anymore, since they are so common.

I am walking home from the market and see a crowd gather. I walk over to see a young girl sitting on the curbstone. She is about twenty and has beautiful thick black hair. Her dark eyes are large but sunken—they are like two pieces of coal. Everyone is amazed at her prettiness; a woman of beauty is so seldom seen now. She sits there, staring and chewing lice that she picks from her hair. Someone whispers that she's a Gypsy from a nearby town. Her entire family has died of starvation, while she has gone crazy and is just wandering around. I feel sorry for her and can't get her out of my mind.

Misha comes home from the bread line empty-handed. He is so desperate that he starts to cry and scream—yelling for food. Mother tries to quiet him and asks him to wait for Alex and Sonia to come home. She then finds a bone Ida has brought home. He grabs it like a madman, chewing on it furiously. After a while he starts yelling again, and mother sees that he is going mad. An hour later he lies stretched out with the bone still in his hand, dead. He lies in the house for three days, and as he becomes swollen he begins to look like he once did. We all realize how handsome he was. On the fourth day, a man takes him away, the same way father was taken away—thrown in a wagon, soon to be covered up by other dead bodies. There are no tears except from mother. The rest of us feel very little for life now; death is a blessing.

The days of the famine drag on without any sign of relief. People begin eating horse meat. There is talk that in some parts of the country, people are digging bodies from graves. This is denied, since no one has actually witnessed it. Some people hear of packages coming from the USA, and this gives them some hope. Everyone keeps praying that they will receive a package next.

The Sbritsky family is now reduced from nine to six; we go on struggling. It is amazing how Mother holds on to life under these circumstances. Day and night she keeps thinking of her lost son, Dmitri, hoping he will come home; we all need him so much now. Other mothers wait for their boys, only to hear that they are dead.

A new crisis has come to our family. Neda is walking in the streets while it is raining and storming, hoping that someone will give her something to eat. She is cold and weak from hunger and collapses in the street, not far from home. Mr. Kapaloff finds her and carries her to the house. She is unconscious, but fortunately she is wearing Ida's fur coat, which is twice her size, and it keeps her body warm.

It is impossible to get a doctor; they all work for the government and are not available in these parts. Mother is frantic. She doesn't know what to do when she sees her child come out of the coma. Neda is lying on a little wooden cot with Mother beside her, on her knees, begging her to say something. Finally, the child asks for food. Mother cries, "Yes, yes!" and runs out to beg from some neighbor. She goes from door to door, only to find that others are in far worse condition than she is. She hasn't been out of the house for a long time, since she doesn't have the energy. Her child is sick, and she begs and cries for a little farina or tea. She calls the neighbors who refuse her "cruel beasts," not realizing that they have nothing themselves. She refuses to listen when they say they would be glad to help if they only could.

Finally, she comes to Mrs. Kapaloff, who digs her hand into a trunk to reach for a little farina. Mother cooks it as fast as she can and begins feeding her child, who is now gasping for air and breathing very heavily. As she feeds her with a little spoon, the food is coming back as Neda's mouth slowly closes. Neda dies quietly and peacefully. Mother cries: "This food, or any other food, would never have helped her. She died from pneumonia. That's how my child died! What has God got against me? First it's my husband, then my son, and now my little girl. Why doesn't he take me instead?" As she cries we gather around her. Alex and Sonia are crying while I beg mother to calm down. I cover my dead sister's face, hoping that will help. Ida comes home from work with her package of bones. I explain to her what happened, and she runs to Mother, who is weeping violently.

Neda lies dead only one day before the man comes to take her away. It's the same man and the same wagon that took our father and brother away. Where? Only God knows.

David: The Scapegoat Dilemma

Earlier Group Therapy Meeting Continued

5

W HERE WE LEFT OFF: *Hugo talked about how he rebelled and changed his life, yet is still depressed.*

Something prompts David to talk. "When I was a kid, my parents had all sorts of high standards for me, and I went to top schools and all that. No matter how well I performed, my parents made me feel like a failure. So I got used to criticism. It's handling approval that I have a hard time with because I'm not used to it. If I got the best animal on the merry-go-round, I was embarrassed to talk about it because I wasn't sure how to handle it without looking like I was bragging." David is being quite honest. He is trying to learn how to talk in the group so that others will approve of him and accept him.

David continues. "And as far as the shell stuff, I remember when I was a child with my parents yelling at me or telling me things I didn't want to hear—'Why don't you do this? Why don't you do that?'—I'd withdraw into a shell and refuse to talk. Then I'd say loudly and with hostility, 'Leave me alone!' and run out of the house. And I think I still do that and retreat into a shell."

People are attentive and trying to give David a fair hearing, but he's covering a lot of ground quickly; it makes it hard to respond. He doesn't pause, either. Hugo almost stands up to shift position.

People continue to listen to David. They are tired of scapegoating him and are making an effort to be tolerant. David continues: "And in here I feel . . . well, let's just say that after every group meeting, I have a headache." People don't miss David's subtle criticism of them, but they don't know how to respond in a compassionate way; they let him go on. "So even right now, when I came in today, I was feeling defensive and in a shell; I didn't want to get into anything. I would just as soon be passive and let everyone else do the talking. But just listening to you fellows talk—talking about shells—I realized that's what I was doing. It built up my courage to say what I just did. I don't know if it made any sense or not."

"It doesn't matter." Hugo responds quickly, hoping for a normal exchange, but a long, painful pause follows.

David is such an experienced scapegoat that it seems almost impossible for him to alter his role. He has chosen a scapegoat or victim role most of his life. He has nothing good to say about his parents or his childhood. He came from a "yelly, screamy" Queens Jewish family. His parents are smart and expected him to achieve. However, they never rewarded him for good grades. Everyone in the family related to one another in either a distant or hurtful manner. His mother was domineering and critical. She usually called him by his brother's name. His father worked all the time, and when he was home, he had only complaints. David was constantly engaged in power struggles with them and found his own way of rebelling. He would escape to the streets of Queens, trying to find a peer group to substitute for his family, but this venture was also doomed to failure. He was "the fat kid on the block." If he did succeed in pushing himself into a group, his mother would tell him that the boys were no good; he would then search for another group. "You can't trust anyone, and you always have to be ready to defend yourself." His mother's parents were Holocaust survivors.

Most distressing was how David failed to protect himself in relationships. Although his mother had taught him to distrust everyone, he developed a counterintuitive (and unhealthy) mechanism for dealing with his fear. Instead of slowly and cautiously finding out whether he could trust someone, he would "undress" immediately, making himself needlessly vulnerable. He would trust blindly and then be disappointed. He came for psychotherapy when he was so hurt that he didn't know if he could recover. An ambitious salesman, he had recently found out that the medical device he was selling to his clients was defective. He was being sued from numerous directions and saw no recourse. He felt helpless and defeated. David became depressed, developed migraines, and regained the eighty pounds he had previously lost.

No one responds to David. He puts his head down and then lifts it up and rubs his lips.

Cheryl:
Anxiety Attacks

Earlier Group Therapy
Meeting Continued

W *HERE WE LEFT OFF: David shared a history of interpersonal rejection and of withdrawing into a shell.*

Robert turns to Cheryl. "Last week you said that you didn't want to say anything that sounded stupid. You didn't feel that you were on the same level as some of the people in here. I was amazed to hear that from you. I didn't realize you felt insecure about being in a group like this."[4]

Cheryl is flustered and has trouble finding words to respond. Her hands keep going to her mouth as she tries. "I don't know how to explain how I feel. I am always that way in certain surroundings. I don't know. People. I don't know what it is. But then there are other times when I come across as totally secure. I can see why you're confused. When I told somebody at work that I was going to therapy, she went, 'You? Of all people.'"

---

4   This meeting is not described in the book.

It's understandable that both Cheryl and the group would be confused. Her background has both positives and negatives that led her to develop extreme strengths and weaknesses. She was the "baby" of the family, adored by her parents and one of her two sisters. She was always popular in school and had lots of friends. Her life went smoothly until her father got a brain tumor when she was thirteen years old. He died when she was fourteen. At the time she was distressed by the anger she detected in herself. She resented having to spend Christmas in the hospital. She was aware of this resentment and felt that she was being selfish. She also felt guilty that she had never told her father how much she loved him.

As she was becoming adjusted to her father's death, her mother suddenly died of a heart attack. She'd had no symptoms to warn her family. Cheryl was sixteen. Her first thought was, "Who is going to take care of me?" She was furious. Her parents were fifty-one and fifty-four when they died. It didn't seem fair. She went to live with her sister, who tried to take good care of her. However, she herself was depressed and could hardly manage her own life, let alone Cheryl's. Cheryl was on her own.

Cheryl continued to be popular with her peers. She was attractive and friendly and began to enjoy the attention of men. When she fell in love, she was confident she could decide the fate of the relationship, but after six months her boyfriend rejected her, and her self-esteem collapsed. She couldn't stop crying, couldn't sleep for weeks, and began to have anxiety attacks. During these attacks her heart pounded, her hands sweated, and she was afraid she would pass out. She felt close to vomiting and losing control of her blatter and bowels. She thought she was having a heart attack, as her mother had. She raced to an emergency room, where her symptoms were labeled "anxiety."

The anxiety attacks got worse and more frequent as she moved away from her family and friends to a different part of the country. Somehow the sense of security she'd felt in her hometown did not travel with her. She had an adventurous spirit, but she discovered that home was not like the rest of the world; in the real world she felt incompetent. She came from a working-class, unsophisticated family. She didn't go to college. Yet she now had a supervisory position in an accounting firm and was getting promoted at an unusually fast pace. She obviously made a good impression, and people *thought* she was smart, but she lived in fear of "being found out." She also didn't have parents, as other people did. She decided she had better keep her distance from her colleagues. She wondered if she was crazy to stay in the business world, where she felt like a fraud. Yet something inside her insisted that she be courageous and try to understand why she was having trouble coping. As she experienced additional rejections from boyfriends, she was further motivated to seek therapy.

David asks, "You're saying that's a facade?"

Cheryl responds readily. "Well, I don't know, because . . . I do a good job at a lot of things; I know I do."

David is encouraged. "Are you saying you're wearing a mask of normality?"

Cheryl responds, "That's probably the best word you could have used. I definitely don't feel normal like everybody else. I mean, with all the anxiety and everything, I definitely don't feel like everybody else does. I always feel as though I have to fight to be normal." David feels stroked by Cheryl's praise and honest response. By taking his questions seriously, she has raised his status.

"But what's normal?" Robert asks.

"I don't know. I'm not sure." Cheryl pauses and then continues. "When I look at people, I always think: Everybody else is normal. They're happy, and they go about their lives. They don't have a problem in certain situations. They don't feel like they're going to pass out. They don't feel like they're going to die. They don't go to sleep at night saying, 'I'm afraid of dying,' but I do! So I'm not saying that they don't—I don't know—but I don't think they do." She's starting to feel as confused as the others.

It's time for me to intervene. "Something happened, Cheryl, with your confidence in here when Hugo came into the group. Isn't that true?"

Cheryl is taken off guard. She's embarrassed. She takes a long time to answer and then says hesitatingly, "It's true."

"So perhaps looking at that could help you and others understand the things that trigger your loss of confidence. You had said it had something to do with education?"

Hugo is startled by this reference. He starts to rock himself.

Cheryl is struggling. She looks at me and then continues with the admission. "Though I don't know what his education is, so, I mean . . . " She can't find the words and then blurts out: "Number one, I guess, one of the things is that I feel like there are a lot of people that were brought up in homes that were better than mine. You know, with families that had more . . . " It's hard to get the words out.

" . . . with . . . more . . . money. And therefore people probably had better educations, or a little more stimulating life growing up than I did." This is so hard for her to say. It almost seems too much to expect that she will have to hear responses on top of it.

Robert is astonished, "You feel that way in *this* group? About *us*?" He points to each person in the group to make sure she means everyone, including him.

"About a few people. Yeah."

"Oh." Robert is stunned.

"I feel that way all the time, though. I mean, it's not just this group." Cheryl tries to minimize the impact on others.

I rest my hand on my chin, "So what is your fantasy about Hugo and his background and his education and his finances?"

I nod my head encouragingly. Cheryl trusts me and responds. "I feel like he probably grew up in a nice house and went to college. His family probably had good friends—people who owned businesses. I grew up in an apartment, and my mother and father made $160 a week. They didn't have any friends; they just had each other." Cheryl pauses for a while, feeling exhausted; she wants the meeting to end.

"How does it feel telling that to the people here?" I ask.

"It doesn't bother me." Cheryl shakes her head. "No."

Robert is still astonished, since he always finds Cheryl somewhat intimidating. He says, "You know, you've told us about—somewhat about—your childhood, but I never heard that part before. It sounds like you're kind of ashamed that you come from that situation."

Cheryl hesitates and then says in a low voice, "Sometimes."

Robert is moved and saddened. He feels for Cheryl and wants to stay close to her. "Well, I've always envied the way other people were raised or the families they came from. I've always been envious and jealous." Without realizing it, he points his finger at Cheryl. "I always felt they had something better than I had. And I've gone through life feeling that way—feeling envious and jealous. I wished that I had something better than I did. Now I realize that what I really wanted was time with my father. When I look back on it, I see that I didn't have any good quality time with him; we were always angry at each other."

Cheryl joins him in sadness. "Yeah, well I didn't have any time with my parents, either. They both worked and nobody was affectionate."

Tim chimes in, sounding angry and challenging. "I don't see why you single Hugo out. I mean, what has that got to do with anything?" The male competition for Cheryl is subtle, but now it's up front.

Robert moves as though he were hit and slides as far away from Tim as he can and still remain in his chair. He crosses his legs, putting up a barrier between himself and Tim.

Cheryl quickly meets Tim's stare. "I didn't single him out. Oh, I did sort of, in a way, but it was wood on fire. It wasn't just Hugo. If it were only Hugo, I wouldn't have felt that way." Cheryl blurts out and laughs at the same time: "It's you and him (Robert) and Hugo, okay?" Cheryl feels like dying of embarrassment. Others sense this and join her laughter. The men are grinning; their faces change color.

"You mean we're intimidating?" Robert is still completely disbelieving.

"I'm trying to be honest," Cheryl says sincerely.

"That's good," says Robert.

Hugo begins talking in a serious, slow voice. "I don't think I have a background that's much different from yours, actually. My parents never made much money; they both worked, and there wasn't a lot of affection at home. There weren't a lot friends around. I think about the only thing that you said that's real, according to my background, is that I did go to college."

What Hugo didn't say was that he was brought up in the backseat of his parents' car, even sleeping there in a cardboard box when he was an infant. His parents lived like hobos, slept in their car, and drove from town to town across the United States. His father would take a job for a few months and then go on to the next town. His mother thought the traveling would be good for her son. When he was of school age, they settled in one place for a year or two—but never long enough to establish roots or make some money. Hugo was an only child. His mother was afraid to have another; she might have a girl, and you have to watch girls.

Tim squirms. He is still feeling angry and irritable and chooses to direct his diatribe at Cheryl. "I don't think background has anything to do with it. I think the original thing you said about not feeling like you could articulate things well may be the reason you feel insecure. And you too, Elizabeth. I think that must have to do with your feelings of inferiority. I'm standing out on a limb here, but I don't see that background has a whit to do with it."

Separation

1967

I learn in social work school that siblings are supposed to separate. I tell Arnold this and after graduation, we go our separate ways. Jerry and I marry and go off to Germany. Arnold opens a café called the Non-Violent Workshop in the middle of a white, conservative town in nearby Orange County. My parents work hard to help him set it up; before we know it, the city shuts down the restaurant because Arnold is letting homeless people sleep there.

During a visit to Chicago, where I am now living, Arnold tells me that he would like to travel in Europe. I tell him that he should go to Israel instead because we're Jewish and it's our homeland. He says, "Okay, but first I want to go to Europe." I tell him that he has to write to me because I'm going to be worried about him. He says, "Don't you realize that I worry about you, too? You're not the happiest person in the world, and I have to live with that. I guess we each have our cross to bear." I am stunned. What is he talking about?

Arnold's Poem

1967

Across the lands of ancient times,
A modern mortal walks,
    alone.
No hope, save that eternal one,
    Is hidden in his breast.
No joy,
No love,
No succulent spring
Has borne him to this place.
He comes as a horse around
    a turn and heads on down
    the home stretch.

Elizabeth: Feeling Invisible

Earlier Group Therapy Meeting Continued

9

WHERE WE LEFT OFF: *Cheryl shared her insecurity.*

Elizabeth is surprised to hear Tim mention her name. She keeps feeling that she's invisible in the group. She has been sitting quietly. Instead of the boyish overalls she has to wear for work, she is wearing a cheerful sundress. It's feminine but gives her a childish appearance. She has short blonde hair that forms ringlets around her face. She is preoccupied with her weight and sees it as her biggest concern. She will go to any extreme to control it, including vomiting up her food before it's digested. She thinks about food constantly. Sometimes when she is in the group, she sits back and imagines everyone in the room as part of a hot fudge sundae. Tim is the nuts because he is hard; Linda is the cherry because she takes up little space in the group but adds a special something; Robert is the chocolate ice cream because dark colors are male and his presence is substantial; Cheryl is the vanilla ice cream because she is feminine; I am the hot fudge sauce because I cover everything and my influence is felt in every crevice. These are her private thoughts, which she has shared with me over the phone in between group sessions.

As Robert and others are sharing their secrets of impotence, she is thinking that her secrets are much more unacceptable and disgusting. For example, putting her vomit in a heavy-duty trash bag and driving around the city looking for a dumpster far from home to drop it in. Or the time the dog found the vomit and ate it. No one could ever understand. Sometimes she'd think, "The world is my toilet"; other times, "the group is my toilet"; other times, "my family is my toilet."

Little does Elizabeth know that it is not her weight at all that is her motivation to binge and vomit. Her emotions are what she wants to avoid. Any time she perceives a hint of negative feeling, she quickly binges and vomits to numb her emotions. It works as an anesthetic, the way a drug does.

The only subject more painful to Elizabeth than her weight is her track record with men. She is twenty-nine years old, and no man has stayed with her for more than three weeks. She has only blind dates and one-night stands. Recently she has joined a few dating websites. Typically, she initially gets a good response from a man, and they embark on a meaningful email correspondence. She then emails him a picture of herself from the waist up, and he continues to be pleased. Then comes the total body picture. As soon as he realizes she's "fat," he abruptly stops writing. Since Elizabeth has been in the group, she has been trying something different to prevent rejection: telling a man up front what her weight is. It appeared that this strategy was going to work with the new man she'd been emailing with. He wrote that her weight was no problem, and they had the most meaningful correspondence she'd had so far. They emailed each other every other day and shared many thoughts. They began to plan a meeting halfway between their two cities, which are a hundred miles apart. Elizabeth was sure "this was it." But the man was not being truthful. As soon as he saw the picture of her total body, he abruptly stopped emailing her. Time after time, every few months, a painful rejection from a man repeats itself. Elizabeth yearns to be loved for the person inside her. She wants a boyfriend more than anything in the world.

When I interviewed Elizabeth for the group, I asked her about her childhood. She answered by telling me about her grandmother. Her grandmother was from Silesia, the part of Poland that the Poles and Germans always fought over. She grew up in an idyllic family with loving parents and a beautiful home and garden. All this changed in 1939 when she was six years old and the Germans invaded. Her grandmother had to go through a "racial purity" test in which people in white coats measured her head and nose. She was alone when the first bombing came. She sat on the steps of her house, watching truckloads of dead bodies pass by—arms, legs, and heads—all in a pile on the trucks. Their town was on the escape route for the German army after the defeat at Stalingrad. The family spent days in the potato cellar. When she came up to look around, she saw hundreds of people torn apart, dying, screaming, and moaning. The town was almost completely destroyed. The Russians "liberated" them and made the residents leave, so she walked with a pack of women and children through the front lines. She was alone and stumbled over dead bodies and bomb craters. A group of drunken soldiers raped women in front of the children.

Years later her grandma fell in love with and married a man who'd had similar experiences. They wanted to free themselves from the Russians and Communism. They had a young son and had to leave him with relatives so they could escape. The plan was that he would follow. For three years they waited for their son. They could not look at a child without crying. Then a miracle happened. During this excruciating time, Elizabeth's mother was born. Elizabeth's grandmother clung to her daughter—her salvation. The group is not privy to this history.

Tim says to Elizabeth to help prove his point, "Remember when you were saying that you felt like what happens to you in your life isn't important—as important as what happens to the other people around?"

"Yeah." Elizabeth blushes.

"Well, I know how you feel," Tim says.

Arnold's Postcards
from Europe

1967

10

'm on a tour of Heineken's brewery today. Free beer and cheese. My motorcycle broke down in Amsterdam, and I'm waiting to have it repaired. I'm on my way to Israel now. Next stops are Paris, Venice, Florence, Rome, Istanbul, Beirut, Israel . . . Amsterdam is the finest city in Europe for my taste so far. It is very atmospheric, with a wonderful canal system and friendly people. I met Doug Harvey by accident here. We went to the museum and discovered the finest paintings the world has ever known. We couldn't believe that the paintings of Jan Vermeer were done by a human hand. There are also Rembrandts, Van Goghs, and Cezannes—all outstanding masters in their own right.

• • • • •

I met a Moroccan last night who is most outstanding. A poet, philosopher, and just an ebullient personality. We are becoming good friends.

• • • • •

When God made the Danish, he took a glass of milk and let the cream rise to the top; it's of the cream that he made the Danish.

• • • • •

I'm in Napoli waiting to leave for Pompeii. I'll spend the evening in Torrente and then go to the Isle of Capri for a day and on to Brindisi, where I'll take a boat for Greece. Italy is of course a marvelous country, and Michelangelo: what a giant, what an absolute giant! However, Mr. Vermeer, in one miraculous moment of history, even surpassed life itself. The result is the painting *Young Woman Reading a Letter*. Holland is a wonderful place. Amsterdam one of the few habitable cities. Bologna in Italy is a masterpiece. Paris reminded me of a cross between a Napoleonic recruiting poster and a beaux arts convention.

• • • • •

I'm now in Sori, a suburb of Genoa, Italy. It's very beautiful. I've come here from the French Riviera, a real-life fairyland. The Alps rise from the coast, and houses and villas are nestled cozily amidst them. I spent the night on the highest point, overlooking Villefranche and Nice, under a magnificent fortress. I arrived too late for the hostel, and it was the most beautiful sight I've ever seen. I've met some very fine people of both sexes in my travels, and am having a very nice time.

• • • • •

The natural beauty of Europe is amazing. I often spend my days in a beautiful grotto by the sea, reading poetry and writing down my scattered thoughts, until the day when I am capable of more.

• • • • •

I had spaghetti in a little Italian place, and I saw all of Michelangelo's faces but David. Missing you all very much. Looking forward to Israel.

The Triangle: Competition for the Love Object

Earlier Group Therapy Meeting Continued

W*HERE WE LEFT OFF: Tim told Elizabeth that he understands her feeling that what happens in her own life is less important than what happens in other people's lives.*

Tim turns from Elizabeth to talk to Cheryl. "It seems like you're five steps above where you ought to be in the world. I mean, in terms of the lifestyle you live and the job you have and all that. And you're in constant fear of being exposed. Like, if you . . . "

Cheryl interrupts him with laughter. She is giddy because she can't believe that Tim is so accurately putting her feelings into words. "That's true! I know what you mean." Cheryl is bubbly.

"This thing about being exposed. You feel like a fake." Tim continues to read Cheryl.

"You could very well be right. Yeah, because I'm amazed. Yeah." Cheryl still cannot get over how empathy feels. It's a relief to be understood. It feels wonderful.

Robert works himself into the action, competing with Tim for Cheryl. "So do you not make as many friends because you're afraid that you might be exposed? That some of your friends might find out that you really aren't what you . . . "

Cheryl immediately corrects him. "No."

Robert tries again. "Or are you just finding it difficult to find people to become friends with? People that you want to be friends with?"

"Yeah. Well, yeah."

"Because I know that's a big issue." Robert is letting her know he has been carefully listening.

"Because I'm picky, too!" Cheryl sounds adamant. "I don't have a difficult time making friends, per se." Her tone changes, and she says slowly, "I have a difficult time . . . finding deep friendships."

I respond: "Is there a difference with men and women?"

Cheryl stares and pauses a long time before she answers. "Yeah."

I continue: "One of the things that's striking is that you're in here partially because you haven't been satisfied with your relationships with men—your feeling that somehow your choices haven't been good—and your feelings of inferiority have come up with the men in here."

Elizabeth rubs her face, and Robert does the same. Robert then starts to wipe his brow. They know my pursuit will be hard for Cheryl, and they would prefer to avoid conflict. It seems as though Cheryl has been in the hot seat long enough.

Cheryl looks at the floor. She feels caught. She thinks of Linda, who isn't present. "I haven't put Linda in the same category. So I don't know."

"Of feeling inferior?" Tim asks.

"Yeah," Cheryl answers slowly. She takes some time to reflect, and no one interrupts her silence. "So I don't know." She takes more time. "I'm trying to see a connection, but I don't."

Various people start sentences, but none of them finish. They are trying to help her but don't know how.

"The reason I have more of a hard time with men is because I have a hard time not being attracted to them, as opposed to just being friends." Cheryl is using her hands in broad gestures; her hands are helping her get the words out. These facts are hard for her to admit even to herself, let alone share with the men and women in the group.

"So how is it for you with the men in here?" I am not letting her off the hook.

Cheryl is shaking her head as she listens to the question. She waits a long time to answer. "Well, it's in here, so it's different."

I still don't let up. "But we do have attractive men and attractive women in here." I pause. All eyes are upon me, and I sense that people need a moment to digest what I'm saying. "It's natural for people to be sexually attracted to one another." I want them to know that all feelings can be experienced and expressed in the group. Since most of their families have trouble dealing with feelings, I need to encourage their expression without judgment and with acceptance. I want them to have a reparative family experience.

When Cheryl realizes what I am suggesting, she starts to laugh, in protest. "I'm not answering!" She laughs again—a hearty laugh. "What's the use?" she exclaims.

Robert starts to talk. He also has a strong response to what I'm suggesting. Cheryl continues to be fidgety and restless as she listens to him. David and Elizabeth shift in their seats to look at Robert, trying to give Cheryl some relief from their gaze.

Robert talks slowly and methodically. He starts by directing himself to Cheryl. "Well, I was just going to say that . . .Well, that originally we didn't hit it off. At least I didn't hit it off with you. The main reason was because I was afraid of you; I thought that you were a philosophical individual who liked to talk in circles. And I have never been able to handle an individual like that. Okay?"

Cheryl sits back in her chair as she realizes that Robert is going to talk for a while. She starts to relax, even though he is talking about her. Hugo has one foot on the coffee table in front of him. He looks at it and rolls it slowly from one side to another to the rhythm of Robert's words.

"All my life I've avoided people like you, so I was putting out negative vibes to you. I didn't want any part of you. Actually, I hoped at one time you wouldn't stay in the group—*prayed* you wouldn't stay in the group—but that's all gone now because I feel it doesn't matter. I mean, you can be as philosophical as you want; it doesn't matter; it's not going to hurt me. In fact, I'm learning to appreciate it once in a while." Robert takes a deep breath and then blurts: "Once you get started ,you really roll!" A laugh pops out.

"How do you feel, Robert, about what I was saying to Cheryl? I noticed you came in pretty fast to change the subject." I'm not giving anyone a chance to avoid looking at what's going on in the room right at the moment. I know that this facing of current feelings is the hardest thing group members can do. It's much easier for most people to talk about their past than it is for them to tell one another exactly how they are feeling in the moment. Yet it is only through examining these prevailing feelings that people will grow and have healthier intimate relationships.

All the group can do is laugh; this is the response to my question. What else can one do when one is thrust into no-man's-land—a land where you don't know the rules? Robert and Cheryl lead the laughter, and everyone else follows. I even smile, empathizing with their exasperation.

When the laughter dies down, Robert starts to talk again. He is accepting my challenge. "Whenever we . . . we get close to sex, I start . . . " He pauses. "I don't know what it is. I find it difficult to talk about it in a group. I don't find it difficult to talk about it with a close friend or whatever. But I find it difficult to talk about in a mixed crowd. Not a crowd—the group. It's always been difficult for me. I've always been very shy about that."

Robert proceeds to talk slowly and carefully, with frequent pauses. "And I know it stems from my home life. We weren't supposed to talk about sex at all. My wife, Sally, has brought me out of my shell in that respect. We're open and loving and honest about all of that. And nothing surprises me anymore, but I find it difficult, especially . . . " He turns to Elizabeth. "Now, I could probably talk to you about it." He looks at Cheryl sitting across from him. "But I'd find it very difficult to talk about it to you . . . *BECAUSE I'M SEXUALLY ATTRACTED TO YOU.* And that's difficult for me to say, too."

Cheryl shrieks, "Oh, my God!!!" Robert has done the forbidden. It feels the same as if he had dropped his pants in the middle of the floor.

"And that's it." Robert laughs too. "It's as honest as I can be." He stops, but people look as though they are depending on him to continue. They let him take a long pause. He starts stroking the top of his thigh as he continues. "I always had a difficult time when I started dating, and I didn't start dating until I was in college."

Hugo takes his leg off the table, looks at his foot and bends it awkwardly to adjust his sock. He has trouble finding a comfortable position. Elizabeth looks up at Robert and then lowers her head; she plays with her hands on her lap.

Robert persists. His legs open and close. He rubs his thighs with the palms of his hands. Occasionally, he opens his palms to the group, asking people for understanding. "And every date I had drove me up the wall because I didn't know, I always wanted to know—look in that crystal ball and say, 'Is this gonna be the one I'm gonna marry?' I went through this every date that I had—it was terrible. I'd go two or three times and about the third or fourth time I'd say, 'I know this is the one.' And then I'd break off the total relationship—never speak to the person again." He lets his eyes meet Cheryl's. "I think there's a deep-seated fear in me that I didn't want to let you know my deep-down, dark feelings that I'm sexually attracted to you, because then I would feel compelled to break off any relationship with you; I wouldn't talk to you in here anymore." Robert's hand is now resting on the inside of his thigh.

Cheryl understands. "Exactly."

Robert continues: "I know there'll never be anything on the outside, but in here I didn't want to break it off."

"Yeah," Cheryl adds empathically.

I address Robert. "So you're asking the same question as Cheryl: How can you be friends with somebody of the opposite sex and be sexually attracted to them yet keep it a friendship?"

"Exactly," Robert echoes.

Suddenly everyone starts talking at once. There is a lot of energy released in the room. Cheryl's voice stands out. "It's possible—as long as you don't let him or her know," she says seriously.

I clarify: "It's like you can have friends you're not attracted to, or you can have lovers. But how do you have something in between?"

Everyone's hands go over their mouths, including me. I am identifying with the group's conflict. I remember my own therapy experience when I focused on the same issue. "It's a strange question," Tim comments.

Hugo perks up and says boldly, "You just take a risk, and you say: 'Listen, I'm turned on by you and I'm horny, but I'd like to be your friend.'" Robert is delighted, and he and Hugo chuckle.

"What about the fact that we have to be friends in here? What do we do about that?" I ask.

"Oh, I didn't know you were talking specifically about in here," Hugo comments.

"Yeah, let's keep it in here," Robert mutters softly and then giggles under his breath.

I continue, this time firmly. "So it's one thing talking about how you feel—it's another thing acting on it. We're here to talk about the feelings, not to act on them. But that may be a very different kind of friendship for the men and the women in here."

Elizabeth's eyes dart around to catch a glimpse of each person as he or she speaks. Her presence is easy to forget.

"See, that's what's been very difficult for me all my life: talking about those particular feelings that I have toward people," Robert exclaims.

"Toward people or women?" I ask Robert.

"Especially women."

"Because men can feel attracted to each other, too," I state factually. It's important to state that we all have a combination of homosexual and heterosexual attractions.

There is a long silence. It seems to last forever. Everyone is stunned when Elizabeth starts to talk; each person freezes in position, except for Cheryl, who slowly moves a finger across her lip.

A pressure has been building inside Elizabeth that is not detectable to anyone. The long silence gives her a chance to put some of her feelings into words and rehearse them in her head.

Elizabeth turns to Robert, who is sitting next to her. "I think what you said really bothered me." She laughs to try to soften her rage. "Just the fact that you can talk to me like I'm one of the guys, but you can't talk to her about it." She darts a look at Cheryl and then pauses. "I guess what bothers me is that sometimes I don't feel attractive enough to men." Her voice starts to crack and then she starts to sob. The tears don't stop, and her nose doesn't stop running. She decides to continue in spite of it and chokes on tears and mucous in her throat as she tries to talk.

"Sometimes at my job I feel like one of the guys, and I try to compensate for that. I guess what it boils down to is that I sometimes don't feel attractive enough. And I'm always . . . " She pauses and reaches for a tissue. No one moves. "It's like when I meet guys, I'm always making reasons or excuses for what I look like and . . . deep down I know that it's what's inside that should really matter, but it doesn't."

Hugo touches his forehead as though he is pointing to the locus of his pain. Robert sits motionless with the others, but if *at that moment* someone had come along and offered to cut off his balls, I think he would have agreed.

The silence continues.

Finally, Cheryl turns to me and says angrily, "This is why I didn't want to answer the question about sexual attraction. Because I think it hurt . . . " She pulls her hair as she searches for the words. "It would hurt people's feelings to answer that question. And I don't see a good point to that!"

"I really envy Cheryl," Elizabeth says tearfully. She's crying hard, but she pushes the words through. "Because she's . . . " Elizabeth bends over and reaches for another tissue. "Sometimes people say to me, 'Oh, you're a good person.' But they never say, 'You're attractive.'"

Elizabeth sobs harder. It's not all right to vomit in the group, but it *is* all right to sob. It is not an ordinary sob. All the residue from her disappointing group therapy experience is being dumped in the middle of the group—right where Robert dropped his pants when he told Cheryl that he was attracted to her.

Hugo shifts in his chair and slowly pulls down the sleeves of his shirt. He looks as though he is in pain and that if he moved too fast, it would hurt more. He settles in his doubled-over "thinker" position.

Elizabeth has blown her nose and is ready to continue. "They just say, 'You're a good person.' Sometimes I wish I was just normal. I wish I was thin because I would be different."

There is a long silence, and the only sound in the room is Elizabeth's sniffling.

Tim keeps feeling that there is something not right about what is going on. He breaks the spell and questions Elizabeth. "What do you mean you compensate at work?"

Elizabeth continues to talk through her sobs. "I get my nails done and try to dress up. I try to look different from the men because I don't want to be treated like one of the boys. You know, in my work, there are mainly men, and my uniform is masculine."

"Oh, I see."

Elizabeth continues to talk and cry in the group; deep inside she feels the group is as rejecting of her as her last almost-boyfriend-by-email. In fact, it feels to her at this moment that the group embodies every rejection and misunderstanding she has ever had. Her parents are very old-fashioned. When she had a crush on a boy when she was thirteen, they thought she was doomed to become a prostitute. She feels a longing to be understood and accepted but has given up on it. At least in the group, where it's safe to express anger, she can vent the rage that she feels the group members deserve. Every painful interaction in her history is being played out in the group; the members are as bad as anyone she can think of in her life.

Elizabeth starts to repeat herself through her tears. "I try to dress up somewhat. I don't like to be treated like one of the guys. I'm *not* one of the guys. *I'm a girl!*" She uses her hands for emphasis. "But sometimes when you're in the kind of work I'm in . . . " She reaches for a tissue. "It's like sometimes some of the guys at work . . . Well, I guess it's normal for them to check out the girl runners and stuff. I mean, you're sitting there in the truck with them and you feel like . . . I don't know the word . . . you just . . . it hurts."

"Well, how do you feel when someone does give you a compliment?" David asks.

Elizabeth answers, "I don't believe it."

More long silence. Everyone looks paralyzed.

David picks up the ball again. He is talking cautiously and even stumbles over a few words. His head is resting on his hand; he moves his hand a little away from his head in order to use it to add to what he's saying. He hasn't moved his eyes from

Elizabeth for some time. "Earlier, when we first came in, I complimented your dress. Did you think I was lying?"

"No, you probably meant it." There's another long pause as Elizabeth reaches for more tissues and blows her nose.

Elizabeth continues. "When I wrote that ad for the dating website and I wrote 'attractive,' I questioned it. I tried to compare myself to other people—I'm not even sure . . . " She cries harder.

Another long, painful silence ensues. The atmosphere feels torturous. David turns his head to look to me for help. I don't respond to the invitation. He sees that I'm calm. I'm attentive. My eyes are going around the circle, and everyone is aware of my personal gaze. They all sit and wait for Elizabeth—giving the message that she can sob for as long as she needs to.

"I don't know what more to say," Elizabeth continues, feeling the group pressure to keep talking. "This guy that I was emailing—I finally sent him a photo of myself. He had a picture before, but it was only a waist-up shot, and he kept saying . . . " She sniffles. "We had this kinda disagreement about why I wouldn't send him a full picture. So finally I said, 'Okay, I'll send the picture.'" Everyone is looking at the floor as she talks. It is painful to listen; looking would make it worse for her and them. "And . . . I sent it. I thought it was a pretty good picture. And now he hasn't even written or called or anything, so I figure that's why." She pauses a while, and no one says anything.

People are still staring at the floor.

David finally breaks the silence. "Before, when you were all talking about . . ." He stutters for a moment and then proceeds. He is addressing the whole group. "When you were talking about the cross-relationships in here, I guess Elizabeth and I were the only ones who were omitted. A lot of times in a group situation, I feel lonely and isolated, and it sends me into a depression. And . . . a little bit of that happened here when Elizabeth and I were the only ones who weren't mentioned in the cross-relationships."

No one sees Elizabeth bristle violently inside at the low-status David pairing himself with her.

"Yeah, but I put myself in the same category as both of you when I was talking about how I felt." Cheryl's voice is soft—gentle but firm. She wants to show David that they share similar feelings underneath. The high-status group member tries to align herself with the weakest so that the group will remain whole. It's beginning to feel as though there has been an earthquake in the room, and the rift is widening.

Cheryl looks directly at Elizabeth, who is sitting across from her. Her voice starts low but quickly becomes more confrontational. She tries hard to let some warmth come through. "Elizabeth, can I ask you one question? When David said what he did to you about your dress, and he said, 'Did you think I was lying?' And you said 'No, you probably meant it.' Don't you do exactly what you're saying everybody else does?"

"Do what? Putting your . . . "

"Looking at people according to whether they're attractive or not?"

"Yeah, I'm probably guilty of that," Elizabeth answers honestly.

"You know, that's a hard thing for anybody not to do. It's all in certain people's eyes. I mean, there are a lot of people I think are attractive that my friends go, 'Oh, wowee, are you kidding me?' But I'm just saying you do it too, so I don't like you judging people for doing it, because *everybody* does it. You know? Including you!" Cheryl is loosening up. Her voice is strong and clear. She looks directly at Elizabeth with great feeling and conviction. She repeats to Elizabeth: "Including *you*."

Everyone makes an effort to stay calm. There is fear that the group might disintegrate or that the catastrophe will worsen if people are not careful. Suppose Elizabeth dies (leaves the group) from Robert's assault? Or suppose she kills Cheryl out of jealousy (Cheryl leaves the group)? Suppose Robert, Hugo, and Tim kill one other as they compete for Cheryl (they leave the group)? Of course, these fears are unconscious.

"We all do," David comments on the heels of Cheryl's outburst. "What I was getting at before was that in the hallway or here, wherever, very often, I just give Elizabeth a friendly greeting, and she is sort of in a shell. And I've never been able to understand exactly why."

Cheryl is shaking her head as David talks, still trying to absorb and recover from her emotive expression to Elizabeth. It would mean so much to her for Elizabeth to see her point. As she absorbs all of this, she decides to let David continue.

"It might be because at the first group meeting when Elizabeth was here, I gave her a greeting from the garage, and she thought I was trying to pick her up or something like that."

Hugo recrosses his legs, checks his sock a bit abruptly, and then crosses his arms, hugging his chest. He doubles over as though he were just hit in the gut. He stays in this position. Only Cheryl is looking at David as he talks.

Cheryl has had her break, and she is now ready to get back to Elizabeth. Her voice is full of passion, and her face animated. "And the other thing, Elizabeth, is when you say you compensate—well, *everybody compensates*. I polish my nails, I wear dresses, I go out and buy five thousand dollars' worth of clothes to look better than somebody else—who looks better than I do!"

David takes Cheryl's cue and talks directly to Elizabeth. "I think Hugo paid you a very good compliment a few weeks ago when he said your honesty and openness were refreshing and rare."

Hugo doesn't budge.

Tim is practically jumping out of his seat. His voice is alive and seems to counter Hugo's paralysis. Those who had been looking at the floor, including Hugo, raise their heads to hear Tim. "I have a little problem with this; I think everyone is trying to say, 'Cheryl, it's just in your head.' And I mean, I don't know what to say, Cheryl, because . . . "

"Tim, do you mean Cheryl or Elizabeth?" I ask.

"I'm sorry, I'm sorry—Elizabeth. That everybody's trying to say it's just in your head and . . . "

"That's why we're here, isn't it?" David laughs at his own joke. I suppress a giggle.

Tim ignores David and tries to complete his thought. He is sitting across from Elizabeth and looks directly at her. "The reason I'm so quiet about this is that the cold, hard fact is that people do this kind of judgment, and you probably *have* been the butt end of a lot of callous judgments. People have probably done exactly what you think they have—judged you by your weight and by your appearance. That's . . . "

Cheryl interrupts and blurts out, "I'm sorry, I can't let you go on . . . "

Cheryl and Tim start talking at once. They are both getting more upset and trying to control themselves.

Tim prevails. "Look it, it's a matter of attitude! I don't say it all equals out. I just said it's a cold, hard fact. I'm not saying it all equals out!"

Everyone's face is up, looking at him. Hugo sits erect and open. Tim continues. "I just hate to see us . . . well, I don't know what to say or do, either! I mean . . . I'm sure you have been . . . Well, there *are* standards. Like you said, what's inside people should matter. And I really agree with that. But unfortunately, it doesn't. And so a lot of people get the short end of the stick. I think we're trying to bury that fact and say, 'Oh, no. Well, everybody does it, so, you know, why should you take it personally?'"

Cheryl interrupts. She can hardly stay in her seat. "I don't think so. I don't think that's what we're trying to do. I don't think we're trying to bury it."

Tim needs to explain more: "Well, I got that impression. People are saying, 'Elizabeth, I gave you a compliment. What's your problem?' I sympathize with Elizabeth. I understand." He looks at Elizabeth, who has slowly pulled up her sleeves and is periodically lifting her head to look at him as he talks. "You know, the way you told the story about that email guy—well, I wouldn't doubt it if the asshole did throw your picture away. That's possible. I mean, it probably isn't just in your head, and now the thing is . . . "

Cheryl butts in excitedly, "But the other thing is, is that she left herself open for that!"

"How?" asks Robert, confused.

Cheryl's voice is getting more high-pitched. "Because she went into the relationship without the picture, and the guy lives a hundred miles away!" She catches her breath. (Hugo starts to smile from odd relief but hides it behind his hand.) "I've done stupid things too. And people have rejected me too." Her voice is shrill.

"Oh, I see," Robert responds.

Cheryl continues: "I've been the brunt of a helluva lot of rejections myself. So just because I look better than somebody else is not to say that I haven't been the brunt of things, either." Cheryl's voice is cracking. "So that's what bothers me about what you're saying, Elizabeth." Cheryl is trying hard to be empathetic, but Elizabeth won't look up to meet her gaze.

Cheryl can't let Tim finish and says, "That's why I'm trying to explain. Granted, everybody's got a higher or lower degree of 'it,' but unless you're going to do something about it, then what are you going to do???"

Tim answers: "Okay, I don't know, maybe I'm wrong. I just had this impression that everyone was trying to tell Elizabeth, 'Oh, there's no problem. I gave you a compliment. You're not really overweight.'"

David defends himself. "I didn't say that. I wasn't trying to say that."

"I'm just . . . kind of . . . you know . . . I don't know. Okay, you didn't, whatever. You complimented her dress or something. I mean . . . " Tim pauses in exasperation. "So what??? What has that got to do with this guy she sent the email to who didn't give her a fair chance because she's overweight?"

Robert shifts and moves as far toward the wall as he can and still stay in his chair. He turns his head away from the whole group. Hugo does the same.

Tim's tone softens. "I just . . . I'm just trying to . . . " He stops to find some words. He looks at Elizabeth, and she looks up at him. "I mean . . . I kind of feel for Elizabeth . . . And David, I'm just not convinced by the things you said—that it's all okay."

Elizabeth looks at David as he begins to respond, and then she puts her head down. David says slowly, "No, what I'm trying to suggest to Elizabeth is that it's her attitude toward herself and her attitude toward people in general. She may be setting up barriers for herself." He pauses. "Because . . . *there are a lot of people who aren't Barbie dolls who get married!*" David exclaims. I can't hide my smile.

"Fine. But what happened in here?" I ask. Everyone looks up at me, startled to hear my voice, including Elizabeth. "Is it because Elizabeth put up a barrier that Robert is more attracted to Cheryl than to Elizabeth?"

Hugo is compelled to speak: "It's real interesting to me that there's a lot of comparison going on in here between people. And that's exactly what goes on in real life and it's real helpful to know that . . . "

Cheryl objects, "Yeah, but don't you . . . "

Hugo continues. "I mean, it's certainly helpful to know how people perceive you, especially if you're a sensitive person. So it's a reflection of your life, but does that get to the core of the issue as to how each person feels about him or herself?"

I ask, "How did you feel, Hugo, about what just went on?"

Cheryl leans forward toward Hugo, with her hand staying over her mouth. Everyone's eyes are on Hugo, except Elizabeth's.

Hugo starts talking: "Well, okay, I was really focusing on how I felt about the issue of attractiveness. And the way I reacted to that was that there are lots of times when I don't feel attractive. I can't imagine that there's anybody in this *whole* world who always feels attractive, unless he or she is narcissistic. But I can certainly identify with having people think that I'm not attractive. I don't know what to do with that. You've got to deal with people, and there are times when people think you're attractive and other times when people don't think you're attractive. Sometimes in my life I feel a lot less attractive than I do at other times in my life. I just don't know. I mean, that's an issue that goes from being *this* big to *massively* big." He illustrated with his hands. "But I sure can identify with Elizabeth. I know all the symptoms: retreat, withdrawal. You start saying, 'Nobody's any good. I don't want to take risks with anybody.' And then there are people you look at who you think are humongously unattractive, yet there they are out there, right up front up, taking risks!" He has loosened up and is squirming openly in his seat. He starts to laugh. "Shit, I don't know. Christ, it's like everybody's got this thing!"

David interrupts Hugo, "It's the St. Francis of Assisi type of story." (Cheryl plays with her hair as David finishes.) "You feel sorry for yourself because you have no shoes until you find someone who has no feet."

Hugo says to Cheryl, ignoring David, "But you also said that we all have it at different levels, and there's always someone prettier or . . . "

"Right," says Cheryl.

Hugo continues: "And that may be true, but it doesn't help you deal with the . . . "

"No, it doesn't," says Cheryl.

Hugo: "I mean, even if you do put yourself somewhere on that hierarchy, it doesn't help you deal with the fact that there's somebody above you or somebody beneath you. You know, I . . . "

"But I wasn't trying to make anybody feel that way." As Cheryl talks she puts her palm out to Hugo again; it looks like a pleading gesture. "I was just trying to state a fact. You know, to a certain degree, I was trying to help Elizabeth out. She was hurting there for a while. Were we all going to just sit here and let her hurt?" Cheryl is exasperated. "I mean, I didn't know what else to say, to not have her hurt."

Hugo responds. Cheryl is out there, exposed, and he is determined to stay with her. Elizabeth and the others watch. "Yeah, I understand. But believe me, I felt *incredibly* empathetic because there have been many times when I've felt exactly the same way as Elizabeth. On the other hand, I'm not sure it's a bad thing to feel hurt." He smiles and is engaging as he maintains eye contact with Cheryl. "I think the core of the issue for me is, how do I come to like myself enough so that these things don't really matter? I mean, I think if we took a vote, we'd have an eight-to-nothing vote that what should matter is how people feel about themselves and not how they look. What's important is that other people accept me for who I am. But they don't. That is the reality of the issue!"

Everyone but Elizabeth looks at David as he responds to what Hugo just said: "I also find that relationships spring up at the most unlikely places and the most unlikely times. I've grown up feeling needy and deprived as far as affection goes. When I go to a party or a singles group or anything like that where I'm trying to make a connection, I feel like an ass. I feel very lonely in a large group of people. It generally ends up flat, and I feel very bad about myself."

After a few moments of listening, Hugo looks away at the arm of his chair. Elizabeth rubs her neck, not budging her bent head.

David continues: "Then again, when I was going to Overeaters Anonymous meetings every night with the same couple of people in Jersey City, I didn't wear anything special or even put on aftershave or anything like that to go look for someone, because I figured OA is the last place I'd find someone. But all of a sudden lightning struck between me and this lady named Celia."

I move my hand a bit away from my mouth and ask, "Is everybody in here saying that people are equally attractive and have equal kinds of problems in terms of . . . "

"I haven't heard that at all." Hugo can't let me finish. Elizabeth reaches for a tissue. Robert stretches backward. Everyone moves and then starts talking at once.

David's voice is the loudest: "I think some people have a harder time attracting others. Perhaps this is what Cheryl and I are saying."

Cheryl leans on her crossed legs and rocks herself.

After some clamoring by others to get the floor, David continues: "And I'm not sure if there's any magic formula in how to break that down."

Elizabeth begins to stroke her hair.

I take the floor. I am aware that it is almost time to end the meeting. "So maybe another question that hasn't been addressed is how much you *want* a lot of people to be attracted to you. How *comfortable* would you feel if a lot of people were attracted to you? That answer might explain some of the differences among you."

Members look at me, puzzled and transfixed. Hugo sits back, crosses his legs, and folds his arms.

Robert still has his head as far from the group as he can get it, but he has his eyes on me. He is tormented. He finds it overwhelming to face the parallel between his hurting Elizabeth—a young, naive woman—and his ex-wife's and daughter's accusations that he watched pornography with his daughter. I am still not sure whether Robert is innocent. His daughter's story is convincing to the expert psychologist who evaluated her. The young girl has been graphic about how the penis looks and how it grows in size and how it is used to rub against another person's skin. I am hoping I can get some clues by observing Robert in the group.

Robert turns to Elizabeth and speaks to her, even though she continues to look at her lap. "I'm sorry that I started what I started, if I started this whole thing. Elizabeth, I've always felt that you're more like . . . Well, I could be your father—there is a big age difference. Whereas I know Cheryl is closer to my age—I'm still a few years older . . . but . . . well."

I ask straightforwardly, "So you think if Elizabeth was Cheryl's age that you'd be equally attracted to Cheryl and Elizabeth?"

Robert is confused again. I keep leading him into dangerous territory. "No, I can't say that. I'm not equally attracted to everybody."

"Why do you feel responsible for hurting Elizabeth with your honest attraction to Cheryl?" Hugo challenges Robert. Everyone perks up and starts to move.

"I know. I feel responsible for it," Robert admits. He is actually torturing himself with guilt.

"But *wouldn't you?*" Cheryl says angrily to Hugo. Her face is flushed.

People are starting to talk fast. If they don't speak quickly, they won't get a chance.

"No, not for the comment he made," Hugo insists.

Cheryl turns to Tim and attacks: "No—*you* wouldn't either! *You* wouldn't have felt responsible."

"No. But that's a loaded way of putting it," Tim protests.

"I mean that I wouldn't have felt guilty about it," Hugo clarifies.

Tim continues: "No, because Cheryl . . . I mean Elizabeth . . . " Cheryl smiles quickly at his blunder, but her smile disappears quickly as Tim explains: " . . . because Elizabeth said something honest. She said what was on her mind for a change."

Cheryl is still challenging Tim. "But even the one time you said something two weeks ago, and you only *barely* said it, off tone, and I got upset, you felt responsible! So why wouldn't you feel responsible now?"

Tim protests. "I just wouldn't call it 'responsible.' I felt like I'd made a mistake or something."

"Okay. Well, okay." Cheryl looks around at the whole group. "So maybe I'm using the wrong word."

"Well, I'm not saying that Robert *is* responsible." Cheryl is still defending herself. She looks at Robert. "All I'm saying is that I just want to know how you feel."

Hugo responds, instead of Robert: "I don't get the specific thing you're asking about."

"Because *I* would feel responsible if it were me, even though I might not *be* responsible!" Cheryl has finally expressed herself to her satisfaction.

Tim tries again to make his point to Cheryl, while Hugo rubs the top of his thighs and then settles his hand on the inside of his thigh. "That was an honest thing that Robert said, and it was fairly innocent, and I don't think . . . I think you don't feel it was right for him to be honest."

"No, it just, it just . . . " Cheryl babbles.

Somehow everyone knows that Elizabeth is about to speak, and they give her a long time to ready herself. "When Robert said what he did, I could feel my nose getting real sensitive and that what he said was kind of hitting something deep in the back of my mind." She points to her brain for emphasis. She smiles shyly as she looks at everyone.

Members sit frozen as they sense that Robert is going to respond. Elizabeth looks down but then looks up at him as he talks. "I don't know you well enough to know that was going to set you off—which, personally, I'm glad it did. Because I learned more about you today than I ever did. And I think everybody else has, too." He seems to be speaking more for the group and the group's goals than for himself.

"We have to stop. We'll continue next week," I say.

Robert and Elizabeth smile. Cheryl reaches for her keys and purse matter-of-factly. David follows Elizabeth out the door and chats, trying to engage her. Tim is the last member to leave the room. He sees that I trip as I take my first steps.

I am proud of the group members. They are now able to grapple with feelings of love and hate. The meeting started with people talking about their discomfort with their own hostility—an essential part of every human being. They searched for a way to express their anger without causing a cataclysmic rupture in their relationships with one another. The men captured the drive that strives to connect with a love object. They allowed themselves to compete for Cheryl. Cheryl followed my lead and furthered the process. It is important that they all participate in this competitive struggle. We all need to be able to compete for what we want: a job, a loved one, and so on. Elizabeth and David are hurting the most at the moment, but I believe they will learn new coping mechanisms and be able to get their needs met in the real world. If they can survive the group, they will be better prepared to face life's obstacles. This is the hardest part of the group therapy experience, but this is the part that is going to help them the most.

I am pleased that Robert and Cheryl both took on the role of Emotional Leaders, showing a great deal of courage. I am pleased that Elizabeth was able to reveal to the group the pain that she carries within. She expressed some of her beliefs about men, and now they can be tested against reality. David seems more integrated into the group than ever before. The group is working hard to incorporate Elizabeth, the Defiant Leader, and David, the Scapegoat Leader. The members often articulate what I am thinking, so I don't need to make many interventions. I was taught, "Do not do what the group can do." Members typically accept confrontation better from peers than from the group leader. Everyone in the group is bravely saying what he or she is feeling at the moment. I appreciate that this in an especially hard task for Elizabeth, since she is feeling so vulnerable.

12

Self-Examination

When Elizabeth doesn't show up for the next group therapy meeting, I'm surprised to find myself short of breath—a somatic warning that something disastrous might have happened. It's the same feeling you get when a punctual friend is late, and morbid possibilities race through your mind in a second's time. Perhaps the last meeting was too much for Elizabeth. All my theorizing is useless if I lose the patient. If Elizabeth doesn't return to the group, all of us will be traumatized. Members might experience their exposure of their feelings at the last meeting as killing off someone they cared about. This is their biggest fear. No one articulated this concern over Elizabeth's absence. I colluded with members and also avoided the topic.

I have a rough night. When I wake in the morning, I know what I need to do. I remember what I was taught: "It is expected that therapists have emotional reactions to patients. It is the emotional involvement that makes the therapy work. What you are feeling now has something to do with your past, and that is why you are so upset. You must search for what Elizabeth's behavior represents *for you*, in your unconscious. Only in this way can you separate out your own issues from hers and be of help to her." The teachers that I looked up to were those who were brave enough to look at their own inner conflicts and projections. They were therapists who were curious about *their own* inner lives as well as their patients' and studied the interaction created between them. These mentors never stopped exploring and learning. I want to be like them. Decision made. I'll go back into therapy.

Thank goodness my therapist, Dr. Susan Brand, is still practicing. I haven't been in therapy in five years, but knowing that I could always go back to see her has always been a comfort to me, and I schedule an appointment. I'm aware that very early separation anxiety is getting reignited. One would think that such anxiety dated back to waking up and not being able to walk when I was four years old and being removed from my home for four months—but I have no memory of being frightened then. Instead I remember being curious and trusting all the adults around me. I was probably copying my optimistic, pragmatic mother. Nonetheless, this experience caused a weak link in my "feeling-secure chain." When my father left for California two years later, the chain broke, resulting in a buried insecurity for the rest of my life. Talking this over with Dr. Brand will help me clarify my strong reaction to the possibility that Elizabeth is leaving the group.

The next day I dial Elizabeth's number. Her machine answers. Elizabeth is listening to the message and hesitates before picking up the phone. When Elizabeth finally speaks, my fears are confirmed. Elizabeth refuses to return to the group. She has already spoken to another therapist, who specializes in weight loss, and has arranged to work with her. Elizabeth has decided that her weight is her biggest problem, and if that is resolved, she'll be popular and happy. The group meeting was a horrible experience for her, she said. She came to group to be helped, and instead she got the worst rejection ever. And to confound it, David—disgusting David—flirted with her after the group. He mentioned that they have a weight problem in common. She found it mortifying to think of being paired with David.

A rush of heat surges through me; I know that means fear. I do my relaxation breathing and find my calm, professional voice. Then I ask Elizabeth if she'd be willing to meet with me privately to discuss what the last group meeting meant to her. Elizabeth is reluctant but finally says, "I'll come, but only if you *promise* not to try to talk me into coming back to the group." I agree that I won't pressure her to stay in the group. But I know that it's important for her to go to one last meeting to say good-bye—and I hope to persuade her. *At this moment,* I feel that parting with Elizabeth would be the worst thing that could happen to me and the group.

I'm nervous about seeing Elizabeth. I don't trust that I'll think clearly—for Elizabeth's benefit—because it seems to matter so much to me that Elizabeth stay in the group. It's as though I can't live through the pain that the group members and I will experience if Elizabeth leaves. It feels like an imminent, unnecessary, irrational tragedy.

I have learned in a situation like this, with the feelings I have, that I need to turn to my peers for help as well as to my personal therapist. My colleagues analyze the clinical challenges Elizabeth's behavior presents and suggest that I strongly confront Elizabeth about her resistance to group therapy.

From My Father's Book

13

1921

S pring finally comes. The grass is green, and the trees are in bloom. The people start coming out of their dreary homes into the sunshine. They gather a few of their belongings and bring them to the market. They try to exchange them for food with some of the peasants who have enough to trade. A bony cow, horse, or dog is occasionally seen. It is a great surprise to observe how some of the peasants have held on to these animals. I was heartbroken when our dog, Tango, died. He was a red-haired Russian Chow whose great-grandmother was bought by the old Mr. Sbritsky. The Sbritsky family has kept these dogs for generations; their Chow dynasty ended with the death of Tango.

Once again the people flock to the river to bathe their wretched bodies. We go at night, so no one can see one another. Fathers and sons and mothers and daughters are separated by only a few feet. During the day we wash our clothing. Parcels from foreign countries are coming in more often; this accounts for the happy looks on some people's faces. The Lubanka family, the poorest of all before the famine, is enjoying life anew. They are the first family in the Dome (our little group of houses) to receive a parcel from relatives in the United States.

Our little town now shows some signs of prosperity; an air of relief and hope is apparent. The dead are no longer buried in mass graves. No one eats *machucha* anymore, since there is flour and sugar from America. The new crop is coming along nicely, the sunshine is bright, and the birds are singing. It's the kind of spring the people have dreamed of for a long time.

Mother receives her first parcel from her sister in New Jersey; we are so happy. We gather around the large mahogany table while Mother opens the parcel, her hands shaking. Her face is too solemn to show any emotion. She is thinking of the others who are not here to witness the occasion. When she sees the clothing, shoes, and food, she smiles slightly, for she now knows her children will have something to eat and clothes to wear. She immediately sells the shoes at the market; they are too large and too good for the summer months. Then she pays her debts and shops for flour, sugar, and condensed milk. She runs home to bake bread. She dresses the children in these unusual clothes. She tries to cook as she once did and fix up our home, but it's too late. The will is there, but the strength and soul are missing. The package has come too late as far as she is concerned. Her 140-pound frame is now reduced to 90 pounds. Her pretty face that was once white as alabaster is now yellow and wrinkled. Her deep blue eyes, which reminded one of the "beautiful blue Danube," are now sunken. Her stomach has shrunk from lack of food. Her heart is shattered by constant thoughts and scenes that are still before her: the loved ones who perished and the sufferings of those who remain. She tries to eat the fine food from America. We have plenty now—in fact, more than we need. More parcels come, this time from Mother's brother-in-law, who is a rabbi in New York, and another from her sister-in-law in Chicago.

As Mother opens these packages, she is sad and brokenhearted; her thoughts are with her husband. If he were only here to enjoy the things his sister and brother have sent them. He spoke of them before he died, assuring his wife that they would not fail them. She also thinks of his sister in Elisavetgrad, whom he hated because she continued to refuse to give help, even though she could have. Mother had sent the children to her after Father died, believing that being religious, she might feel sorry and offer to help her nieces and nephews. She turned them down, only to die a few weeks later, leaving all her belongings to her son in America.

These thoughts keep repeating themselves again and again in Mother's head, making her ill. Ida calls a doctor, hoping he can cure her, but the doctor says there is nothing he can do. She lies in bed murmuring to herself and sometimes gets hysterical. After much agony, she goes into a coma and never comes out of it.

The neighbors come to see our mother, weeping and praying, whispering how good and brave she was. The children are bewildered. Mrs. Kapaloff helps Ida arrange the funeral. Ida spends almost all the money on the funeral; it is expensive. She sells most of the clothes and even sells some of her personal things and mine to pay for the expense.

Mother lies in the house for a whole week before an undertaker comes. This causes us all a lot of misery. Our mother lies on the floor, as is the custom, with two large candles on either side of her head, which is covered with a sheet. The weather is warm, and the body swells up to three times its natural size. We sleep in the next room, all cuddled together. Alex and Sonia cry in the night, saying they are afraid. They cry during the day, saying they want their mother. I try to comfort them while Ida cooks with tears in her eyes. It's a miserable week for us, particularly at night.

I am now twelve, and Ida is sixteen. We have awful nightmares and can hardly sleep. The last few days, no one comes around, as the odor of the dead body becomes sickening. When the undertaker finally arrives, he puts Mother in a wooden box, alone in the wagon, unlike our father, brother, and sister. We are glad that we can bury her decently. Ida walks on one side of the wagon with Mrs. Kapaloff beside her, while I walk on the other side, holding the box with one hand and wiping my tears with the other. Alex and Sonia follow in back of the wagon, holding hands as usual. The hearse moves up the hill slowly toward the cemetery, which is five miles from town. Alex and Sonia grow tired and weary.

The box is lowered into the grave, and we all fall on the ground, yelling and weeping. Ida starts tearing at her hair. After the grave is covered with sand, I begin looking around for something to identify our mother's grave from the others. I finally find a little bush and push it into the sand with pebbles around the roots to keep it firm. After staying a while, we kiss the grave and then walk home slowly. As we go over the side of the hill, we lose sight of the grave where our brave and devoted mother lies.

14

Primeval Man

Maybe my deep emotional reaction to Elizabeth stems from the fact that we can look at any human being as a prism: we can look into one person and see everyone else. The Hindus said that India is a network of gems and that each person is a crystal that reflects all others. We are all variations of the same themes. If we compare our DNA, we would see little difference.

We are all like the Hindu god Shiva, who has the power to destroy or create. As Bhairav, he is menacing and cruel. He wears a necklace of skulls and usually holds a trident (the symbol of lightning), a sword, a bow, and a mace topped with a skull. As Pashupati, he is lord of the beasts—a sweet shepherd of animals and humans. As Rudra, he is a corpse. As Mahadeva, he is peaceful and great. We are also all like Shiva's consort, the goddess Devi. As Kali, she is the "dark one," whose stomach is a void and can never be filled. She craves blood—of demons, animals, and people. The blood of severed animal heads flows over her body. At the same time, Kali is Durga, who gives birth to all things.

This interconnectedness means that although we can kill others, they can also kill us. So we can all either kill one another and join in collective suicide, or we can renew the pact that primeval man made: join hands with the realization that our survival depends upon it. The only way we can join forces is to face ourselves and forgo our option to project outside ourselves. Can we face ourselves and see that both Hitler and Mother Theresa embody our potential? We can destroy ourselves with violence and hatred, but we also can create great beauty in art, music, and architecture. We can even have a concert for disaster relief, where people all over the world join together to help their "brothers and sisters" in a faraway country. We often act out these various potentials in our dreams, where we might kill as unabashedly as an animal, write as brilliantly as Shakespeare, or save innocent people as heroically as Superman.

If we allow our Hitler side to predominate, we destroy our human race. If we let our selfless and altruistic Mother Theresa side win out, we risk losing our identity and the sense of self-preservation that allows us to maintain our basic self-esteem. Somehow we have to find a middle ground between these two extremes—a delicate balance between our destructive and preservative powers. We must connect with another person and a community with tolerable tension—and for some fortunate people, even equanimity.

Yet there is even more to this nightmarish race back and forth between the devil and the deep blue sea. Within ourselves we have an array of impulses, emotions, and drives that are equally paradoxical, confusing, and overwhelming. Most of us cannot stand to look honestly at ourselves because we fear that what we would see would be too horrible and unacceptable. So we project the evil and ugly parts of ourselves onto others; then we can feel pure and good. It's a simple and primitive mechanism—and it works. A country can feel proud and nationalistic by simply naming an enemy and then putting energy into fighting that enemy. Killing others in this effort doesn't matter because these others are less than human—they are the embodiment of all that we abhor in ourselves.

Freud theorized that men (yes, only men and not women, whom he considered the objects of desire) started to form groups because without them they would kill one another. Although this theory sounds extreme, I think Freud makes a good point that resonates with what I have observed in triangular relationships. He presumed that we all have an unconscious memory of the time when competition for the desired loved object was so fierce that we endangered the survival of the human race. The only solution was for the men to make a pact that part of one's self-interest would be given to the group; the survival of the group then became as important as the survival of the self. It was the group that modified man's basic and total narcissism—and consequently, ensured his survival.

Group therapy leaders expect members to have an unconscious awareness of these stark human realities. They consider it normal and healthy for group members to project bad qualities onto those outside the group so that they can affiliate comfortably—and thereby ensure the survival of the group. They expect the healthy group to go through stages. Only when the group is firm and strong will members be able to see some of these frightening elements within themselves. The group's ability to confront its fears will take courage and will represent a huge achievement.

In the same way that we create enemies by projecting the bad onto the other, we create gods by projecting our own goodness—our divinity—onto the other. But when we do so, we diminish ourselves. As the other becomes more godlike, we become weaker and therefore more dependent on that other person.

As the small therapy group is forming, it can coalesce easily if the members externalize their hostility and direct it at people or groups outside themselves. It is too frightening for a group of strangers to affiliate if they directly consider the dangers inherent in both themselves and others. Each person would face his own ability to hurt others and others' ability to hurt him. Will he be accepted? Rejected? Scapegoated? Each person would think of every negative experience he has had with others and be too frightened to affiliate.

There has been, is, and always will be a struggle between our wanting to connect with another person and join a community and our wanting to be separate and maintain our individuality. The psychologist Harry Guntrip has eloquently described the human torture of the schizoid person, who is caught between the danger of losing his or her sense of self by merging with another person and the danger of dying by withdrawing from other people. If we move too closely to another person or a group, we risk being swallowed up and annihilated. We can lose our identity and our own will—the two things that we use to define ourselves and that give our existence meaning. We risk *psychic* self-destruction. But if we retreat and run away from people, we face a different hell and a different road to self-destruction. We are lonely and lack the stimulation we need from other human beings to stay alive. We need contact with others to stay healthy—not just collaboration but also affirmation of our basic self-worth.

What a challenge it is to form a relationship with another human being! We need this connection to feel special, unique, and worthwhile. It gives life meaning. But how do we get past the godlike or despicable parts of ourselves to allow this connection to happen? If we project these parts onto our partners, they become even more dangerous than they really are, and our fear magnifies. Whether we face another person as our enemy, another small group as our group's enemy, or another country as our country's enemy, we are in a terrible bind because we're ultimately connected to our enemies. Our fates are intertwined.

Some of us are aware of this delicate and precarious balance when we choose someone reliable to trust and we allow that person to care for us as though he or she were a parent and we were a child. We realize that we are giving up some of our autonomy and diminishing our age and power, but we do so because we need a dose of unconditional maternal love as sustenance for the pressures we face. To minimize the danger, we've used our best judgment to choose someone safe. We have learned to differentiate between a realistic assessment of a trustworthy person and the projection of our fears and ugliness onto others. We take the risk of joining in sexual union. Here we expose ourselves and become vulnerable—and momentarily defenseless. But because we've chosen someone safe, our fears transform into excitement and sexual pleasure.

Arnold's Postcards from Israel

1967

'm living at Ein Gev Kibbutz and studying Hebrew and working. I'm very popular here and have many friends of both sexes, intimate and casual.

Miss you all very much.

• • • • •

Tomorrow I leave the kibbutz for a few days for Rosh Hashanah. I'll be staying with a Moroccan friend of mine and also a very good friend from India. It is difficult for me to write because my life is composed mainly of work and study. I've had some minor fling with at least half the girls studying with me, but nothing serious. Actually, I just got through with a rather ridiculous affair with a girl who gave a wonderful appearance, but was really rather crazy.

What Happened?

1968

16

This is what I make of the communications Arnold sent me from Israel. He had his first sexual experiences, his first affairs, his first relationships with women. Some were not so good, but he survived them. He sounded a bit giddy—but all right. He was writing, and he was all right.

He was not in Israel long before he realized that the Israelis were the establishment and the Arabs, the underdogs—and Arnold always sided with the underdogs. The Arabs were also different and exotic, and he could learn more from them. He considered them more spiritual.

The letters and cards stopped. I will never know for sure what happened next. All I can do is piece together a picture from a one-page letter that my uncle obtained from the American embassy in Israel; my mother's daily reports to me about what Arnold was saying to her and to his doctors; and finally, what I know in my heart about my brother.

A mud hut in Eilat in the south of Israel became Arnold's home. He lived there with his Arab friends. He learned their language quickly and adopted their accent, even when he spoke English. They smoked hashish daily. Being with the Arabs was intoxicating. It was like joining the Indians in the movie *The Broken Arrow*. He had found his niche with society's noble underdog—and he was euphoric.

The hashish was stronger than he realized. He thought he had perfected the art of drug taking, but the new environment excited him to the point that his judgment was affected. He stopped paying attention to how much he smoked. The more he smoked, the more blissful he felt as he luxuriated in love for his Arab roommates.

The Israelis arrested Arnold and his Arab friends as they were crossing the Jordanian border with drugs. We never found out whether he was crossing into Israel or into Jordan.

He was in the Beersheva jail for a month. The guards treated him worse than his friends because it was a special insult that a Jewish boy from the United States would commit such a crime. He was isolated, deprived of food, and beaten.

Of all the fates he could imagine, this was not one of them. He felt rage but had no outlet. The isolation, the lack of connection with another human being, led to a despair that was deeper than anything he had ever known. There was no getting away from this despair. There was no humor. There was no one to say, "Some things are worse than death." Purest cruelty was thrown in his face.

Arnold lost his mind. He became psychotic, and his rage created ever more horrible nightmares. He didn't have a therapy group where he could talk about his small hurts and angers so that they wouldn't pile up and cause a psychic explosion. He hallucinated that the Jews were out to castrate him. They were coming in droves. He had to find his Arab brethren to save him. He was terrified.

The jailers notified the American consulate. An American Jewish boy was ill. Money had to be obtained from his parents. He had to be sent home. He was given a room at the Jerusalem "Y" while arrangements were made.

He continued to hallucinate: Jews were chasing him with knives. He had to escape; it would be easy, since he was not supervised. He ran as fast as he could, crossing the border to Jordan, yelling, "My Arab brothers, save me! Please!" No one shot at him. The Arabs sheltered him and then did not know what to do with this American Jewish twenty-five-year-old young man, who had an Arab accent and was clinging to them for safety. He calmed down in their presence. He felt safe and rested; the sounds of the Arab language lulled him to sleep.

The Jordanians turned to the UN Armistice Commission for help. The commission helped transport him first to Israel and then onto a plane headed for New York.

No one in the United States was told that he was psychotic. When he deplaned in New York, he looked unbelievably handsome. His skin was bronzed and his small, normally deep-blue eyes shone a light, bright color. He was a raving lunatic. He was frantic because the Jews were still coming after him with instruments to castrate him.

Sonia, our father's little sister, picked him up at the airport, excited about meeting the younger version of a brother she adored. A shock of pain and recognition went through her when she saw this bronzed, lunatic, dear nephew of hers. She had perfected the art of never thinking about her childhood. Suddenly, the worst of it was before her.

Arnold changed completely when our mother arrived from California. The frightened little boy recognized his mommy. He begged her not to leave his side, and she promised. They slept in the same room at night and then made the trip to California. He trusted her completely. He was a good boy and would do anything she said. She was like the earth—it was the one thing that was solid and would not go away. If he held on tightly, maybe he could get grounded. Gravity would take hold.

She took him to the city hospital and then to Norwalk State Hospital. She visited him every day and baked chocolate chip cookies for the staff and patients. But it was hardly a cheerful scene.

He was put on Thorazine and was like a vegetable. When he was taken off the medication, he had torturous hallucinations again. His only relief was when he hallucinated going back to Israel with his little brother, Gary (the prince) by his side; together they would get revenge. Back on the meds and back to a vegetative state. It was hard to know which state was worse or better. Words screamed in his head:

I want to pray!
> but there is no God.

I want to cry!
> but the tears won't come.

I want to die!
> but I have but one life.

My mother says, "Life is what you make it."
> God, I wish she were right.

After being on the medicine off and on for some time, he had moments of clarity:

I have thought the thought that precludes thought.
I have felt the feel that cannot be.
I have longed for the chance to be free.
But now I am drowning, for I know what it means to be.
Nonexistent God, can't you see why so many turn to thee?
Why do I see in everything mockery?
Because I stand outside them.
Let me in. Oh, please, let me in.
I have asked once too often.
I no longer need to get in nor even want to get in.

He could hardly believe what he thought might be true was really true. But in those lucid moments, he was committed to discovering reality.

I am engulfed in a sea of hopelessness
> so absolute and complete.

I question the validity of the statement
> that absolute cannot be.

Why write? I already feel it all. I guess
> I want to communicate my sorrow.

He suddenly saw the truth before him. His whole life was a mockery. What had become of the young man who was trying so hard to understand and help the world? His parents, Ivan and Gazelle, had suffered so much. They were always tormented souls. He wanted so much to help them. The grand ideas he had about "making a difference," joining a revolution in Brazil, making a fortune—*were sincere*. He was the Lamed-Vovnik in André Schwarz-Bart's novel *The Last of the Just* (1959), a man who carried the burdens of humanity.[5] All his dreams and hopes had turned to dust. How can you possibly put dust back together to make a person again? He couldn't even think straight for long. To get any relief from the torture, he would have to take medicine and become a vegetable. What kind of choice was that? All of his desires to be one with the Arabs—the noble underdogs—months of work wasted—months of believing with your whole heart and soul and then to face the fact that it was bullshit.

I have become hard as a rock, cold as a stone,
And I yet attain to be flesh and bone.

He had to think and act quickly while his lucidity lasted. He had a goal now, and this time he had better achieve it. Given that his life was a mockery, his death should not be. It had to be one where he was in control. He had to be thorough and effective.

He started by being a model patient so that he could get a leave. He was a pro at manipulating people. It felt good to see that he had not lost this power. He laughed at the thought that his young psychiatrist didn't know that he could see through his questions about winning at blackjack. "The guy thought he could fool me and appear benevolent while he obtained information he wanted to use himself."

Arnold wrote to me in Chicago, saying he was feeling better and hoped I was having and would have a happy life. When our father finally visited the hospital, Arnold took him for a walk, put his arm around him, and said with all the love and sincerity he could muster, "Dad, all this is not your fault. Believe me. Don't

---

5   Schwarz-Bart's novel explores the ancient Jewish tradition of the Lamed-Vov. According to this legend, thirty-six "just men" (Lamed-Vov) are born in every generation to take on the burden of the world's suffering. The Hebrew letters *lamed* and *vov* represent the number *thirty-six*. A Lamed-Vovnik is one of these thirty-six just men.

worry about it!!" Our father was comforted, but he couldn't understand how he could have survived what he did and his son, his carbon copy, could not. Arnold didn't have to say anything to our mother—a look would suffice. She had shared this misery with him. She knew that it was more than any human being could bear. She would understand.

Taken in by Arnold's fine-tuned social skills, the doctors quickly recommended a leave. Our mother was skeptical, especially since they would have to leave him alone with his little brother while they went to work at the luncheonette. The doctors insisted he'd be fine. She did not agree, but she had only a high school diploma; she couldn't argue with such highly educated people. So Arnold came home, and she told Gary to stay home from school and keep an eye on him.

As soon as our parents left, Arnold started to work on Gary, saying that he should want the best for his big brother. He just wanted the feeling of being alone with his own thoughts. In the hospital he'd had no privacy. Gary was reluctant to go against his mother's wishes, but Arnold's persistence was no match for a sixteen-year-old who idolized him. Gary left the house and came back a short time later.

Arnold immediately hunted for his favorite quilt. He kept his concentration focused on the task at hand. His only thought was to be effective; this was the only way to justify his existence. Without hesitation, he turned on the gas jet by the fireplace, put his face over it, and covered his head with the quilt. As the gas engulfed every orifice of his face, he was deeply satisfied with himself. He could feel himself gently being put to sleep. He could feel it working. He had planned it well. It never occurred to him that the house could explode or that his dear baby brother could be ruined for life. At the moment he felt most free, when he rose as far as he fell, he was as lethal as an ax-murderer.

A Note
from Jerry

17

1968

Arnie's mind, which he freely and frankly exposed to us, vacillated between the noblest idealism and the most profound gloom. In moments of enthusiasm, he would literally vibrate and glow with an electric energy that excited all of us, no matter how far-fetched the object of his enthusiasm might have been. And we would all share in his depressions, albeit unwillingly, for they were inescapable. He was constantly torn between such passionate involvement in the world and such complete withdrawal that in the end he could not remain whole. Society and Arnold Abrams could not—try as they might—tolerate each other, and only we who knew his untapped potential can truly gauge society's loss. Arnold once said, "Man is an island—in an archipelago." There is now a gaping hole in that archipelago.

After

1968

Arnold's high school friends come to our house and ask if they can have the quilt Arnold used to cover himself; they want to make a shrine for him. Perhaps they will start a new religion. One young man says, "I feel like I have seen the history of the Jewish people being played out through one person."

There is no funeral. This family, still in transition from war and poverty, has no organized way of expressing itself. It is a socially and culturally isolated family—a part of no community. The father is agnostic, and the mother voices religious platitudes that are expected but have no meaning. The parents have no friends, community involvement, or hobbies. The only thing the family instinctively does is take a few days to do nothing—except talk about Arnold.

Arnold was right about our mother; she did understand. She explained to others what he had communicated in his look. And in a strange way, I understood also.

I now know that there are some times when you have a nightmare that seems real. When you wake up, for a moment you believe it *did* happen, and the horror stays with you. Then you realize it was a dream and feel a tremendous sense of relief. There are other times when the reverse happens. You wake up only to remember that the nightmare occurred in real life. You say to yourself, "It's not a dream; it really happened." This sequence repeats itself morning after morning; you know you have to face the horror all day long. You feel a kind of torture that hurts so deeply that you know you can never find words to express it, so you don't try. It stays private. It is your personal pain. There will always be a part of you that only you will understand.

You have only one life. For some people life is a heaven on earth; for others, a hell on earth. Yet for most people, life is a combination. You sense that the "good life" is fragile. Somewhere inside, you are aware that in an instant, your life can turn from heaven to hell. You try to ignore it, try not be conscious of it, but the back-burner anxiety remains. Then a stranger pushes you to the ground, steals your wallet, and runs away—and you feel as though someone has run sharp fingernails down your face. Or a friend you trusted suddenly turns on you with unwarranted rage, and you realize how close the netherworld is.

Arnold's death changed me. This had to happen, because he was part of me. I had always assumed that when I lost my father, I would have his carbon copy, my brother—a lifetime of security. We now know that the brain is plastic; it grows new neural pathways as we process great losses. Thus when we lose a part of our identity, we are able to grow a new piece—but no one can believe that in the moment of grief.

A Letter to My Twenty-Six-Year Old Self

19

1968

E
ven after forty-five years, I have difficulty putting into words how you feel right now at twenty-six-years old, having lost your "almost twin" brother. Just like your parents, you don't miss a beat functioning. No one would be able to detect a change in any of you, but you walk around feeling as though someone had taken a knife and sliced you open. The emotional pain is so strong that it feels like physical pain; the pain is in your chest, around your heart. It feels as though your insides are bleeding, but no one can see the blood. You know that your life is permanently altered, and you don't know exactly how. You are too stunned to cry. You know it will take a lifetime to believe your brother is dead. You know that you will need psychotherapy with a very special therapist. You know that you have fully experienced your parents' strength for the first time. They did not fight with each other; they sat for days and talked about their feelings. They were not depressed, but sad. They were as comforting to you as they had always been—no luxury of self-absorption or self-pity for them!

You all pieced together a story based on a one-page report from the consulate, what Arnold told his doctors at the hospital, and his postcards from Israel. It was such a foreign story that it was hard for any of you to visualize it. Clearly, Arnold was having the time of his life on the kibbutz. Clearly, he loved his Arab friends, feeling an expansive oneness with them. I suppose Israeli guards in a small town would be provoked by this: an American Jew calling the Arabs and not them his brothers.

There are things you will never know, and these things will always haunt you. How could Arnold go over the edge with drugs when he was always so calculating and careful with them? Somehow it was part of bonding with these friends; his love for them was as strong as anything he had ever felt. Well, that will be your fantasy. If only you could meet these men who were his kinsmen. You will never even know their names. You wonder what happened to them after they were arrested.

Can you imagine meeting the love of your life and then having your world turn upside down—from ecstasy to hell? Arnold once wrote in a poem that the higher you rise, the farther you fall. He was right. Another thing that will always bug you is how he could have become psychotic. Even if he had been tortured, as his doctors believed, other people are tortured and survive. His own parents lived a kind of torture and survived. Knowing him, I think he must have taken his jailors' assaults extremely personally, whereas your father saw his torturers as persecuting randomly and even felt lucky that he and three of his siblings had been spared. I believe that Arnold at twenty-five years old felt he had failed in his life's mission: to make a difference. He suddenly was helplessly at the bottom—at the mercy of others. When he finally became lucid, he saw his life as a sham—even laughable. How could anything matter when you realize that all your perceptions and instincts were not what others perceive as "reality"? Even his sacred promise to help his sister take care of Gary forever no longer mattered.

Deep in your heart, you know that your father's life in Ukraine was not only a part of your father, but of Arnold as well. Arnold's life seems like an offshoot of our father's. This is what you believe now, and you will always believe it. Some mysteries are just too hard to explain without sounding foolish.

In fact, you too were born into your parents' tragedies—your father's horrific experiences growing up in and escaping from Ukraine, your mother's extreme childhood poverty. When you moved to Monterey Park and started going to other people's homes, your sense of wonder was the same as that of someone who has just arrived off the boat at Ellis Island. You benefitted from your parents' survival instincts, idealism, and ability to love their children, but these qualities were not enough to equip you and Arnold to navigate in the new world.

Retirement and Divorce

20

1974

M y father always said that when he turned sixty-five, he was going to do everything he had always wanted to do: visit Russia, dance, ride his bike, work out at the gym. I would always have the horrifying thought: What if he doesn't live to sixty-five? He would never reap the rewards of working like a donkey in the coal mines. There was one aspect of his work that I know he enjoyed. His last business was a tiny lunch counter opposite a port. Here he would cook in front of the customers and educate the truck drivers, sharing the latest information from *I. F. Stone's Weekly*. At any rate, he kept saving his money for retirement.

As the years passed and he approached his sixty-fifth birthday, he became sexually impotent with my mother. She thought: "This is my chance! I don't have to worry about losing him, since no one else will want him now. He finally needs me." She decided that they should move to Leisure World in Seal Beach, where they would have many wonderful activities. He went along with spending the money on a condo there, but when it was time to move, he said he wasn't ready. She excitedly moved there herself and was absolutely positive that he would follow her. He didn't. Instead he moved to a tiny condo near the beach in Torrance, where he had a bike path and a pool outside his front door and a gym nearby.

Ivan had always had a fantasy that a tall, blonde woman would chase after him—and before long, sure enough, there she was. He couldn't believe it. After they made love, he told me: "This woman brought me back to life!" I knew what he meant.

My mother started making friends immediately, and soon she was a beloved fixture at Leisure World. When anyone was sick, she'd bring over homemade food, and whenever there was community work to be done, she was right there. It was easy to see that she did these things with an open heart and enjoyed giving. "I'm having such a good time," she wrote to me. "I'm popular, just like you were!" The highlight came when she made a best friend. Sissy was young, pretty, vivacious, and full of energy. They went everywhere together and smiled and laughed continuously. I never saw my mother so happy.

Much to my father's dismay, my mother said she wanted a divorce. This meant that my father would have to give her half his money—which meant he had to tell her how much money he had. I thought this would kill him. To my surprise, he survived. There was enough money for both of them to live separately and comfortably.

My mother now had her own money for the first time. My father was always sure she would spend money carelessly if she had it. First she extended her tiny living room; then she bought material to make pants in every color. It was such fun to have choices. She also felt the freedom that comes with not having to cook for a family and just making what she felt like eating. She joined every activity including being in silly plays and traveling with friends. She even took a trip to Israel with friends. She said to me, "I was always afraid to get divorced. I would think: 'What would I do if my car broke down?' Now I know: You go to the corner and say, 'Fix my car.' I was so stupid."

My poor mother had such bad luck. Her best friend just dropped dead. At the time I couldn't think of anything worse happening to Sissy or my mother. I was sure that this would break my mother's spirit. No one else noticed it, but I detected less of a spring to her step. Yet she continued taking life's blows as they came, never letting them push her down to the ground. She put one step in front of the other and continued her march through life.

My Mother, Gazelle

21

1983

I go to the doctor with my sixty-eight-year-old mother. She seems to be in good health, as she has always been. She is here to get reports from the many tests she has taken as part of a checkup. The doctor looks at my mother gravely: "I have bad news for you."

I see him hesitate. I say, "You can be straight with my mother. She's a realist. Just tell her what you found."

"You have lung cancer. You can have chemotherapy and surgery, if you like. I will give you all the pills you request for pain."

"I thought only people who smoke get cancer."

"Not always."

Her mind works quickly. She wants no part of being sick and living. She starts to read the book put out by the Hemlock Society. She giggles as she sits by the pool with her friends and reads her book: "Imagine what they would think if they knew what I was reading!" (It turns out that it is not so easy to kill yourself and do it well.) I sit with her and also laugh at her secret.

"You know, Elaine, I'm ready to go. I've had a hard life, haven't I?"

"Yes, you have."

"I'm tired of it."

"I understand."

"Really? You really understand? It is all right with you if I die sooner rather than later?"

"Yes, it is. You've always said that you would rather die than have a severe illness. You've been active all your life. It has taken me forty-three years, but I finally feel that I can survive without your backup."

"I am so lucky! My friends are all suffering with pain and illness, and their children will not let them die. Have I been a good mother?"

"The best. It's hard to believe that you never said no to me for anything I requested. The only demand you ever made on me was to say thank you and appreciate you. I never wanted to find out what you would do if I didn't oblige. I thought you might kill me. Whenever I hit rock bottom, I could count on you to do whatever you could do to help and to say just the right words to comfort me. I can't even begin to describe your generosity. Remember when Gary came to the house with a friend after your divorce and said that if he only had five thousand dollars, he'd be happy. You shocked him. You took out your checkbook and wrote him a check for five thousand dollars and handed it to him. It was your way of saying, 'Okay, no more excuses. Go and be happy.' His friend was as astonished as Gary and said softly to him, 'Your mother is a saint.'"

Mom continues: "I was jealous of your friend's mother, even though I baked bread for her because she was so nice to you. You said that you wished she was your mother. You could talk to her about deep things. Maybe she would have been a better mother for you."

"I was mean and stupid. I'm so sorry."

Mom says, "I miss Arnold."

"What do you miss about him?" I ask.

"He liked my cooking."

"Mom, I have a secret that I've never told you, and I know you have a secret also. I asked Dad, but he said that you had to be the one to tell me. I always sensed that it had something to do with a baby. I'll tell you my secret if you tell me yours."

"Are you sure you aren't tricking me?"

"I cross my heart and hope to die."

"Okay. I had sex with your father before we were married, and I got pregnant. I found a cheap abortionist, located in the slums. I couldn't tell anyone in my family what I was doing. It would have been a disgrace, and everyone would have hated me forever. When I arrived home from the abortion and slipped into the bed I shared with my mother, I found myself swimming in blood. I quietly cleaned everything up and concealed my illness so my mother wouldn't see. I ultimately recovered and didn't hold a grudge, but your dad always felt guilt—probably always will. Now, do you really have something to tell me?"

"Remember when I was twelve, and you had your first friend, Betsy, and you were so happy? Well, her husband, Joseph, gave me a ride home once. When the car was parked in front of our house, he slowly put his hand on my crotch. I got out of the car as fast as I could. I decided it would be my one and only secret for life. I knew if I told Dad, he would want to kill Joseph, and you would lose your friend."

"Thank you, Elaine. I appreciate what you did. I'm sure your father would have wanted to kill him, and I'm sure I would have lost my friend. Betsy brought joy into my life. We laughed a lot. Remember when she took her false teeth out to amuse Gary, and he wailed in terror? I'm not too surprised about Joseph. He was caught fondling his retarded daughter. When I was a young teenager, a man fondled me in my father's store. I never told anyone. Maybe it happens to all girls at some time."

My mother prepares for her suicide. She tries to think of everything in great detail. She decides that I will need to wash her sheets, tells me where the washing machine is, and leaves me two quarters to put in the slot. She labels all of the pictures on the wall and the furniture with the name of the friend who wants it. She tells me who to call for a memorial service and says that everyone at Leisure World has one, so people will make one for her at my convenience.

My mother has three kinds of lung cancer, and one of them is lethal. It spreads to her brain before she has a chance to kill herself. She dies one month later at the age of sixty-nine. A hundred Leisure World residents come to her memorial service.

Her friends read the Jewish poem "A Woman of Valor," from the Book of Proverbs. I am taken aback that anyone except my brothers and me can see her true worth. I imagine that my mother is as surprised as I am.

My Baby Brother, Gary

22

1968

Gary is the best looking of anyone in our family. I love to look at him. He has a bronzed, surfer's body (he surfs); big gray-blue eyes with long eyelashes; my mother's beautiful smile; and a head of thick, wavy hair that shimmers auburn and gold in the sun. I can picture Gary as a two-year-old playing in the backyard, falling and laughing, falling and laughing—a bundle of joy. When he was a baby, I thought he was so adorable that I sent two snapshots of him to the movie studios. In one he was drooling, and in the other he was wearing a cowboy hat that made a shadow over his eyes. I never heard back from the movie studios.

Gary was possessive of me and loved being the delight of my life. When he was six-years-old, he used all his strength to carry my portable sewing machine for me. I was afraid he would hurt himself, but he wouldn't let me take it from him. When he was nine-years-old, I took him to day camp with me; he was a camper and I was a counselor. He hugged me hard when another little boy wanted to dance with me.

He was painfully shy, but he forced himself to dance with me the whole time so no one else would.

As we sit in the living room talking about Arnold after his death, Gary sits in the adjoining den, listening. I go in to talk to him every few hours, day after day, but I only get one-word responses. He refuses psychotherapy or the opportunity to talk to anyone else.

Gary is good-looking and social, and he is a talented artist. But he is missing the strength of character that would allow him to label and nurture his wounds. He is missing the survival instinct that his mother and father possess.

Gary gets through high school and settles in Studio City, which straddles the line between Hollywood and the Valley. He designs tee shirts and pop art for a gallery in Studio City that is owned by his friend, a leader in the Jewish community. Before long, Gary is part of the cocaine-snorting Hollywood jet set.

At home he screams at us at the drop of a hat. It's hard to have a conversation with him. He finally asks me for help and says that he has to stop the drug use. A trusted psychiatrist colleague of mine prescribes Haldol. Gary starts to have weird facial tics as a side effect of the medication. He no longer looks beautiful. I complain to the doctor, but the doctor is worried about something else. He can't figure out why Gary is not responding to the medicine by becoming calmer and more rational. He wonders if Gary is still on cocaine.

Gary comes into my mother's hospital room and starts screaming at me. He walks out.

"I'm sorry that I have to leave you with this, Elaine."

"Don't worry. I'll take care of him."

"I know you will."

Los Angeles Times,

September 10, 1986

23

Slain Man Is Identified as Missing Studio City Artist
By Patricia Klein, *Times* Staff Writer

The body of a man found shot to death in a Fontana field last week has been identified as that of a Studio City artist who disappeared with an associate, who also was found slain execution style, Los Angeles police said Tuesday.

The body of Gary Abrams, 35, was found at about 10:50 p.m. on Sept. 3 in Fontana, shortly after his friend and employer, Marshall E. Brevetz, was found shot to death in the El Sereno section of Los Angeles.

Abrams, bound and gagged, was taken from a vehicle in the 10700 block of Oleander Avenue and shot several times in the upper body, said Fontana Police Capt. Sam Scott. . . .

Brevetz, 47, owner of Framed Art Posters in Studio City, was found shot to death in El Sereno at about 9:15 p.m. on Sept. 3. . . .

Earlier, police said they were investigating the possibility that Brevetz's killing and Abrams' disappearance were drug related. Brevetz, a former recording studio owner and business manager for entertainers, was paroled in 1983 after serving 15 months of a three-year sentence for possession and sale of cocaine.

Kathryn Owens, a friend of Brevetz, said earlier that Brevetz had telephoned another friend the night of his disappearance and reported that he needed $30,000 to pay a group of Colombian drug traffickers. "I need to get 30 grand for these people by tonight or I'm a dead man."

Trying to Understand

1986

24

What *do* I think I know about this death?

I know that Gary watched his friend being shot and then was in the trunk of a car for one and a half hours.

I know that Gary was in the wrong place at the wrong time.

I know that the police said to me that the three men who did this escaped over the border and probably would never be found.

I know that I am grateful that my parents are dead and spared one more unfathomable tragedy.

I know my heart is breaking.

What I *don't* I know about this death?

I don't know what went through Gary's mind as he lay scrunched up in the trunk of a car. Was he in shock and not thinking at all? Is that possible for an hour and a half? Did he think, "I should have listened to my sister and stopped using cocaine?"

I can't bear to think anymore about how it would feel to be in that trunk—the first moment—the last moment.

I am in the deep section of a swimming pool filled with sand. Gary is two years old and in the shallow section. I feel the sand under me sinking. I panic because I know Gary is little and the sand could rise and cover him. I work my way out of sinking sand and run to the shallow section. He is under the sand. I yell for people to help me dig and rescue him, wondering how long he can survive under the sand. I wake up.

PART 4
THE WINNING TICKET

If I was pushed down and someone picked me up,
Which would be more important?
—Arnold S. Abrams

From My Father's Book

1922

1

The city of Elisavetgrad takes on a new life as the Soviet government becomes well established. This government is under the leadership of Lenin, who is the commissar of the people, and Trotsky, who is the commissar of the army. The country is set up as a workers' government ruled by the Soviets; private property is abolished and confiscated. Now all the people work for the government.

We find for the first time in history a party composed of workers who start ruling themselves. Law and order are established, and for the first time an insult to any race is considered a criminal offence. Churches are abolished; all gold and things of value are taken by the government. They are used to form the workers' social clubs, libraries, and schools.

Most capitalists and even workers are not in full accord with this type of government, but they have no choice. Freedom of speech and press are stopped. Nobody can criticize the government or form his own party, but this does not affect most people because they never knew what freedom was like. Most fall in line and support the change of government. A new nationalist feeling begins to spread, and only four years after the revolution, people enjoy social and economic freedom. This is an amazing achievement given the backwardness and deprivation of czarist Russia.

Four children are left in the Sbritsky family. We find ourselves facing this new government as orphans. It is up to Ida, who is now seventeen, to guide the children through life until they are old enough to take care of themselves. Fortunately, she has a kind heart. She tries to be authoritative in order to control her brothers and sister. She had a little schooling, but most of her knowledge comes from experience. She has learned a little about cooking by helping Mother and improves rapidly through actually doing it. She finds it very hard to discipline the children; they feel that they can do as they please, since our mother and father are not here. Mrs. Kapaloff comes often to visit and sympathizes with Ida. She suggests that Alex and Sonia, now seven and five years old, go to the new orphanage. They will get good food and discipline. Ida does not like the suggestion; she cannot see herself parting with them. But she knows it would be for the best—she has little money to pay the rent, and the parcels from America are used up quickly.

The greatest problem that people are now having is locating relatives here and abroad. The war in Europe and the revolution here separated many families. Ida finally discovers that our mother's brother is in Kiev. He was always the pride of the family. His name is Solomon, and he is tall and powerful. He wears a goatee and mustache, which make him appear distinguished and handsome. He is a lawyer who works for the government and has a high position. Ida obtains his address and sends him a letter telling him of our misfortunes and that we want him to come to Elisavetgrad to help us. His reply is cold, saying he is sorry to hear what happened, but he cannot come because he is busy with work and does not have the money for the trip. He offers to ask his sister in America for help; maybe she can bring us to America, where we will be happy. Ida weeps as she reads the letter. Seeing that our own uncle has turned us down (even though our mother spoke so highly of him), Ida finds no alternative but to follow Mrs. Kapaloff's advice. Alex and Sonia are getting wild and disrespectful. She speaks to them about the orphanage, telling them that they will get plenty to eat there and that it will not be long before we leave for America.

The word *America* quiets them; people are talking about it constantly. They say America is a paradise, where you can find gold in the street. Sonia asks me, "What is in America?" I gently say, "It's wonderful, honey. There you can have all kinds of toys just like the Rosenfeld children had: roller skates, bicycles, dolls, candy, cake, and everything your heart desires." Sonia smiles happily and immediately agrees to go to the orphanage for a while, and Alex replies similarly after he hears my story. I feel guilty; I wonder if what I told them is true. Those who went to America have never come back to verify these rumors, but we all pray that our relatives will call for us. Like everyone else here, I want to believe it. I lift my little sister in the air and kiss her as I bring her down.

The next day we prepare to go to the orphanage. It is heartbreaking for Ida and me, but we agree that it is the best thing to do. Upon reaching the great black gate of the home, we have to show our credentials to a young man in uniform who is guarding the entrance. I act as spokesman, and the soldier assures me that the children will receive the best of care. He stresses the point that Alex will be taught a trade; that makes me happy. I get the visiting hours straight. We kiss and hug the children, reassuring them that we will come to see them as soon as we can. We walk away. Ida and I turn to watch Alex and Sonia enter the new wooden structure; none of us has ever seen anything like it.

Progress is seen all over the city. Schools are being built for the children, and organizations of all kinds are being formed. Folks who cannot read or write join the workers' clubs and the Bolshevik party and get their education at night. Men begin cutting off their long beards. Woven burlap suits replace old, dirty coats. Women begin to work in factories, as the men do, and dress like them also; the only difference is that they wear skirts instead of pants and their clothes are made of khaki instead of burlap. More people wear shoes instead of rags around their feet. All these reforms are slow but steady. There is still plenty of misery and suffering, especially for the old folks, who are religious and don't believe in joining any organizations.

I find myself a free boy; I can do whatever I please. I do not have to account to anyone for my doings. Ida tries to give me some advice, since she is older and feels it is her duty to guide me. I refuse to listen to her because I feel that I can take care of myself, and I know right from wrong. I go back to my old business of selling cigarettes—this time Soviet brands. I meet my old friends, many of whom are boys of the street. They try to influence me to participate in vices such as stealing, visiting prostitutes, and getting customers for the prostitutes. The only vice I indulge in is smoking. I do not even like to smoke, but all the boys smoke, and I don't want them to make fun of me. Also, I am selling cigarettes, and it would not look right if I did not smoke. I am small for my age and serious, never smiling. Smoking makes me look more manly. I have lived in a nightmarish world; my childhood was over by the time I was seven, when I started to sell candy. Now I think like a man, work like a man, and live like a man.

I teach myself how to read and write Russian. I begin reading books and pamphlets about the revolution and the Soviet government. My mind craves knowledge all the time, but I can't get into a school. I take every opportunity to talk to people and ask them all kinds of questions.

I become someone who dreams of America day and night—the land of paradise that everyone speaks about. I lie awake at night visualizing myself as a millionaire bringing my family name into prominence. I will be kind to people and help people in need. But then I think that if it were paradise, there would be no one in need. I hear that even shoemakers in America are rich. This is strange, since shoemaking is considered the lowest type of work in Russia.

Many times I hate the thought of leaving my native country, even though I have suffered so much here. There is a place in my heart for this home, even though my loved ones have died of starvation, and my oldest brother went to war, never to return. Yet I have faith in this living hell that I call home. I can feel part of me rebelling at the thought of leaving. Maybe it's because my ancestors were happy and successful here. Since we never heard otherwise, I believe that my brother gave his life for this country. I want to see this cursed land flourish with progress, love, and understanding under this new government. I wish this country would turn into a paradise instead of my having to go to a strange land for happiness. A new nation could be born here, just as misery ends for the mother who gives birth to a beautiful child. She enjoys the smile, the bright eyes, the tiny pink body that she will see grow up.

We finally receive a letter from Aunt Martha telling us that our Uncle Nathan in Odessa is coming to get us and bring us to America as soon as all the arrangements are made and the tickets are bought. We are very happy. It is the first time since the death of our parents that we are certain something good is about to happen. We wonder if our uncle from Odessa resembles our mother.

The next Sunday afternoon, we go to visit Sonia and Alex and tell them the good news. Alex is playing in the yard with the other boys while Sonia stays with the nurse who takes care of the younger children. Alex has a lot of complaints. He says that they are watched every minute of the day and cannot do the things they do at home. If he refuses to obey, they beat him, especially at night, when he refuses to part with his little sister. "Oh, I wish I were out in the street and able to do the things I want to do and be free!" Sonia stands close to him, holding his hand and verifying everything he says. I feel sorry for them. I know they want the freedom I have. I promise I will take them home soon and that our uncle in Odessa will come to take us to America. Alex refuses to listen, saying that if we do not take him home now, he will run away. I get angry and say that if he does such a thing, we will not take him with us to America. This quiets him.

Although we hear these complaints, we notice that Alex is putting on weight. The nurses admire his good looks but say he is too tough to handle. Sonia is very tiny and slim and does not gain any weight, but she looks healthier. She shows signs of deprivation from the famine. She is still pretty and lovable, looking very sad at times. Ida understands the reason for her sadness—she misses her mother and Ida. Both the children have shaved heads to prevent lice; they wear gray uniforms that are the same for boys and girls (and despised by Alex). Visiting hours are over. Ida and I hug them both tightly, telling them that we will come for them soon and to be brave in the meantime.

Two weeks later, in the middle of the night, Alex walks into the house. I am not home yet, and Ida is amazed to see him. She grabs him and immediately asks what he did with Sonia. He replies, "She's still there. I ran away alone. I could not take her because I knew she would cry, and then they would hear us. I left that prison last night and I roamed the streets looking for food, and I finally decided to come home because I was afraid that they would catch me." Ida feels sorry for him, since she knows that the orphanage is not as good as it should be. She hurriedly gives him some borsht that was left over from supper. When he is through eating, she puts him to bed, happy to have him close to her again.

The next day we are faced with a problem. Two officers come to take Alex back. I plead with them, telling them that I make some money now. This does not satisfy the officers. Finally, I produce the letter showing that our uncle is coming very soon to take us away. The letter is satisfactory, and the officers say that we can also take Sonia home. This makes our little family happy. While Ida is preparing dinner, I rush to bring my baby sister home.

Sonia is surprised to see me. She smiles and kisses me when I tell her that I have come to take her home. She tells me in her cute way how she missed Alex, and when she cried for him, they beat her. I hold her close to me, realizing how much I love her. We run home as fast as we can, so we will be in time for hot borsht. Sonia is very glad to see Alex; they have never been separated before, and now they will be together again.

The Sbritsky children are beginning to feel content again. They have plenty to eat, and it is nice and warm in the kitchen. I put on a wool sweater that came from America and a long pair of pants with patches that I picked up in the market. I pull my cap over one eye, and with my cigarette box, I am on my way out for business and night life. Winter is on its way, but it is unlike other winters, since the people are better prepared.

With our hopes high, we wait for our uncle to take us to the New World. The only thing that mars our happiness is the memory of our loved ones who are gone and who were so vital to our life and happiness.

I am growing up and making older friends who are able to tell me what's going on in the world. Reading the newspapers, I learn how to understand the political and economic situation of Russia. The news is vague, and the country still appears to be unsettled.

Ida keeps writing to different organizations and political bureaus, inquiring about our brother Dmitri's whereabouts. The answers are all alike: "We can't find him; he must be dead." These bureaus never make any attempt to locate the missing; they are disorganized and inefficient.

I am always out in the street, tramping the sidewalks, looking at the newly erected buildings and comparing them to the old, shattered ones. I hang out with boys who are homeless and ignorant. I like that in the company of these hoodlums, I do not have to be a follower. I feel sorry for the boys who have to go home as soon as it is dark, but it does hurt me that I have no parents who care about what I do. I am no different from any other child of twelve who craves a mother's love. Business is unusually good. I have enough money to buy a piece of salami, cake, candy, and even ice cream. I never dreamed I would taste these things again.

I do most of my business in front of the theater that shows motion pictures for the first time. I manage to go in during the show without paying. I become friendly with the operator in the projection room, which is visible from the street through a window. Hundreds of people watch how the projector is operated, and the boys look at me enviously as the operator helps me up with my cigarette box into the little projection room. The room is hot and stuffy, but I don't mind. I watch in amazement, wondering what it is all about. For this valuable friendship, I supply both the operator and his girlfriend with cigarettes. *The Black Mask* is playing, a serial that is very exciting. I watch almost every night. The last show goes on past midnight, and many times I fall asleep. Not that I want to—I just can't keep my eyes open.

I hang around different theaters, getting to know the actors, ushers, and operators. I surprise the neighbors and my sister by mimicking the famous comedians and dancing the latest steps. We are starting to forget our past and have some fun. Ida cooks and jokes around, smiling as she watches me mimic the actors. Alex and Sonia are always playing in the street. Alex keeps managing to get into fights, while Sonia is getting prettier and sweeter by the day. I explore the night life everywhere, except on the main street, where my father's jewelry store was once located. The street is now lit up with bright lights. My heart beats fast as I walk hurriedly to avoid it.

2

An Insight

I embark on a significant journey of self-exploration to understand my panic about Elizabeth's departure from the group—most of it at night when my defenses are down. One night I thought I was going to cry, but what I heard were grunts, as though my crying vocal cords were rusty. I discovered that I was holding myself as Hugo does, so that the pain could be contained. Emotional pain really does feel like physical pain—right in the chest. Soon real sobs came out. I felt that the sobs were like Elizabeth's: wails over isolation, misunderstanding, rage, longing. I sobbed for Arnold's pain, my father's pain, my grandparents' pain, my aunts' and uncles' pain. I sobbed for the cushion that was never there—the cushion of extended family and generational support that protects you from being shattered by life's blows. I imagined Elizabeth and we sobbed together, using the same box of tissues. I took Elizabeth by the hand, and we cried together for little-girl-Linda, who wasn't allowed to have any negative feelings; and for little-boy-Hugo, who grew up in a box in the backseat of his parents' car; and for little-girl Cheryl, who thought she was selfish;

226

and for mean-little-girl-Elaine, who threw girls in the swimming pool blindfolded; and for Tim, whose parents couldn't face the truth; and for Robert, the man who looked like a mannequin and might be watching child porn with his daughter. Oh my God! I forgot Gary—my dear, beautiful, sweet, jovial baby brother! He had such a short, tragic life. "Why didn't Gary listen to me and stop taking drugs?" I yelled to myself. Elizabeth also might not listen to me!

Just as I thought I could not bear another moment of anguish, I had an insight. My pain has to do with a final separation *THAT IS NOT SUPPOSED TO HAPPEN!* For me, Elizabeth's announcement was unpredictable. I thought she was doing well and was going to follow my guidance and have a good life. I was caught off guard. It is another death *that is not supposed to happen*. My father was not supposed to lose his father at age nine and his mother at age eleven or his sister and his brothers. Arnold was not supposed to have a psychotic break at twenty-five and commit suicide. Gary was not supposed to be murdered at thirty-five.

In a dream I imitate my mother when she was at the end of her rope. I stand up, raise my fists and let out a blood curdling scream. I feel light and slowly lie down on the floor. A calm envelops me, and I wonder if this is how Elizabeth feels after she vomits. Elizabeth said that it helps her sleep. In the dream I close my eyes, and everything and everyone is swimming in one pool: Elizabeth, Arnold, Grandma, Dad, Hugo, Tim, David, Madame Marushka, Neda. The devils are dancing with the saints. Work, home life, past and present are all mixed up. I fall into a deep sleep. I wake up refreshed and with more clarity.

I admit to myself that in my heart, I believe that if Arnold and Gary could have had group therapy at the right time in their lives, their deaths would have been prevented. Whether or not this notion is true is not important; it can never be tested. Given this hidden belief, it becomes urgent for me to keep Elizabeth in the group.

Fortunately, I am realistic; now that my beliefs are conscious, I know how to separate out my own emotional beliefs about my brothers from Elizabeth's fate if she does not return to the group. Sure, she would lose an opportunity, but it's her choice, and she may not be ready for what the group has to offer. It's too bad that a group for bulimics doesn't exist in this town; it would be better for her to be with other young women who share her problem. Actually, a weight-control program will help her start to get control of her life. It's a good first step. It's clear to me that Elizabeth uses her weight as a resistance, and it will take a great deal of courage for her to test relationships without it. *Elizabeth is not going to die like Arnold and Gary if she leaves the group!*

I continue to think about last night. I now see my own problem with separation anxiety more clearly. I keep wondering if this anxiety is universal. Is it my unconscious link to all human experience—past and present? Perhaps all humans have been dealing with anxiety about separations that are not supposed to happen. Could this be an aspect of what Jung called the collective unconscious and what Freud referred to as our collective memory of primeval man's struggle for survival?

Arnold made us laugh, but he was wrong. (Could this be why he was so funny?) It's not that we should all hold hands *and* drop dead; we must all hold hands *or* drop dead! The difference of one word is the difference between life and death. Arnold is dead, and I am alive. I can think, write things down, help others, have sex, laugh, and wail in pain. I have a future. But *I miss the future that I thought was mine!*

3

A Confrontation

Elizabeth has agreed to come in for an individual session if I promise not to try to talk her into coming back to the group. She is on time for our private meeting. My goal for this session is for me to be present with her and put aside my own inner conflicts. First I say that I want to understand what made her last group session so painful that she missed two meetings and has apparently dropped out of the group. Of course, my hope is that she will decide on her own to return.

Elizabeth says that she does not belong in the group. She is younger and inferior to the other members. She has an eating disorder that others do not understand. Everyone pairs her with David, and she finds this degrading and humiliating; she cannot stand his flirtatious overtures toward her. She reminds me of my promise not to talk her into coming back to the group. I reiterate that I just want to understand her better.

I ask Elizabeth more about her history, since that might help elucidate the painfulness of this event. I am particularly interested in her sexual development.

Elizabeth was an early developer, and she hated it. Her mother would never discuss sex with her; she sent her to her godmother for information on menstruation. When she was fourteen, she went to a coed school. She had a crush on a boy. Someone found out and humiliated her. After that, she went to all-girls schools and had little experience relating to boys. She always felt awkward around them.

Elizabeth's parents are very religious Catholics and only have sex for procreation. Her father works for the church. Her most disturbing and complex relationship seems to be with her mother. Her mother was the "good" girl. She was a virgin when she married. She never wanted to go to college or have a career. She was a devoted mother and housewife. Elizabeth wanted to follow a different path than her mother: she wanted a career *and* sex. She figured if she waited until marriage to have sex, she might never have any. So she took advantage of the opportunity to have one-night stands. Inside she felt she was committing a sin. Without being aware of it, her judgment of herself became even harsher than that of her mother. I can see how she unconsciously used her eating disorder to keep herself away from men—and safe from more guilt.

I comment that it seems as though Elizabeth sees only two alternative ways to be a woman. She can be like her sisters and mother and have a home and only have reproductive sex with a husband, or she can have a career and be a "whore." I tell her that there must be other options. Elizabeth also seems to split men into two categories: sex objects or boring companions. I ask Elizabeth if she ever thought she could discuss her feelings about men with the men in the group. Elizabeth says she would die first. I use this reaction to point out that she still seems very uncomfortable with men and that she cannot have a relationship with a man until she sees men more as people. She also seems painfully troubled about her sexuality.

I point out that Elizabeth does not mention the role that I played in the group. I imagine that she did not experience me as supportive or empathic. That is indeed correct. She is particularly angry with me for not protecting her from David.

I voice again how struck I am by the parallel between Elizabeth's personal problems and how they are being played out in the group: discomfort with and sexualizing of men, accepting a limiting role for herself, competition with Cheryl as the sister who is different, and resentment of the nonempathic and unhelpful therapist/mother.

Something else is troubling me. It seems to me that Elizabeth is enraged with everyone in the group, including me, and that she has chosen to treat all of us exactly the way she thinks she has been treated by men and by her parents. She is, therefore, dumping us precipitously and breaking a contract with us, just as men have done to her. I want her to know that I now have a good idea how awful Elizabeth feels when men reject her because she is doing the same thing to me and the group. I say, "It feels awful to be walked out on with no notice—with no chance to process a good-bye—and it is also enraging."

Elizabeth is a bit shocked by this exposure. She has never quite looked at herself as evil, like the men who have rejected her. She also does not know how to deal with my anger.

I pick up on her discomfort. Without realizing it, my voice starts to rise and have a pleading quality. I remind Elizabeth of our first intake session. She wanted help with her weight and relationships with men. I explained that these would be difficult problems to help her with and it would take time—at least a year. There would be times in the treatment that would be especially difficult because her worst fears would be reenacted in front of her. She would want to flee. But these times would be the most important times to stay. In fact, she should almost be glad when these times occurred because she would know that a core conflict was being stirred up. If she stuck it out, she could have a real personality change. These were the turning points. But she would have to go through the rough spots to come out on the other side.

I give Elizabeth a penetrating and loving look. In my look I am saying: *"PLEASE TRUST ME! PLEASE BELIEVE ME! I CAN HELP YOU MAKE YOUR DREAMS COME TRUE! DON'T LEAVE OUR FAMILY! GIVE US A TRY!"* I tell Elizabeth that I have experience treating people with eating disorders and that there are no shortcuts to dealing with the conflicts and feelings that are generating the symptom of overeating and obsessing about weight. Most often, repressed rage (and not knowing how to handle it) is a big part of the problem. If she wants to get better, she will have to face that in addition to being a victim herself, she is an angry young woman who victimizes others. Elizabeth can switch therapists or join another group, but eventually she will have to face these issues. At some point she is going to have to change her pattern of running and face herself, no matter how much it hurts. She will see that as much as others have hurt her in the past, as a free adult she herself is now putting up the largest barriers to her happiness. I assure her that the women I have treated with her problem got better. I remind her that she was binging and purging two times a week prior to joining the group, and for the six months that she has been in the group, she has only binged and purged once.

I try to pull back when I begin to hear myself sounding more like a revivalist preacher than a therapist. I finally say, "Look, Elizabeth, I really care about you, and I really care about the group. It's hard for me to see you do something that is destructive to yourself and the group. If you could just come and say good-bye, you would be doing something different from what you've always done in the past. You would be taking a step in changing a lifelong pattern."

Elizabeth says, "You've given me a lot to think about. I never looked at things the way you put them. I never thought I'd ever say this, but I think I could come to the group one more time. I did make a promise to give notice when I was ready to leave." Tears of relief well up in my eyes.

Elizabeth does indeed come to the next group meeting—and she decides to rejoin the group after all.

From My
Father's Book

4

1922

buy an old American turtleneck sweater, a pair of long pants, and a hat that looks like a chauffeur's cap. I am proud of my outfit. It is late at night, and I am standing with a bunch of my friends from the neighborhood. We are all smoking and looking into the cracks of Mrs. Jacobson's windows. We watch prostitutes being intimate with the soldiers. It is a very clear night; the only light is coming from the full moon. It is one of the most beautiful nights in a long time. I am leaning on the brick wall of the house with a cigarette in my mouth. I look like a hoodlum. We hear heavy footsteps approaching us, and as we look up we see a man approaching us. He is neatly dressed in a black coat and fedora, and he carries a portfolio under his arm. We are sure he is a government man, and we shudder. Government men are the only ones who dress neatly and carry portfolios. I act as the spokesman while the other boys back up, afraid the man might arrest us for being out so late. With a daring voice I ask what he wants. The man quietly answers that he is looking for the Sbritsky children. "I am a Sbritsky!" I proudly answer.

The man hugs me and tells me that he is my mother's brother, Uncle Nathan, and has come to take her children to America. He asks, "Why are you dressed like this? Why are you smoking? Why aren't you asleep, you poor child?" I say nothing, thinking only of my uncle's presence. I will be saying good-bye to my homeland. I look down on the ground and realize that I will never walk on it again. I look up at the beautiful sky that lights up the little homes in the Dome; they look so friendly now.

I take my uncle home, where Alex and Sonia are sleeping and Ida is reading. I come in saying, "This is our uncle from Odessa!" Ida jumps up and throws her arms around his neck, tears coming to her eyes. I wake Sonia and Alex. We gather around our uncle, telling him everything that has happened in those miserable, unbelievable days. Our tears are plentiful, and our cries are loud. We all sit around the table, which is covered with a red cloth, and discuss plans for our departure.

We start to feel strange—different from the people we are leaving behind. Our uncle tells us that he has moved from Odessa to a nice home in Ekaterinoslav (Katherinatown), about five hundred miles from Elisavetgrad. We are going to take the train there and wait until the trip to America is planned. The next day the neighbors—who always welcome a stranger to this inner part of Russia, where civilization is so far behind—come to see what's going on. Our uncle's strange appearance and talk make them feel as if they are listening to a worldly scholar and a great government official. In reality he is a printer for the government in his town. The neighbors never question his real occupation; they just sit and listen with wonder as he speaks of the change in the government. The neighbors who are ill or ashamed to be seen because of their ragged clothes peek through our windows (which are stuffed with rags to keep the cold out). We sense people's jealousy of us. Some of my friends say, "You are lucky to have your mother and father dead so you can go to America!" This enrages me, brings tears to my eyes, and leads to a fight.

It is a bright, sunny morning with the bitter cold sweeping the countryside; the snow is high above the knees. We are packing our few belongings. One is a valuable watch that my father gave to my mother on her birthday. It is the one thing my mother would not sell. I am arguing with my uncle because he wants to take the little Swiss watch. My uncle insists that he will keep it for safety. I am finally convinced that his intentions are honorable and that he will give it back to us when we are older.

We all treasure this watch; it is the only piece of our mother that we can hold on to. My mother comes to me in my dreams, asking me to take good care of Alex, Sonia, and Ida and to try to forget her.

I put on my new boots from America with pride. It is a sad departure. We walk slowly through the snow. Uncle Nathan holds on to my free hand; my other hand is carrying a large bundle that practically covers my whole body. Ida follows close behind, holding both Sonia's and Alex's hands. It is bitterly cold, and we are bundled with blankets and old furs. We keep turning our heads, staring at the broken-down structures that were once our happy home. Uncle keeps quiet as we turn and sniffle. We wave good-bye with frozen hands. I am the most pathetic because I am sentimental; I love the open spaces and my freedom and cannot bear to leave my friends. For a moment I feel like running away.

We lose sight of the streets that are so familiar to us. We reach the train station; it is a large, old, one-story structure. It is made of red bricks, and a wooden sign hangs from the roof with big golden letters spelling *Elisavetgrad*. I am the only one who has seen this station before—I was seven and sold candy here. Now I am almost thirteen. My uncle cannot believe it when I tell him.

As the children cuddle up in Ida's lap in one corner of the station, I roam off to look the place over for the last time. Uncle Nathan leaves us to inquire about the arrival of the next train. When he returns, much to his annoyance, I am not there. After searching a while, he finds me near the rails. He reprimands me severely. I am stung by this scolding. I have a morbid feeling as I sense my freedom slipping away.

Alex and Sonia have fallen asleep, and Ida is dozing off when we return. I sit on the trunk near them. I am wide awake, thinking about the past and future.

The train comes rolling in at three a.m. through the heavy snow, like a huge monster. Uncle Nathan hurriedly wakes the children. There is a great deal of excitement at the station as people rush to board the train. The train stops for just half an hour, and everyone is panicky. If they miss this train, they will have to wait a month for the next one.

We settle into our crude berths, the top one for our uncle, and the lower one for us. Each consists of a straw mattress, a pillow, and a brown army blanket marked *USSR*. It feels heavenly to lie down on this bed after lying on the cold cement floor of the station. Alex and Sonia fall asleep immediately, while Ida and I sit up, blowing our hot breaths against the frozen window as we look out. I am amazed by the way the trees move as the train hurriedly passes them. Though I know it is the train and not the trees that move, I find it very interesting that it appears this way.

So far everything is new, and the exciting things I have heard about are right before my eyes: the wastelands, the roar of the stormy wind, and the deep snow that could cover the tallest man. I now know why people get frozen to death in the outskirts of the city, only to be found in the spring when the snow melts away. It is the first time I have ever ridden on a train. The roar of the engine frightens me, and the noise of the whistle surprises me. The new faces on the train make me curious; I hardly take my eyes off them. As the sun appears on the horizon the train slowly enters Ekaterinoslav. This town is named after Katherine the Great. It saw very little of the revolution and famine because it was one of the first small towns to establish a Bolshevik government. It was stable enough to keep out the looters, bandits, and other menacing powers that crippled the other towns before the Bolshevik government could establish itself everywhere. The town is industrial and well planned, with many parks and nice brick buildings in the business center. We look around and find it more beautiful than our own city. My real surprise comes when I meet Aunt Rose. She is young and beautiful, and her eyes are as dark as a Gypsy's.

I love my Aunt Rose, and my feelings for her confuse me. It is more than just a craving for a mother's love. I sit up late into the night and stare into her eyes as she sews dresses for Sonia that make my sister look like a little doll. It is on these nights that I start to talk to her about my experiences. Some nights the thought of her keeps me awake and almost drives me mad with frustration, particularly when I hear my uncle enter her bedroom. Like a beast, my jealousy rises. I cannot bear the thought of another man with her, even though he is her husband. I picture Uncle Nathan going to sleep with her and touching her naked body and doing things to her. I remember what I witnessed through the peephole in Elisavetgrad and make up my own imaginary acts. I want to kiss her, hug her, and touch her milk-white skin. I know not to share these thoughts with anyone. Many times my aunt looks at me curiously, as though she is wondering why I watch every move she makes.

I am beginning to enjoy a life where I do not have to carry my heavy wooden box filled with cigarettes and yell at the top of my lungs on bitter-cold days. I am free to walk the streets and enjoy the different sights and fresh air and sunshine. My only duty is to bring a hot lunch to my uncle at his workplace, the government printing plant. I watch with wonder what machines can do. I never saw newspapers printed before and never thought an opportunity like this would arise—I can actually see the machines in action. I look forward to lunchtime so I can look around and ask questions. I want to work there. I ask my uncle to let me do something in the plant, anything at all, but it is against the rules.

Walking in the park, I meet a girl that I like. I ask Aunt Rose for money to buy her candy. I grow very fond of this girl. We meet every night at sunset and timidly hold hands as we walk through the park. We say little to each other. I just turned fourteen, and she is twelve. We are children, but we are aware of our hearts beating faster than usual when we are together. She is short and chubby, and her cheeks are always red. I like to look into her eyes; they are unusually blue. We talk of the revolution, each recollecting the facts that we can remember. I spare her details because I want to forget them. Our affection grows as we stroll through the park every night; we begin to hold hands more tightly. She keeps telling me that she likes my Mongolian eyes and my black, curly hair. I marvel at her milk-white skin. Some nights we go to her backyard. I come close to her and feel her lovely skin. On one special night, when the stars are bright and the moon is full, I touch her cheek and can't resist kissing it. It is the first time I have ever kissed a girl. I blush as a thrill goes through me. The little girl bashfully moves away with wonder in her eyes. I try to explain my actions, telling her that I am leaving for America the next day and that the kiss is the way I want to say good-bye. I tell her, "I will always remember you when I am in America." She comes close to me, and looking into my tiny eyes, she replies, "You are so different from the other boys. I like you and wish you didn't have to go away." Suddenly we hear a loud voice that brings us out of our trance. It is Aunt Rose calling me for dinner. I give my dear friend another quick kiss and run away. I feel sad to part from her, but I am happy again when I realize that we will finally be on our way to America.

Harry: Under the Table

Current Group Therapy Meeting Continued

WHERE WE LEFT OFF: *Toward the end of Part 2, Tim and Robert clashed and then found their commonality. Tim revealed his sexual problems and helped Robert with his. (Part 3 flashed back to an earlier group therapy meeting.)*

As Elizabeth talks, she plays with her blonde curls and then strokes her hair gently. She expresses herself slowly and hesitantly. This is her second session back in the group. "I guess in a lot of ways everyone can relate, as far as parents go. They are from such a different generation than us. I guess a lot of people feel that their parents never taught them about sex in a good way. It's hard to get involved with someone in a relationship when the things you were taught were not positive or sex wasn't dealt with openly, as though it was too dirty to talk about. My parents never talked about sex. I consider myself as coming from a loving family, but they showed their love primarily by providing for us and trying to protect us from going to hell."

Cheryl rubs her ear, and Linda readjusts her head on her hand as she listens to Elizabeth.

"But it was like sex was . . . " Elizabeth pauses and then comes out with the words. "Sex seemed . . . dirty . . . and bad."

Hugo sits forward, trying to meet her halfway with his body.

Elizabeth continues. "I guess in my parents' circumstances . . . Well, I have a hard time thinking about them even dating, let alone having sex. I can't believe how straight they are."

Cheryl and Hugo smile at Elizabeth. Harry sits up high—he is almost standing—and settles into a different position. Hugo scratches the top of his leg to the rhythm of Elizabeth's words and then rests his hand on the inside of his open thighs.

Elizabeth has everyone's attention. "But maybe in their generation, sex was basically to have kids. I don't know if they could even say anything about enjoying it. They would never share something like that with their kids."

"Probably pretty strong Catholics, too?" Robert asks, smiling.

"Very strong. My dad, I mean, he should have been a priest. That's what we always told him: 'You should have been a priest, Dad.'"

"That's what the church dictates: you only have sex for children," Robert adds.

Linda chimes in, "And you're not supposed to have fun."

Everyone starts talking at once. They have the freedom to experience sexual impulses that their parents did not have. The meeting is beginning to feel exhilarating.

"It's so weird. My experience is exactly the opposite of Elizabeth's." People look at Harry, puzzled but amused.

"Oh, really?" someone says.

Harry elaborates. "My family is from India, and they grew up Hindu. Have you read the *Kama Sutra*? Have you seen pictures of Hindu temples? They're covered with images of people copulating in different positions. My parents, well, I mean, I used to come home and find those two. Or I would hear or smell them—under the dining room table." Harry takes a breath. "The table is made of burl, and the base is a root ball, so it looks like a tree."

People start to smile, then someone bursts into a giggle, and soon the whole group lets out a gale of laughter. I am afraid of completely losing control, laughing, and try to swallow some of it. After a few minutes, we all use our strength to collect ourselves so that we can continue to talk.

"A-a-all ri-i-ight!" yells Robert.

Harry adds matter-of-factly, "I guess the reason I'm saying this is so you don't think that it would have been such a positive experience."

Tim is the only one who doesn't look amused. He is even looking at Harry with suspicion.

Harry continues: "I want to correct all of you if you think, 'If only my parents had been more open about sex, maybe I would be a little freer myself.' That's not always the case, 'cause I don't feel like . . . Well, I think for me it was just the opposite. I was so shocked so many times that it made me a little nervous."

I can't help smiling, even though I know that sexual excesses aren't good for children. I seem to be the last one to get serious. Members must be picking up on my delight.

"Yeah, but did they talk to you about sex?" Robert asks.

"Indirectly." Harry pauses. "The thing is, I noticed a pattern when my mother came to visit last weekend. My dad was going out of town for the week, so my mom stayed with us. I noticed she was doing a lot of nice things with my wife, but she was commanding me, 'Do this! Do that! Do this!' I cooked this big meal for them. We went out, she took my wife shopping, and all *I* heard from her was 'Get that! Drive carefully! Do that!'" He snaps his fingers with sharp hostility as he imitates her commands.

Everyone is sitting quietly, studying Harry as he talks. "She was being nice to my wife, whom she doesn't even know well. Well, my mother died when I was young—I don't remember her much—and my dad remarried, so she is actually my stepmother, but she raised me. I am the person I am largely because of her. She's got some good qualities . . . Well, we were talking about these crazy, different things that we never realized. And she says, 'You know, I only have one regret: that I wasn't able to marry your father earlier.' She didn't know my father when my mother was alive. I looked at her, and I thought to myself, 'Is she saying that she wishes my mother had died earlier so she could have married him? Is that what she's saying?'" Harry is indignant.

Elizabeth scratches her eye. David cracks a knuckle on his lap. Uneasiness stirs around the room.

Harry continues: "What impressed me is that she's tactful and considerate to almost everybody but me. I can do this! I can do that! I can fix the car! I can cook for her! And *she* can tell *me*, 'I wish your mother had bitten the dust earlier than she did.' And I thought to myself, 'Even if I'm over the fact that my mother died, that's a terribly tactless thing to say.'"

Hugo makes a standing-up motion as he talks and leans toward Harry. "She could have been expressing an awful lot of love for him. I mean, that's the way I would interpret what she said. She just wanted to have all that time with him."

"That just happened to be the way you took it," Linda says to Harry.

"I agree with you—that's a possibility. And in all probability, I think that's what she meant. But when I looked at her after she said what she did, there was this half glimmer of recognition on her face that said, 'Oh, I realize what I said.' And it wasn't, 'I didn't mean to say that.'"

"Why didn't you ask her?" Hugo asks.

"Well, the unfortunate thing is that this is a topic that can't be discussed in my family. I never saw a picture of my mother, and my father refuses to talk about her. And my mother—I mean my stepmother—acts as if I were just created."

Tim scratches his head as he puzzles over what Harry is saying.

"That's terrible!" says Cheryl with great empathy. Cheryl knows the horror of losing a good mother before one is grown up. So do I. I lived with the consequences of my father's loss of his mother my whole childhood. He was not able to have a reparative therapeutic experience. He remained damaged—never able to love a woman generously and without conflict. His inability to share resources or compliment his wife put tremendous strain on the entire family. It is not surprising that his two sons may have been broken by the legacy of this loss. Once Arnold picked up a stray dog, named it, and instantly fell in love with it. Our father made him give it away. Ivan didn't want to lose another beloved dog. Because Ivan was not willing to take this risk, his son had to endure the painful loss of a pet. Ivan avoided noticing his son's shattered heart when he made him give the dog away.

Harry responds with increasing irritation. "It just pisses the hell out of me. It really makes me mad. I would like to confront her, but she's a very . . . "

Robert is sitting at the edge of his chair, involved. "Why confront her? Why don't you confront your father with that?"

It is a relief to have advice to give when there is such a horrible transgression to face. I know many people suffer because they feel they have to erase the image of a dead beloved. Other cultures have rituals to deal with this, knowing that one generation builds on another. To ignore the foundation can make a house vulnerable to collapse.

Cheryl also sits forward. "Yeah, I would," she says.

Robert continues to advise Harry. "Get alone with him. It's really none of your stepmother's business. That's the way I feel about my first wife. She died. I don't discuss her with anybody." Then Robert mumbles, "Your dad is probably as upset as you are." It is hard to fathom the hurt of such loss for long, especially when it reminds you of your own.

"My dad is irrational when I talk about my mother. I found out later that she died in a really unhappy way, and he just . . . Well, he's never discussed it with me. He's never told me how she died. He doesn't accept the fact that she's not here with us anymore."

Cheryl talks firmly even though her hand is in front of her mouth. "But he *owes* it to you to discuss it. Hard as it may be, you owe it to yourself to discuss it with him."

"I think you're right. And I don't mean to be going, 'Yes, but,' but I tried. I thought a good time to do it was ten years ago, when I went to college. I had to fill out this form. I didn't know if my mother got cancer or if she was run over by a truck."

Elizabeth wiggles in her chair as though a shiver has just run down her spine. She would rather not hear how cruel life can be. She does not want to face her grandmother's suffering in Poland and how it damaged her mother. I wonder to what extent this legacy relates to Elizabeth's dysfunction. I will keep this in mind as I continue to work with her.

Harry is aware that he has captivated his audience. "She was a nurse, and I thought when I was little . . . Well, I just thought she went to work, and the shift kept on going and going and going. Anyway, I said to my dad, 'Here's this form that asks about what happened to your parents. I've always wondered what happened to my mother. I know that obviously she's not here with us anymore, but what happened?' He was absolutely furious. I thought he was going to beat me up. He grabbed the form out of my hand, filled it out, and mailed it. I never saw it. I was never able to ask any relatives because he took them . . . I had no contact with my mother's family after she died. They all were just gone—vanished. My older sister disappeared too. I was only eight. My mother had two children from a former marriage (their father had died) who were fifteen and sixteen. They ran away from home when my mother died. I found my sister two years ago, but no one knows where my brother is."

"Have you ever thought about trying to find the death notice?" Hugo asks. It is so much easier to ask a question than face the horror of Harry's story. Harry is talking about it somewhat lightly, but I hear the nightmare. Such separation is everyone's nightmare, including mine. Arnold's and Gary's abrupt departures are still a nightmare. My father's sudden losses still affect me. I am prone to terrible separation anxiety, as was apparent when Elizabeth threatened to leave the group. I also panic about money, thinking I am going to starve if I don't have enough.

"I did. And . . . " Harry starts to talk very slowly, as though each word is precious. " . . . I found the rest of my mother's family . . . which is the premiere experience of my life."

"When did you do that?" Linda asks.

"About four years ago."

"I don't agree with the way my dad has acted, but I think I understand him better now. I try to accept that he cannot deal with my mom's death. I'm not going to change what happened twenty-four years ago. I don't think he's going to be reformed. He won't tell me about it."

Linda readies herself to gently confront Harry on his projections (the parts of himself that he wants to disown). This is an important part of the group's work, and Linda is taking the lead. I admire members when I watch them accept this challenge. I think: Projection is such an antiquated, primitive response to our inner torment. There has to be another way. The survival of our planet depends on it. Doesn't anyone think it's odd that the Japanese could be our enemy in one decade or century and our friend in another?? Or the Germans?? Or the Russians?? Children should be taught about this in school: the dangers of black-and-white thinking and an enemy (us vs.

them) mentality. They should learn that the larger the group they join (society), the more vulnerable they are to supporting cruelty.

Linda takes her hand away from her mouth and puts both hands on her knees. Everyone stares at her. "One thing keeps sticking in my mind: your interpretation of your stepmother's remark."

"My what?" Harry asks.

Tim follows on the heels of Linda. "Because when you said what your stepmother's remark was, I took it in a different way. I interpreted it completely differently from the way you interpreted it. Why did you react that way? There are any number of ways you could interpret that remark, because it's just an off-the-cuff remark. She may have looked taken aback because it's one of those remarks that can be taken wrong five hundred different ways, and she probably knew it the minute she said it."

"Then why couldn't she just tell me she was sorry?" Harry retorted.

A number of people start talking at once. Linda repeats Tim's question: "Why did you take her remark the way you did?" Harry is being educated about the ways of the group: Look at yourself—self-reflect.

Cheryl answers excitedly instead of Harry: "Because everything is so unresolved!"

"Yeah," echoes Elizabeth.

Cheryl turns to Linda and continues to speak for Harry. "I took it the same way that you took it when Harry first said it. But after hearing the rest of his story, I can imagine why he would be defensive."

"Yeah," agrees Elizabeth, who remembers her grandmother's horrible tale.

Cheryl looks at Harry. "I can just imagine why you would be very defensive, if nobody told you . . . "

"Particularly when I'm not allowed to talk about it," adds Harry. He continues: "And I'm excluded. My father and stepmother are Indian. They are tall and have small eyes. I am short and have big eyes like my mother, who wasn't Indian. It seems like a small thing, but it's not. When my stepmother was at my house, I thought to myself, 'You've got some nerve. You come to my house. You order me around. I'm your little slave, and on top of that, you have the audacity to say something that maybe you didn't mean to say but was still cruel. And when you do realize it, you don't say, 'I'm sorry. I didn't mean it that way.'"

Linda is sitting with an open stance in front of Harry and starts to talk to him. "But how would she know how you took it if you didn't say? See, if you had said to her, 'Look, when you said this, I felt this way,' then she could have said, 'I'm sorry' because she would have realized what was upsetting you."

I help out. "We seem to be talking here about forbidden things or bringing up forbidden topics." I face Harry. "Your reaction shows that it's not only forbidden to talk about your mother with your stepmother and father, but also with yourself." I add to myself: 'Yes, let's look within. Let's take responsibility for ourselves.'

Harry smiles like a secretive little boy and says, "I think about my mother every day. I still do. I like to talk about her with other people. That makes me feel really good. I don't know why, but it does."

"Do you have any pictures of her?" Robert asks.

"Yes, yes. When I found the rest of my family, they gave me all the pictures." He hugs his chest dramatically to show how precious they are. Linda hugs her thighs in resonance. Everyone is glad he has pictures—something to hold onto.

"How sad," I think. "I have pictures too. They help a lot. One of my worst fears is that I will forget Arnold and Gary, but I haven't. Now I know you never forget your departed parents or your siblings. They live as long as you do. There is a way of staying attached, even after they die. The *relationship* stays inside you."

"Did they tell you how she died?" Robert asks.

"Oh, yeah. She was dancing with my father at a nightclub, and she dropped dead in his arms . . . No one knew it, but she had a brain aneurism that was quite large, and it just burst, and she died immediately."

"Ouch," Robert says spontaneously. "No wonder your father doesn't want to remember." He rubs his foot back and forth along the floor. The nightmare is inescapable.

A long silence follows. Horror and sadness fill the air.

From My Father's Book: The *Polonia*

1923

6

A t sunrise the baggage is being loaded onto a wagon while our aunt and uncle go to bid their neighbors good-bye. I am drowsy from a sleepless night. I sit close to my sisters and brother in one corner of the train. The train is old and rolls at a slow pace into the city of Riga, Latvia, where we are to change for a train to Libau, also in Latvia. From there we will take a boat across the Baltic Sea that will lead us to the rough Atlantic Ocean. We will be taken to Ellis Island, where our Aunt Martha will meet us and take us to her home in Bayonne, New Jersey. Throughout this entire journey, my thoughts travel faster than I can digest them. We are all so excited. When we arrive in America, it has been only one year since we left our town of Elisavetgrad, but it seems like a much longer time; we have seen so many different things in such a short time. Our future seems bright and exciting.

We get off the train at Riga. The custom guards examine our baggage and passports. We stop at a small hotel, and after dinner we decide to explore the city. I am becoming a young man, so after much discussion, my uncle lets me wander around alone. I walk through very narrow streets—so narrow that only a few people can walk abreast. The streets are clean, and the roadways are neatly paved with cobblestones. I see people from all walks of life with different dress and mannerisms. The store windows display expensive wines and liquors and all sorts of delicacies. One window appeals to me so much that I stand in front of it for ten minutes, wondering how the delicious- looking things taste. I drink in all the beauty of the new architecture as I look up at the tall, slim buildings. I want to question the strange people who pass me by, but my uncle warned me not to talk to anyone.

Our stay here is short, and the children enjoy it. As they take pictures for their passports, they feel a sense of importance when the street photographer makes them pose. The sunshine is bright in the park where they go every day, but their hearts are full of envy because the children there have toys and games. Sonia is the baby, and because Aunt Rose loves her, she deprives herself of necessities to buy her a doll. Alex tries to play with the doll, but Sonia objects.

After a month's stay in Riga, we go to Libau. The train is much faster and more modern. We reach Libau at sunset. A cab takes us through the dark streets to a hotel near the Baltic seaport, where we will take the boat to America. We wake early to see our new surroundings. Uncle Nathan and Aunt Rose share our excitement; this is the farthest they have ever traveled. The hotel is a three-story building for three classes of people. Each family is given one room consisting of a sink with running water, two steel cots with two pillows, a gray mattress filled with straw, and two brown army blankets. The room is freshly painted, and the sunshine streams through the large windows. At night the cold breezes from the sea sweep through the closed windows. Our little group begins to get a taste of contentment in these clean and friendly surroundings.

There are many people here from all walks of life. After breakfast we all go out to the large yard, which looks more like the yard of a private estate than that of an emigrant hotel. The lawn is neatly trimmed, the flowers are in bloom, and the trees are covered with blossoms.

In the afternoon my aunt unexpectedly tells me to get ready, as we are taking the boat to America at two o'clock. My heart begins beating fast, and beads of perspiration appear on my forehead. The hour is finally approaching when we will leave for the land of the free, where gold is found in the streets and everyone is happy. These are the things I have heard many times, and now I will find out for myself.

The *Polonia* is ready and waiting at the pier. It is an immense steamer, the likes of which I could never have imagined. The ship is freshly painted, and it shines brightly in the afternoon sun. There is much excitement—yelling, weeping, and laughing. My uncle grabs me by the arm while Aunt Rose carries Sonia and Ida follows with Alex. We step onto the large deck of the ship among cheers and cries. The whistle begins to blow, and we all look around wildly to see if our loved ones are with us. As the *Polonia* slowly moves away from the pier, the people on board wave their handkerchiefs to their friends; their emotions are intense. Some of these people have left their homes and farms because they were persecuted for the crime of loving their neighbors or believing in God and religion or having the wrong religion or skin color. But all these people are going to America, a free country, with new hope in their hearts—America, where there is malice toward none.

I stand on the deck near the rails with tears rolling down my face and dropping into the sea. Soon I can hardly see the pier, and I begin to look into empty space. I cannot believe that we are on water with no land in sight.

The large, powerful ship moves with greater speed on the second day at sea. The *Polonia* is now approaching the roaring Atlantic Ocean. The wind is fierce, and the ship begins to rock. Everyone is nervous. We have all seen so much since we left our oppressed countries, but the rough sea with the sky overhead and no land to be seen for thousands of miles and sharks following the bow of the ship—all of these are totally strange and foreign. We never even dreamed that such sights existed—waves the size of mountains and sharks the size of horses. The excitement of these sights soon wears off as seasickness overcomes most of the passengers. Men and women lean over the rails, and the lavatories are crowded with people trying to get rid of the meal they ate. The children are lying on their cots, some crying loudly and others suffering quietly. The dinner bell no longer attracts attention. Those who are not sick are tired of the constant diet of salt fish and potatoes. The sailors find it amusing to watch us. For them seasickness is a joke. I don't get as sick as the others. I hang around the sailors, watching them intently. The sailors get used to me, and in due time we become friends. They tell me tales of the sea, and I tell them stories of the revolution and famine.

The weather worsens as the ship fights its way into the fifth day of its journey. A Charlie Chaplin comedy is showing in the main dining room to cheer up the crowd. It makes the kiddies happy, and they forget their sickness to some extent, but the adults find little relief in the funny little man. As the storm grows worse, people begin to worry. The captain orders all the passengers to their cabins. The entire crew works on deck, and lifeboats are made ready to be let down at a moment's notice.

The storm calms down as dawn approaches. Those who fell asleep wake up to a beautiful day. After sixteen days, the *Polonia* finally heads into New York Harbor. Everyone goes on deck to watch for the symbol that these miserable people and orphaned children have come to find. We are all worn out, and many are sick because their weak bodies could not stand the strain of the long trip. One man is not here to witness the scene. He died on the tenth day of the journey, and his body was thrown into the sea—a sight that is still fresh in everyone's mind. A newborn baby is in the arms of his mother on the lower deck. The upper deck is jammed with everyone waiting anxiously. Finally a tall man yells, "There it is, there it is!" pointing his finger into empty space. In a few minutes, everyone can see the figure as a shadow; it becomes clearer with each minute. We all start laughing with joy and shouting as the Statue of Liberty comes clearly into sight. We gasp with surprise at its tremendous size and the outstretched hand holding the torch. Some smile, some cry, some sigh with relief, some are nonchalant, and others are astounded by its presence—but we all have one thing in common, and that is great happiness. We have searched for happiness for a long time, and in seeing the Statue of Liberty, we feel that we will find it here in the land of liberty and freedom. We are all welcome here, no matter what our race, religion, or creed.

The *Polonia* slowly moves toward Ellis Island, where everyone is immediately examined and quarantined. The children impatiently want to see our American aunt and uncle.

Aunt Rose is arguing with the authorities because they will not let us disembark. They tell her that many things have to be straightened out before we can come ashore. The problem is that Uncle Bill Abrams (my mother's brother-in-law) did not expect to adopt these orphan children. He already has two children of his own—a boy of thirteen, one year younger than me, and a girl of sixteen, the same age as Ida. Our uncle has a shirt factory and is fairly well-off, but he does not want to take the responsibility of adding four children more to his family. These are his wife's sister's children, and his wife is not anxious to adopt them, either. They had planned simply to bring the children here, keep them until they were old enough to work, and then send them out on their own. But the authorities are taking a different stand. They want Uncle Bill to legally adopt these children, give them his name, and bring them up as his own. They also want his three brothers, who are rich, to sign an affidavit that in case he cannot support the children, his brothers will. Such a signature is difficult to get from them, as his brothers are greedy. They are so money mad that two of his brothers have not spoken to each other for ten years because one cheated the other in a business deal. Fortunately, Uncle Bill is honorable and decent. He persuades his brothers to sign because he is on friendly terms with them, and they like him.

Unaware of what is going on, the children are having a grand time on Ellis Island. The food is the best we have ever eaten. At dinnertime all the immigrants sit around a table that seats fifty people. The table cloth is pure white and changes after each meal. There are five courses of fine food with different recipes for every day of the week. What impresses me most is the napkin each person receives and the pieces of sugar wrapped separately with printing on them (which I can't read). I feel important to be the object of so much attention. I begin to feel that there is some truth to what people say about America. Everyone is treated the same on this little island that is surrounded with bars like a prison. Everybody is given the same food. There is no prejudice or hatred. No one calls one another names as they did in Russia. No one asks us if we are Jews or Christians. These things keep whirling in my mind and make me happy.

After hearing about the trouble Uncle Bill is having, I am surprised at the interest the government is taking in our welfare. The thought of being sent back to Russia never entered my mind before. I thought this government was too good to send anyone back. I don't realize that we *will* have to return the next day if my uncle's brothers do not agree to sign the affidavit.

Aunt Rose comes running down the hall, full of laughter. She finds us scattered around the recreation room, watching people play cards, checkers, and chess. She gathers us around her and tells us that we are to leave Ellis Island the next morning. Her news is greeted with shouts of laughter and tears from all of us, including the new friends we have made during our month's stay.

A guard calls for the Sbritsky children. We are sad and serious. We are about to leave our safe haven to meet the aunt and uncle who will take the place of our dear mother and father and the cousins who will take the place of our beloved Neda, Misha, and Dmitri. Soon our excitement and curiosity overwhelm us.

The Winning Ticket

Current Group Therapy Meeting Continued

7

W HERE WE LEFT OFF: *Elizabeth told the group that her parents never talked about sex and made her feel that it was dirty. Harry revealed that his parents had sex under the dining room table, oblivious to all. He also explained that his mother's tragic death is a forbidden topic in his family.*

Hugo says softly and logically to Harry, "Well, that doesn't have to stop you from telling your father you want to talk to him about your mother."

"What's in it for me to talk to anybody about it?" Harry asks.

Hugo doesn't move from his *Thinker* position as he answers, "Well, I don't know. It just means that you take a risk, and the worst that can happen is that it'll be just like it is now."

Members see that I am about to talk; all eyes turn toward me as I change the subject. The issue of "the forbidden" is a good bridge back to the incident that the group has not fully explored. "It seems as though people here are taking a risk talking about the forbidden. And one thing that has been forbidden in here is to talk about one's sexual attractions." I look at Cheryl, who is sitting across from me. "You're the one who brought it up initially in here, Cheryl, when you said that sometimes it was hard for you to be friends with somebody you were attracted to. I asked if you were attracted to anybody in here, and you got angry with me and said you wouldn't say. Robert then took a big risk and admitted that he's attracted to you."

David looks around the room to see everyone's reaction. Cheryl scratches the back of her neck. Hugo takes his glasses off and then puts them back on.

I continue, speaking slowly, giving people time to digest what I'm saying. "All this talk was forbidden until recently. And it seems as though it may be more than a coincidence that you, Robert, came in here today and brought up your lack of sexual desire. After all, a few weeks ago you made a declaration to Cheryl, devastated Elizabeth, and felt guilty about it." As soon as I had put all this together for myself, I had become pretty sure that Robert was innocent of harming his daughter by sharing pornography with her. People capable of such guilt are usually not transgressors. They punish themselves before they act—even when they have the *thought* of abusing someone. My guess is that Robert's daughter was actually molested, but by someone other than Robert. That's the reason her story was so graphic and convincing to the psychologist. I don't believe Robert mistreated her, except perhaps by overindulgence. "Poor child and poor Robert," I think. "What bad luck."

Robert laughs impulsively and says honestly, "I don't see a connection. The lack of interest in sex was something I just had to talk about today. I promised Sally."

I ask, "How are you all feeling now about the incident with Elizabeth a few weeks ago—in terms of what's taking place in here with us now? Since that meeting Robert says he's lost interest in sex, and during our meetings, people seem to be feeling a lot of discomfort about sex and sexual attraction."

People are frozen. They look at me with questioning faces. I imagine their thoughts: "Therapists are human, after all, and they do make mistakes. But this is a big one. On the other hand, she has really helped me. I am better now. She knows what she's doing. When she interprets other people, she always sounds on target—it's just when her interpretations refer to *me* that they seem far-fetched. She looks confident and that she believes what she's saying. This connection is just too crazy. But I guess I should at least consider what she's proposing."

Robert keeps his hand folded in front of him as he talks. He looks as though he's in a straitjacket. He moves only his two thumbs to help him along. "All I know is that it's something I've wanted to talk about in the group for a long time, but I never had the guts to do it. And that's how I feel about it. I feel much better talking about it." He scratches his shoulder.

Hugo sits up in his chair, turns to face me, and says, "I think there was an inertia that had kind of built up in here. But now things are different. The more open people are, the more accepting we are of one another, and the safer it feels to be open. People are feeling they can be open about anything that they want to. I think that's terrific. We're no longer into bullshit. I'm not sure if it's particularly over sexual issues; I *do* think that it's about openness."

"I think that Hugo's got a good point. The only, the newest person in the group, I forgot your name . . . " Robert says nervously.

"Harry."

"Harry. I'm sorry I forgot your name. The rest of us have been here for quite some time. I have a feeling of trust, whereas I didn't have it before because we kept adding new people. Now we've got a fairly stable, I mean a very stable group. I don't feel threats anymore. I felt a threat from you for a while." Robert turns to look at Tim and for a moment, they both remember their clash. "We went through that stage. Now I don't feel a threat, so I can say things that I wouldn't say before."

I strike again. "I feel that there's a *relationship* between your being able to talk as you are today and what's taken place in the last four meetings." In other words, growth comes from dealing with what is happening right now. If you can be free to express yourself, say what you truly feel, and realize that you're all right, you won't have such a need to project onto others."

Linda rubs her neck. Everyone stares at me, looking puzzled.

Hugo finally says, "I think we're more trusting now, but I don't think it's sexual."

"What is it?" I ask.

"I think it's an openness that's been created."

"By whom? How?" I ask Hugo.

"By . . . " He stops to think a moment. "I don't know. I don't think it's by one person specifically. People have taken the risk of expressing significant pain, and there hasn't been any judgment of that in the group, so that might make people feel that there isn't going to be any pain resulting from being open, and that makes people feel okay about talking." He keeps his hand on his cheek as he faces me. "I mean, what you're saying sounds real Freudian to me, which I think is a dogmatic kind of approach to things. And I don't . . . "

Linda smiles.

"How is it Freudian?" I ask him, unruffled.

"Well, because of the sexual emphasis. All of this energy that's created as a result of a sexual issue. Frankly, it didn't occur to me before you brought it up. And I don't think . . . My reaction to it, is that it's not that. It's an openness that's been created that started from somebody talking about a sexual thing. I mean, there were all sorts of things talked about. There was appearance, acceptance, and friendship. Just because it was between a man and a woman doesn't necessarily make it a sexual connotation. I tend not to think of relationships between men and women as always being a sexual thing. I'm not even sure what happened here. I mean, you're dealing with somebody who can be attracted or not attracted to people for reasons other than sexuality."

Linda starts to talk with her head down. She soon sits up, looks at everyone, and uses broad gestures to magnify her words. "The connection that's been seeping into my mind over the last week or so is that we are getting to a point where we're really listening to one another. We're realizing that we're not alone in our problems and struggles. Some of us are finally getting past the intellectual knowledge of 'Yeah, I'm not the only person with this problem.' Speaking for myself, I now believe I'm not a freak. I didn't believe that before. But now it's in here." She points to her heart. "And I'm getting the feeling that people in here are genuinely sharing their experiences with one another."

Hugo adjusts his glasses, and Cheryl wipes her eye.

Tim follows. "I was in here for a real bitch of a reason." He looks at me. "You asked what good all of us think came out of what happened with Elizabeth in the group and how she's been talking about the reasons for it, and how that's affected what we've been talking about? I got to thinking about it, and I guess the way I feel is that I'm glad you're back, and I'm really glad some stuff has come out." He is looking at Elizabeth.

The members of the group are all crossing a barrier. They are finally beginning to recognize the safety of the group. They are attached—both to the group and to one another—and as a result, they will never be the same again. Attachment makes the neurons in our brains dance around and find new positions, changing the way we think, the way we deal with other people, and the way we recover from trauma. Attachment is like hitting the emotional jackpot. *Attachment is the winning ticket.*

My Father's Good-Bye

1982

know my days are numbered. I almost died of a heart attack two years ago at seventy-one years old. When I was in the hospital, I realized that I never gave Elaine a big present. I said to myself that if I lived, the first thing I would do is buy her a brand-new car. I had fun shopping for it. You should have seen the look on her face when I handed her the keys to a shiny orange Toyota Tercel.

I am divorced now and having the time of my life. I always said that when I retired at sixty-five, I would do everything that I loved to do. I go to the gym every day, ride my bicycle for miles, swim, and enjoy women. I go dancing, and even young women want to go out with me. When I was in the Intensive Care Unit, the nurse told Elaine that I had the most beautiful body she had ever seen. I was on the *Dating Game* TV show, and I came in second. The girl said she liked my legs the best.

It is sad that I have to die. I feel forty years old on the inside and am surprised when I see my age written down on paper. It isn't fair that I have to die. I love life so much!

Here is part of my Last Will and Testament that will be read after my death. I am handwriting it:

If the family wants a funeral, it is okay with me. I can be placed in the slumber room where the family can gather. If possible, you can play Beethoven's Fifth Symphony and/or Tchaikovsky's Seventh Symphony. If not, any symphonic music will do.

If anyone wishes to bring flowers once in a while, they will be for Arnold and me, so we won't be completely forgotten.

I want to live, but there comes a time sooner or later when we all must go. I guess my time is now. The world and life have not been good to me. However, I made the best of it, and I did derive some happiness.

My children gave me some joy when they were small. Elaine has given me much pride.

When Arnold took his life, he took one-third of me with him. It is the worst thing that can happen to a person. All my dreams and hopes vanished. I was so sure when he was in high school that he would be everything I wanted to be and couldn't be because of circumstances beyond my control. I carry this tragedy with me, *plus guilt*, to my death.

Well, this is my last good-bye. Just a few inner thoughts that I want to express before I leave. It has been great in many ways and tragic and sad in other ways, but that's life. So after the funeral, get together and talk and tell stories about me all you want. My family and brother and sisters were nice to me in many ways.

I never thought I would see anyone after my heart attack, but I got another chance. That was nice.

Good-bye for good. I wish everyone—my family, brother and sisters, friends—all the luck and happiness and joy, but the main thing is health. If you have health, you have everything. I found that out after my heart attack. Every day was a bonus. Every day had new meaning. Every day was great when there was no pain and no aggravation.

I hate to leave but my time is up.

Love and kisses to everyone I know.

Ivan Sbritsky Abrams

Arnold Looks at the Face of a Dead Woman

I am at a concentration camp. I am looking at a photograph of a dead woman's face:

It is not bad
    nor good
But something entirely different
    touching you
As you rise as far as you fell
And then
    somewhere else.
Complete peace and serenity.
Wonderful expectant divinity on earth.
Even if things are rough,
    I'll always know it is there.
Completeness of life.
Die in peace.

I Want My Mommy

10

Current Group Therapy Meeting Continued

WHERE WE LEFT OFF: *Hugo said that the reason for the change in the group was that members have become more open and trusting. Members are now attached to one another—they have obtained the winning ticket.*

I ask directly, "Was anybody annoyed with Elizabeth for skipping out on us for two weeks?" I see members are stumped, so I add, "Or have any other reaction?"

"I was worried," Tim admits. Others echo the same words.

Tim elaborates. "Because I think if any one of us really gets so depressed that we can't deal with it and drop out, it injures the whole group. Even though all of us are in here to straighten ourselves out, it's a group effort. So . . . "

I take advantage of Tim's pause, and everyone looks at me. "Nobody was annoyed that Elizabeth gave you a taste of the medicine she's been getting from men? That she would get intimate with you, and then out the door she goes?" I am encouraging them to go even further: Get in touch with that anger and own it! Get in touch with your sexuality and own it! Get in touch with how you long for maternal and adult love and own it!

"Not a bit," Cheryl says quickly, shaking her head. "No."

Robert scratches his arm. "I was more worried."

Linda looks at Elizabeth, who is sitting across from her, and smiles at her. "I felt sympathetic because . . . "

Elizabeth responds to Linda's approach. "I was more embarrassed than anything."

Harry says, "I wasn't here when you had such a rough time, but when I heard about it, I thought: 'God, she must want to just shrivel up and hide under the rug—poor woman.'"

Elizabeth smiles and shakes her head with recognition. "That's how I felt."

"Yeah," Linda reflects.

Elizabeth is wearing a denim suit and sits with her legs crossed at the ankles. She looks directly at everyone as she talks and uses her hands freely. "I figured something important was going on with me inside, because I never cry. Even if something is bothering me, I'll try to cover it up with a smile. It's kind of like wearing a mask. But I knew when I finally broke down that day . . . well, I was more embarrassed than anything. I didn't feel comfortable enough to come back."

Linda is nodding her head up and down to encourage her, the way I do.

Elizabeth responds and continues, "I sought out another kind of help—a weight-control counselor. I guess in a way it was good because the help that I sought out was positive for me. I felt at that time that I was just getting negative . . . Well, I was in a slump as it was, and to get negative feedback in the group was just getting me down further. What I needed was someone to kind of pick me up and say, 'You've got this going for you.' I needed a pep talk, not a put-down."

Linda smiles and encourages her: "Yeah!"

Elizabeth continues, "That's what I needed at the time. And then I saw Elaine."

At the sound of my name, Tim moves his arms. Cheryl rubs her mouth.

Elizabeth turns to me and proceeds to talk. "Like I told everyone last week, she said she wanted to talk to me. At first I didn't want to come. I said, 'No, I don't want to do it.' I didn't want to come back; I didn't want to have anything to do with the group, or anybody, for that matter."

Cheryl wipes her forehead.

"We talked and I cried some more. Gee, you feel so much better after you cry! It's sort of like letting all this bad stuff come out. You know when you make soup and all the crud rises to the top and makes brown bubbles and then you can skim them off with a spoon? Well, I felt comfortable with just Elaine—instead of in front of a lot of people. Because, as I said, I could let everything come out. And I was able to get a grip on what was going on."

I don't give anyone a chance to respond. I have another important question. Time is at a premium now. "Did anybody have a reaction last week when Elizabeth said she saw me for an individual session? It's not typical for me to see one of you outside of group."

I have learned that almost everything that is talked about or acted on in the group has some relationship to members' feelings about the therapist. If members are talking about sexual attraction, they probably have some attraction to me. If members are talking about wanting support, understanding, and attention, they probably want more of this from me. If members are talking about cold and distant parents, they are probably referring to my low activity level.

A number of members have straggled out at the end of a meeting, hoping for a private moment with me. People call me during the week with excuses to hear my voice. Having a therapist sometimes feels like a giant tease. I am the mother everyone wants but can never have. Group members get only a small dose, but it is sufficient for them to grow. When people become conscious and comfortable with their longing for my love and their frustration at not having as much of it as they want, they learn to understand their problematic behaviors better. They learn to understand their need for both dependence and independence—and to take more control of getting those needs met in an intimate relationship.

Tim is the first to answer. "Your seeing Elizabeth made a lot of sense to me."

"Yeah," Linda agrees.

"I felt reassured," said Harry.

"Me too," says Cheryl, shaking her head up and down. "Because you asked us, 'What does everybody think? Should I call Elizabeth or not?' I think I would have been madder at you if you hadn't called Elizabeth." She laughs with some anger just thinking about the other possibility.

Linda smiles and scratches her neck. She strokes both sides of her face before she talks. "Yeah, in the sense of a safety net."

"Anybody feel jealous?" I persist.

Cheryl quickly shakes her head no, not realizing that the men are shaking their head in the opposite direction.

Robert, David, Tim, and Harry say, "I did."

I sigh with relief. The muscles in my face and stomach relax.

Tim says, "I was about ready to call you and demand some individual attention." I feel like cheering.

Cheryl scratches her neck. She doesn't expect this reaction.

"When?" Linda asks.

Tim answers, "When I was expressing the idea that I had done a lot in my life but I didn't seem to be getting anywhere in here. I do have trouble expressing myself in the group; it's easier with one person. Maybe that's why I ramble on in here. I'm nervous—I still am. My heart started to pound in here today."

Robert giggles with recognition and then looks at his feet to gain control. He also would like an individual session with me. Harry sits up in his chair and hugs his knee like a little boy.

I am pleased. A glimmer of longing for connection is surfacing in the group. The healthy psychic structure is based on some positive union with a mother or mother figure (it can even be the group-as-a-whole). If the members can take in what the leader and the group-as-a-whole are giving them—validation and acceptance—they will have the foundation they need for a healthy, mature, intimate relationship. As they feel better about themselves and as their deep need for intimacy is met, they become more responsive to the needs of other people and also become more responsible citizens. If people own their rage, they don't need to have an enemy mentality.

Linda starts to talk. "Do you ever find that when there isn't a group meeting and something comes up or something's bothering you . . . that you find yourself consciously making an effort to be your own group in your head? Or do you save up all your problems for the group?"

I cross my arms on my chest with satisfaction. I say to myself, "Linda, I love you! You are going to explain to the others what is supposed to finally happen here—what makes it possible for members to have a *reparative experience* here and take it with them forever."

Linda continues, "Well, I was just thinking, Tim, because you were talking about needing extra attention. It's come up before for me when Elaine was gone for three weeks." Linda looks at me and then back to the group. She makes sweeping gestures as she talks, as though she is building a sculpture for the group at the same time. "What do you do when there's no group? You can't put yourself on hold. I had this *odd* reaction when we'd been off group for a second week. It was a cool experience in a way. I'd taken a promotional exam at work, and I came in second. I missed the job by one point. It wasn't that I was disappointed in not getting the job, because I'd already made up my mind to go to another farm. But when I got the results, I was really sad. And I thought, 'This is very odd.' It was on a Thursday, and we didn't have group. I was sitting there thinking, 'Why do I feel so sad? What is it that makes me feel this way when these are the facts about the job? What is it?' And then I thought, 'Well, there's no group, so what do we do in group, folks?'" She laughs and rubs her palms with delight.

Cheryl feels her ear and then her hair and then strokes her hair to the rhythm of Linda's words.

Linda continues, "And all I could hear was Elaine's voice in the background saying, 'Now, how do you really feel? Put a word to the feeling that you're feeling right now. What is it in your life that's happened to you that has made you feel the same way?' So I was driving around and I finally thought, 'Well, I remember feeling this way when I'd do badly at school, and I'd go home and say, 'Well, I did badly at school.' In fact, I got thrown out of school at one point for political activity, believe it or not. Most parents would rant and rave and scream and yell and say, 'You naughty child! Now, don't do that again.' My parents, if I screwed up, would show huge disappointment without doing anything. It was kind of like . . . " Linda lowers her voice to a whisper and mimics her mother's cold voice: "'We're very disappointed.' But they would never discuss it. Then I thought: 'I'm having the same emotional reaction right now about not getting this job that I had when I got kicked out of school. I didn't do what I was supposed do. My parents were disappointed, but they would never talk to me about it. And I would feel bad." She presses her hands to her heart. "When I got kicked out of school, I was angry with them for being that way because they weren't listening to what I was saying. And I thought, 'This is what makes me sad. It's this feeling of frustration over nobody listening to me.' It was *so weird*—as soon as I figured that out and made that connection, I stopped feeling sad." She lets out a big laugh. "I thought, 'Wow! That's what happens!' Because I identified it. When I identified what the sadness was and where it came from, it went away. If you know what it is, it doesn't bother you anymore. I saw that it wasn't what was said to me or done to me that made me feel bad—it was what *wasn't* said. It was the *unknown* things that hurt me, that *terrified* me. I can work myself into a blue funk over what *might* happen next week—which is absurd because next week comes and nothing happens. That's why I always hated flying. By the time I'd get to the airport, I'd have written my will. Then I'd get on the plane and be exhausted from worrying. But identifying it—that's what did it. I was driving around the city, tears running down my face, trying to control the sobs, wallowing in despair. There was no group to fall back on. You don't go to group to get a new head. You go to group for support and to learn how to help yourself. We can't be in the group forever, so we have to know how to do it ourselves. It's funny that the key is so simple."

I am sure the members see the smile on my face. I am ecstatic. I believe that once the members experience a good attachment, they will be changed forever. Having a healthy and positive attachment is the winning ticket to accepting the good and bad parts of yourself; you no longer need to project them onto others. You don't have to be fearful of what others can do to you, because you know that basically you're okay, even though you're not perfect—other people also aren't perfect. For each person in the group, every other member represents a piece of themselves. When the group matures, every member is accepted, including the Defiant Leader and the Scapegoat Leader. Thus *when we all hold hands, each person becomes whole.*

I feel that Linda still has more work to do. She may be denying her need for the therapist/parent prematurely. There still may be more love Linda can get from me (and the mother/group-as-a-whole) before she terminates. As a child Linda got into a pattern of never asking for or expecting anything from her mother. I ask her, "Did you feel jealous when I met with Elizabeth outside the group?"

Linda shakes her head. "No. I felt reassured, oddly enough. I thought, 'Well, if something happens where I can't handle it—something where I'm overwhelmed—then that safety net exists for me, too.'" Linda lets out an embarrassed giggle. "It's kind of cool to know I won't be left out."

I address everyone in the group. I purposely look directly at each member. "Does anybody feel like you may want to have something catastrophic happen to you so that you could meet with me individually?" I am acknowledging that the desire for closeness with the mother is so deep that members might be self-destructive to get more of it.

Linda laughs and says, "God, no."

Others register the question and a gale of laughter starts. Robert, Cheryl, and Linda laugh the loudest.

Linda mixes in some words with her chuckles. "Catastrophes, I've got so many. Nothing else can happen. There's no room." She gives it some more thought and then says, "No, it's like making an emergency and going to the emergency room. I don't want to go out and break my leg just to have the nurses be nice to me."

Everyone laughs harder. Cheryl keeps shaking her head and laughing. We can hear Tim's laughter now, and he says, "Linda hit the nail on the head!" They all talk at once and prolong the delight of Linda's image.

Robert says, "There aren't any nurses there to be nice to you." People laugh some more.

Linda adds, "It's like sticking your finger in the socket to see if it really does work." More delight. More fun. The walls are bouncing the roar back to the group.

Arnold joins in: "I like to laugh. You know, really laugh spontaneously. Damn, it's a good feeling."

Note

The group members in this book are composites of various attributes the author has devised for illustration purposes and are thus fictional.

My Wish

In this book one generation overlaps with another. I hope my children will add a layer and my grandchildren, another. For a family that one generation ago was torn apart by war and poverty, I cannot think of a better affirmation of what is best about being human.

Afterword

Dear Reader,

Please go to www.elainecooper.com for

- a place to tell me your story
- photographs of family members in the book
- a blog on generational social trauma
- a video lecture exploring generational social trauma
- a video lecture on finding a therapist
- information on weekend workshops for personal exploration of generational social trauma

I hope to hear from you!
Elaine Cooper

About the Author

Elaine Cooper, LCSW, has forty-five years of clinical practice and thirty years of teaching experience in individual, couples, and group psychotherapy. She is a clinical professor at the Langley Porter Psychiatric Institute at the University of California, San Francisco, School of Medicine and has been awarded the annual Excellence in Teaching Award nine times. Cooper has also taught at Smith College, New York University, New York Medical College, Hunter College, Adelphi University, the Psychoanalytic Institute of Northern California, and the University of California, Berkeley.

A licensed clinical social worker, Cooper received her master's in social welfare from the UC Berkeley School of Social Welfare in 1964. She is a fellow of the American Group Psychotherapy Association and on the editorial board of the *International Journal of Group Psychotherapy*. She is the author of *Group Intervention: How to Maintain Groups in Medical and Psychiatric Settings*, as well as numerous articles and book chapters on group therapy.

Cooper lives in Berkeley, California, where she has a private practice in individual, couples, and group psychotherapy. A regular presenter at local, national, and international professional conferences, she also consults for mental health professionals, including therapists in psychiatric hospitals.

Bibliography

Agazarian, Yvonne M. *Systems-Centered Therapy for Groups*, New York: Guilford Press, 1997.

Agazarian, Yvonne M., and Richard Peters. *The Visible and Invisible Group: Two Perspectives on Group Psychotherapy and Group Process.* London: Routledge and Kegan Paul, 1981.

American Experience: The Great Famine. DVD. Directed by Austin Hoyt and Aiskyuak Yumagulov. Boston: PBS and WGBH Boston, 2011.

Beck, Ariadne P, Albert M. Eng, and Jo Ann Brusa. "The Evolution of Leadership during Group Development." *Group* 13 (Fall/Winter 1989): 155–64.

Beck, Ariadne P., and Carol M. Lewis, eds. *The Process of Group Psychotherapy: Systems for Analyzing Change.* Washington, DC: American Psychological Association, 2000.

Beckett, John. "General Systems Theory, Psychiatry, and Psychotherapy." *International Journal of Group Psychotherapy* 23, no. 3 (1973): 292–305.

Degruy, Joy. *Post Traumatic Slave Syndrome: America's Legacy of Enduring Injury and Healing.* Portland, OR: Joy Degruy Publications, 2005.

Durkin, Helen E. "The Development of Systems Theory and Its Implications for the Theory and Practice of Group Therapy." In *Group Therapy 1975: An*

Overview, edited by Lewis Wolberg and Marvin Aronson, 8–20. New York: Stratton Intercontinental, 1975.

Freud, Sigmund. *Group Psychology and the Analysis of the Ego*. Vol. 18 of *The Standard Edition of the Complete Psychological Works of Sigmund Freud*, edited and translated by James Strachey and Anna Freud. London: Hogarth Press, 1955 (1921). First authorized translation published 1922 by International Psychoanalytic Press.

Guntrip, Harry, *Schizoid Phenomena, Object Relations, and the Self*. New York: International Universities Press, 1969.

Hopper, Earl, and Hiam Weinberg, eds. *The Social Unconscious in Persons, Groups, and Societies*. Vol. 1, *Mainly Theory*. London: Karnac Books, 2011.

Jung, Carl Gustav. "On the Psychology of the Unconscious." In *Two Essays on Analytical Psychology*, 3–119. Vol. 7 of *The Collected Works of C. J. Jung*. 2nd ed. Edited and translated by Gerhard Adler and R. F. C. Hull. Princeton, NJ: Princeton University Press, 1966 (1917). This English translation first published 1953 by Pantheon.

Lonergan, Elaine Cooper. *Group Intervention: How to Begin and Maintain Groups in Medical and Psychiatric Settings*. New York: Jason Aronson, 1982. Reprint edition with new preface 1989.

Rutan, Scott, and Walter N. Stone. *Psychodynamic Group Psychotherapy*. 4th ed. New York: Guilford Press, 2007.

Scheidlinger, Saul. "Freud's Psychology." In *Psychoanalytic Group Dynamics: Basic Readings*, edited by Saul Scheidlinger, 5–14. New York: International Universities Press, 1980.

Schwarz-Bart, André. *The Last of the Just*. Translated by Stephen Becker. Woodstock, NY: Overlook Press, 2000 (1959). First American edition published 1960 by Atheneum.

Schutzenberger, Anne Ancelin, *The Ancestor Syndrome: Transgenerational Psychotherapy and the Hidden Links in the Family Tree*. Translated by Anne Trager. London: Routledge, 1998 (1993).

Siegel, Daniel J. "Commentary on 'Integrating Interpersonal Neurobiology with Group Psychotherapy': Reflections on Mind, Brain, and Relationships in Group Psychotherapy." *International Journal of Group Psychotherapy* 60 (October 2010): 483–85.

———. *The Mindful Brain: Reflection and Attunement in the Cultivation of Well-Being.* New York: Norton, 2008.

Sullivan, Harry Stack. "Introduction to the Study of Interpersonal Relations." *Psychiatry* 1(1938): 121–34.

Volkas, Armand. "Drama Therapy in the Repair of Collective Trauma." In *Trauma-Informed Drama Therapy: Transforming Clinics, Classrooms, and Communities,* edited by Nisha Sajnani and David Read Johnson, 41–68. Springfield, IL: Charles C. Thomas, 2014.

———. "Healing the Wounds of History: Drama Therapy in Collective Trauma and Intercultural Conflict Resolution." In *Current Approaches in Drama Therapy.* 2nd ed. Edited by David Read Johnson and Renee Emunah, 145–71. Springfield, IL: Charles C. Thomas, 2009.

Yalom, Irvin D., and Molyn Leszcz, *Theory and Technique of Group Psychotherapy.* 5th ed. Cambridge, MA: Basic Books, 2005.